Postcard History Series

Kings County

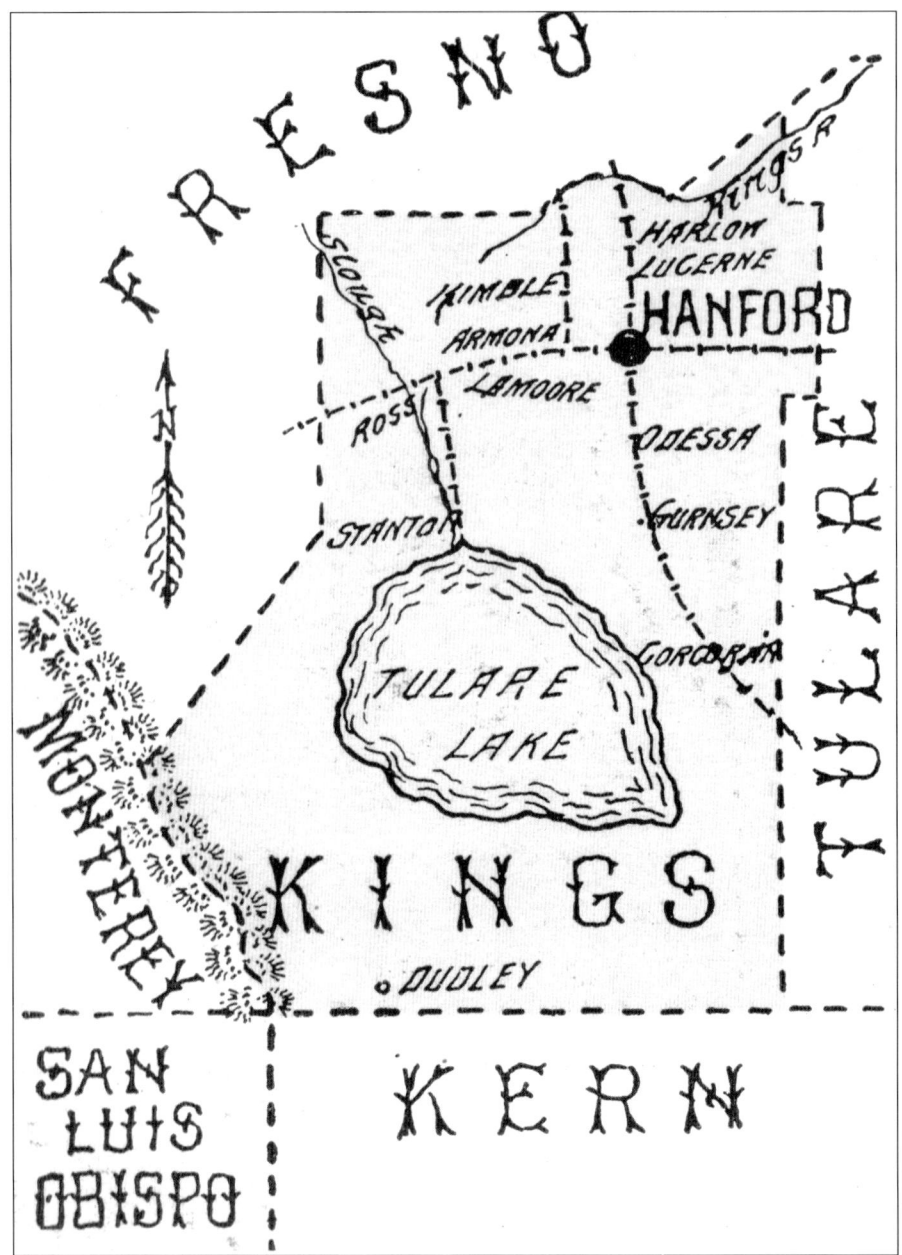

POSTCARD MAP OF KINGS COUNTY. This image was taken from a card that was handed out at the 1915 Panama-Pacific International Exposition in San Francisco. Kings County is located in the heart of the San Joaquin Valley and is bordered by Fresno, Tulare, Kern, and Monterey Counties. It was also the location of the largest inland lake west of the Mississippi.

ON THE COVER: This unused postcard shows a view of the Hanford Hotel from around 1910. Located on the southeast corner of Douty and Seventh Streets, the building was designed by McDougal and Son and was originally named the Aborn Hotel. Today it is home to a local furniture store. (Courtesy Hanford Carnegie Museum.)

POSTCARD HISTORY SERIES

Kings County

Michael J. Semas

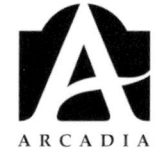

Copyright © 2005 by Michael J. Semas
ISBN 0-7385-3109-X

Published by Arcadia Publishing
Charleston SC, Chicago IL, Portsmouth NH, San Francisco CA

Printed in Great Britain

Library of Congress Catalog Card Number: 2005936984

For all general information contact Arcadia Publishing at:
Telephone 843-853-2070
Fax 843-853-0044
E-mail sales@arcadiapublishing.com
For customer service and orders:
Toll-Free 1-888-313-2665

Visit us on the Internet at www.arcadiapublishing.com

This book is dedicated to my wife, Christine, who feigns a modicum of interest in my hobby, and to my two daughters, Katherine and Sarah, who constantly ask me how much my postcard collection is worth.

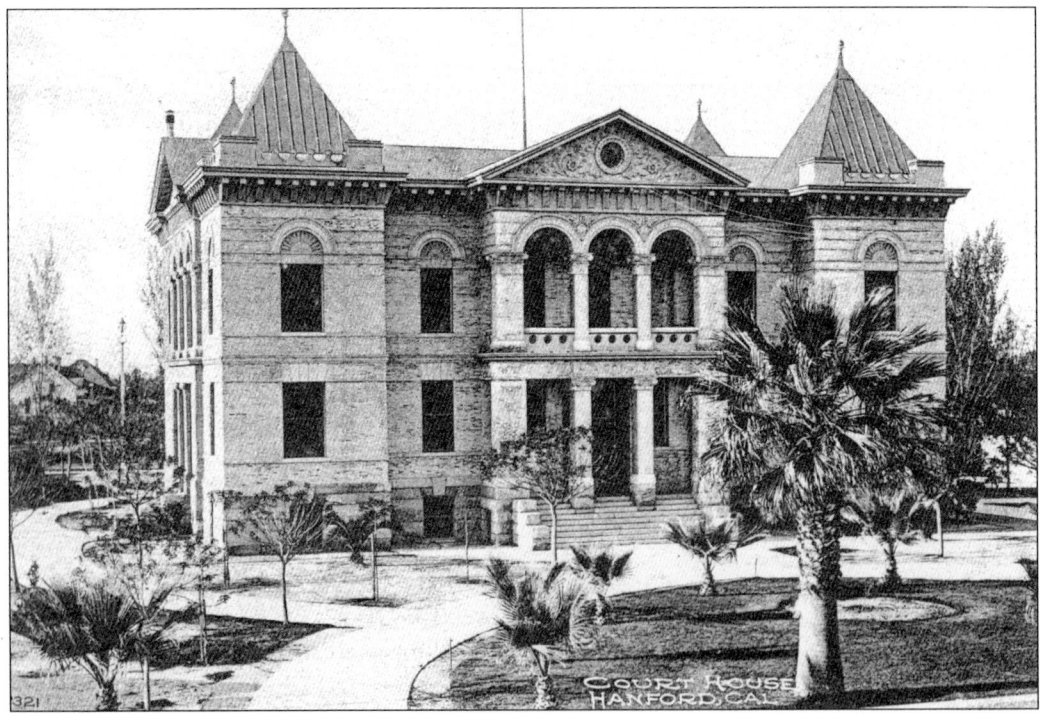

KINGS COUNTY COURTHOUSE. One of the most prominent fixtures of the county is the local courthouse. Located in Hanford, its Romanesque design represented the culture and refinement the early residents of the county wanted to establish for their community.

Contents

Acknowledgments 6

Introduction 7

1. Hanford 9
2. Lemoore 73
3. Corcoran 91
4. Avenal 103
5. Armona and Hardwick 107
6. Agriculture 111
7. Kings Kounty Karnival Parade, 1911 121

Bibliography 128

Acknowledgments

The postcards presented in this book represent the best of several private collections. Every reasonable attempt has been made to provide a fair and complete representation of Kings County. However, postcard images of certain communities are difficult to obtain or the images may not exist. Postcards of the towns of Hardwick and Armona are rare and extremely difficult to come by. Every image that I found depicting these communities is published within these pages. No postcard images of Stratford, Grangeville, Guernsey, or Kettleman City appear in this book since I could not locate any postcards of those communities.

Most of the postcards presented in this book come from my personal collection. Cards not from my collection receive special credit in their captions. I would like to thank Ron Burris, Ron Lerch, James Hickman, Julieann Faulkner, Floyd Bookout, John Reynolds, and Lenora Mann for opening up their private collections for me to use in this book. Joann Gibbons, curator for the Hanford Carnegie Library, was extremely helpful in providing written source documentation for the postcard captions, as well as several images. I would also like to extend a very special thank you to Martha Bentley, who encouraged me to undertake my first foray into the publishing world. Not only did she offer the use of several of her images, she took the time to fact check all the written material. Much of the detail included in this book was obtained from her written work for the Hanford Show Offs.

And now, revisit Kings County when it was young, full of promise, and willing to show off.

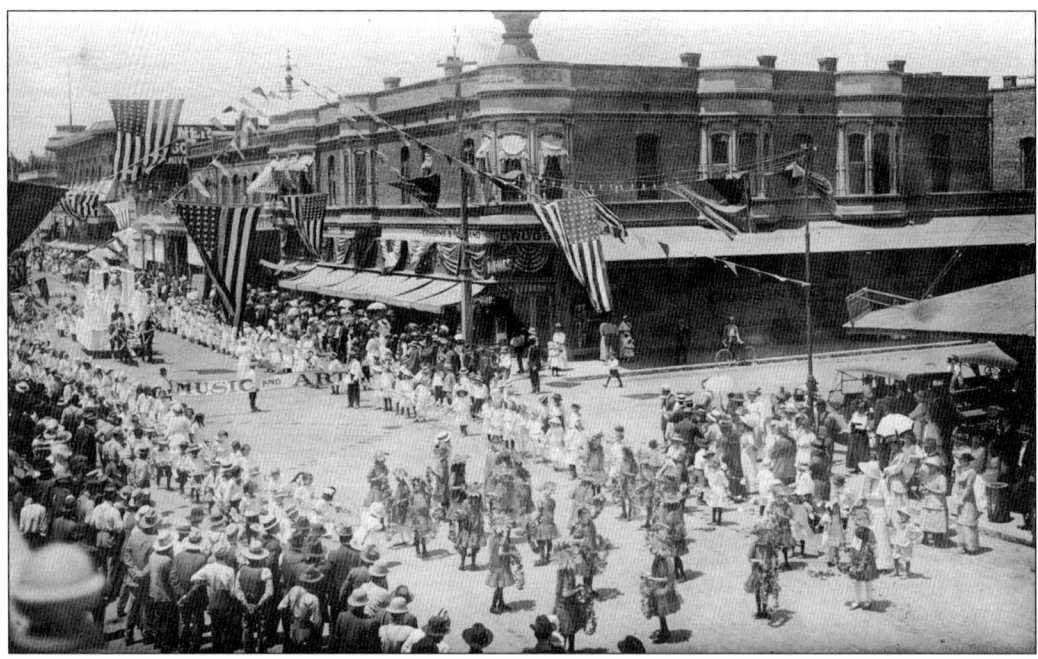

Parade Scene, Hanford. Parades were a common form of local celebration. Each community sponsored and built floats that represented the best that each local town had to offer. Pictured in this 1911 postcard is the northwest corner of Douty and Seventh Streets. The parade shown is celebrating the 18th birthday of Kings County.

Introduction

Kings County was born on May 23, 1893, and by all accounts it was not an easy birth. Originally the western part of Tulare County, the land encompassed the lower Kings River Delta, the western foothills of the San Joaquin Valley, and all of Tulare Lake.

The earliest residents of the area were the Tachi Yokut Indians. "Tachi" is the Yokut word for "mud hen," a duck that inhabited the local area. The Tachi tribe lived around the vast Tulare Lake and depended on it for their survival. The lake teemed with fish and freshwater clams while the shores were home to a wide array of birds and mammals. It was a Garden of Eden.

To the early Spanish explorers, the lake appeared infinitely huge and was a large obstacle to be avoided. The shoreline was choked with vegetation and enormous clouds of mosquitoes would envelop anyone who ventured near its shores. When the winds blew, the friction of the air on the lake's surface would move its shoreline several miles in a single day.

Spain briefly considered establishing a mission near the lake but decided against it when the mission's safety could not be assured. The south valley area was an extremely isolated area. Spain could not commit the resources necessary to maintain a remote outpost for the Catholic church.

The first white settlers to the area were livestock herders. Large pig herds were established on the shorelines where they could gorge themselves on the clams that lived in the mud. Sheep and cattle were allowed to roam the shores and surrounding grassland. Soon the early settlers discovered that the land itself could produce a bountiful harvest. Vast grain fields were planted around the lake and the tonnage harvested was incredible for the times.

As more people settled in the area, they harnessed the waters of the Kings River by digging irrigation canals. With the water delivered by these canals, formerly barren desert land became fertile and productive farmland. The lands became very valuable and Tulare County reaped the economic rewards of agriculture. Towns and settlements such as Hanford, Lemoore, Armona, Grangeville, and Hardwick were plotted out by surveyors working for the Southern Pacific Railroad and lots were sold to eager settlers. The western part of Tulare County took on the name Lucerne, after the lush alfalfa hay that was grown in the area. The area became very prosperous and it was this prosperity that planted the seeds of Kings County.

Almost immediately, the early residents resented the tax drain on the area. The property taxes paid by the area residents were not being reinvested in their communities but were used by the more populated eastern area of Tulare County. Furthermore, all official county business had to be conducted in Visalia, which was a one-way, 20-mile trip by horse or train. Something had to be done.

In 1890 and 1891, several bills were submitted to the California State Legislature to partition away the western portion of Tulare County into its own separate and independent county government. These bills were defeated due to an intense lobbying effort done by eastern Tulare County representatives. In 1892, the residents of western Tulare County joined forces with the residents of northern Fresno County, who also wished to form their own county. The combined representation of these two areas was enough to win passage of a bill that permitted the subject of division to be put to a vote of the people. On May 23, 1893, the election took place and the county was born. The county residents decided on naming their new county after the Kings River, which flowed along the northern part of its boundary. With a final vote of 1,412 to 412, Kings County became the youngest county in the state of California.

In its 112-year history, the county has undergone a huge transformation. Agriculture is still king, but the crops have changed. Grain gave way to fruit trees and vines. Trees and vines gave way to cotton. And recently, cotton is giving way to trees and cows. The dairy industry has become the largest growth segment of the local economy. In 1900, the average dairy herd was 10 to 20 cows, and they were all milked by hand. Today local dairies are being built to house over 3,000 cows. Technology and breeding have created large milk factories that produce more milk in one day than the early dairies produced in a year.

Other industries were also established. Several large creameries and cheese plants were built to process all the local milk. The discovery of oil in the Kettleman Hills in 1928 on the west side of the county created a local oil industry. An oil refinery was built in Hanford in the 1930s to process oil that was pumped in from the west side. In 1959, a naval base was built near Lemoore to house carrier-based fighter jets. In 1964, a tire manufacturing plant was built. Although many of these businesses no longer operate in the area, their influence on Kings County still remains.

In 1898, *Kings County Resources Illustrated* was published. The book stated that the lands encompassed by Kings County were viewed by many outside the area as "nothing more than a sandy, barren plain, suitable only for the growth of prairie dogs, rabbits and wild oats" and the people who settled here "were considered fit subjects for a madhouse." The book went on to dispel such myths by stating "the early settlers of (Kings) County were men possessed by great thrift, energy, and determination, with nerves of iron, and hearts for any fate. Theirs was not a mislaid confidence; how abundantly has the land filled labor's hands with her rich products; how splendidly has Nature, with the combined force of labor and intelligence, transformed this desert plain into a vale of verdure green, a valley of plenty."

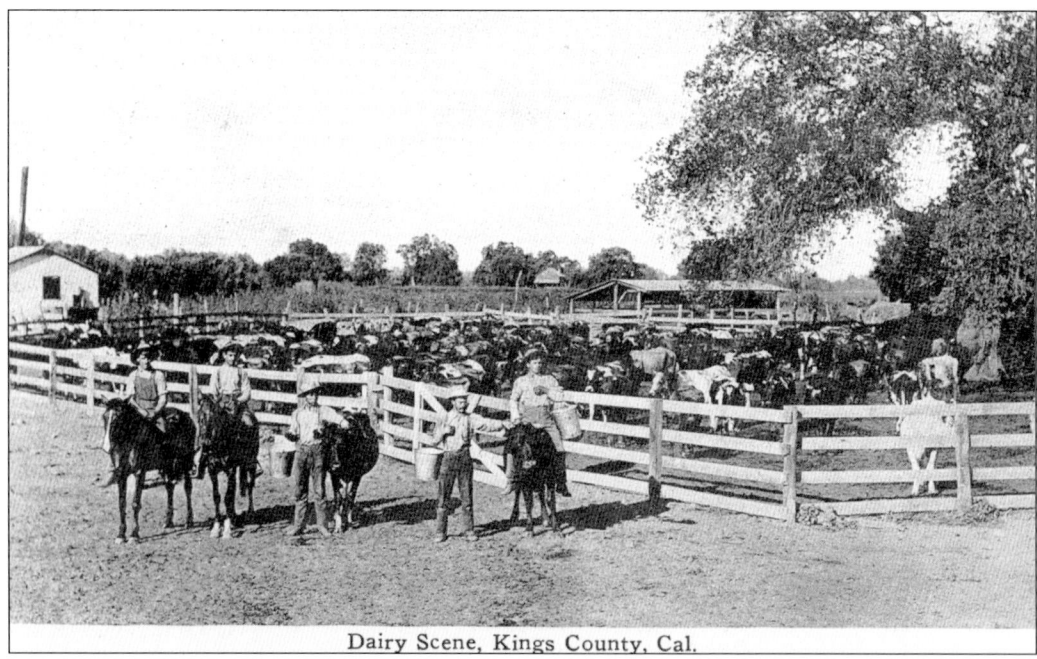

DAIRY SCENE, KINGS COUNTY. Agriculture was and still is the number-one industry of Kings County. This 1910 postcard shows an average dairy. The dairy industry remains one of the most important parts of the local economy.

One
HANFORD

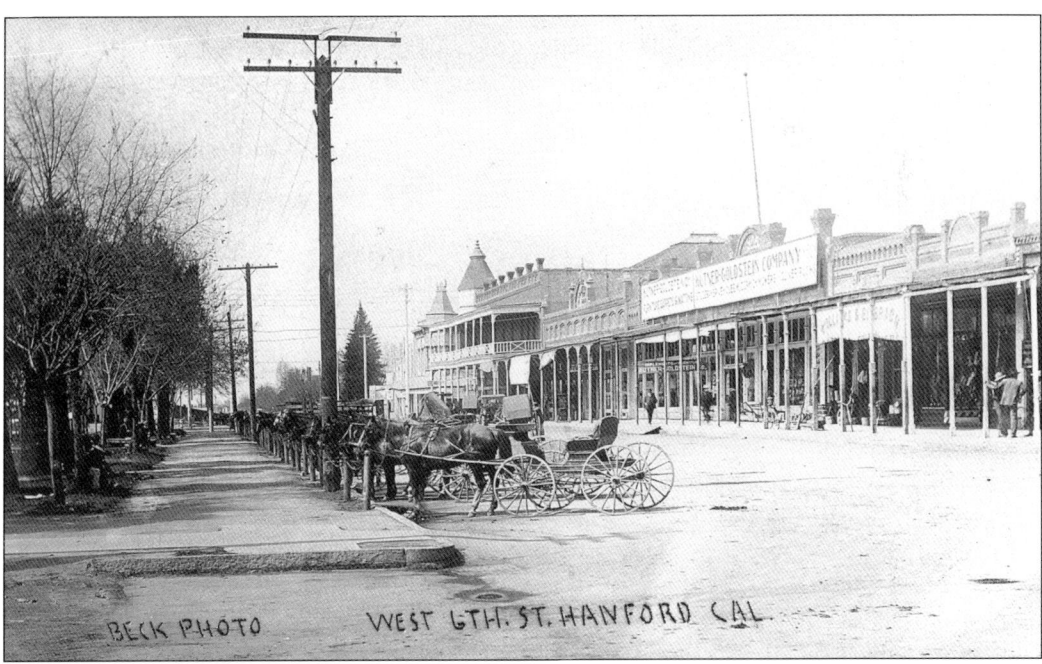

SIXTH STREET LOOKING WEST FROM DOUTY STREET. Pictured in this rare, unsent postcard are the businesses that lined the north side of Sixth Street. A park occupied the south side of the street. Originally named Front Street, it runs parallel to the Southern Pacific railroad line. The building with the large sign is the Kutner-Goldstein equipment store. Most of these buildings still exist today. (Courtesy Ron Lerch.)

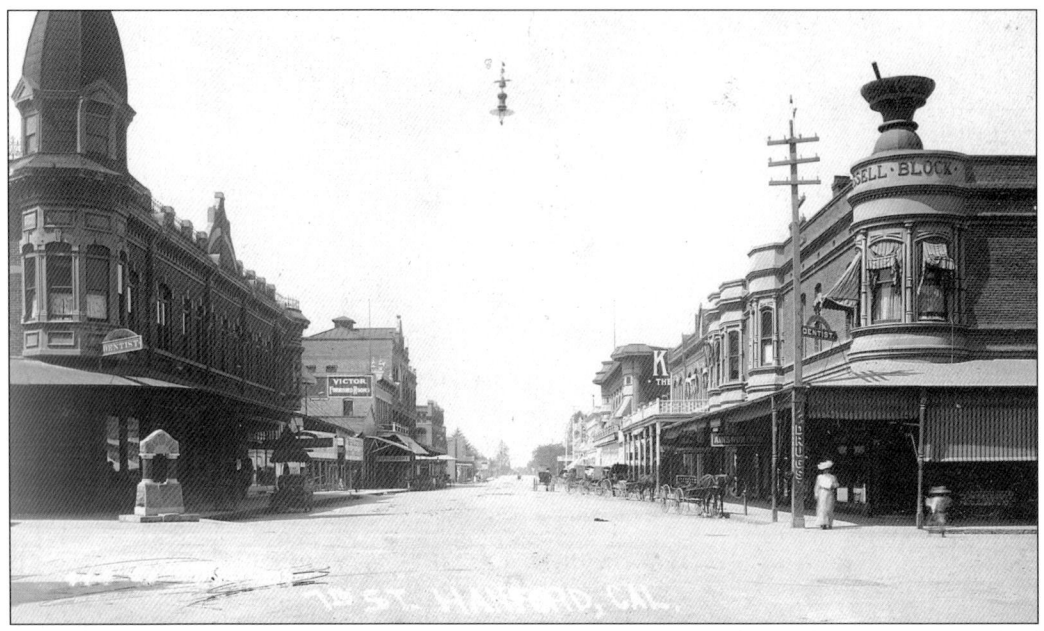

SEVENTH STREET LOOKING WEST FROM DOUTY STREET. This early view, postmarked 1907, shows the corner of Douty and Seventh Street. The building on the left is the Farmers and Merchants State Bank. The fountain in front of the bank was given to the City of Hanford in 1905 by the Women's Christian Temperance Union. Behind the bank is the implement yard for the Kutner-Goldstein Store. Across the street is the Cousins and Howland Drug Store.

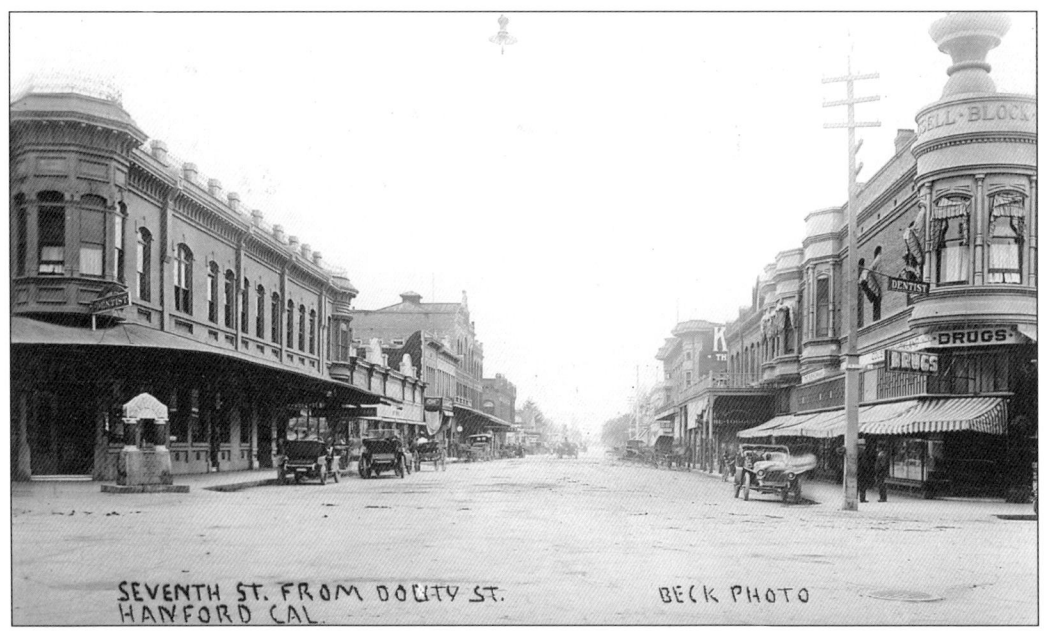

SEVENTH STREET LOOKING WEST FROM DOUTY STREET. This later view of the same intersection shows that the cone-shaped roof on the building on the left has been removed. Automobiles also have become more a common sight. Most of the businesses have remained the same.

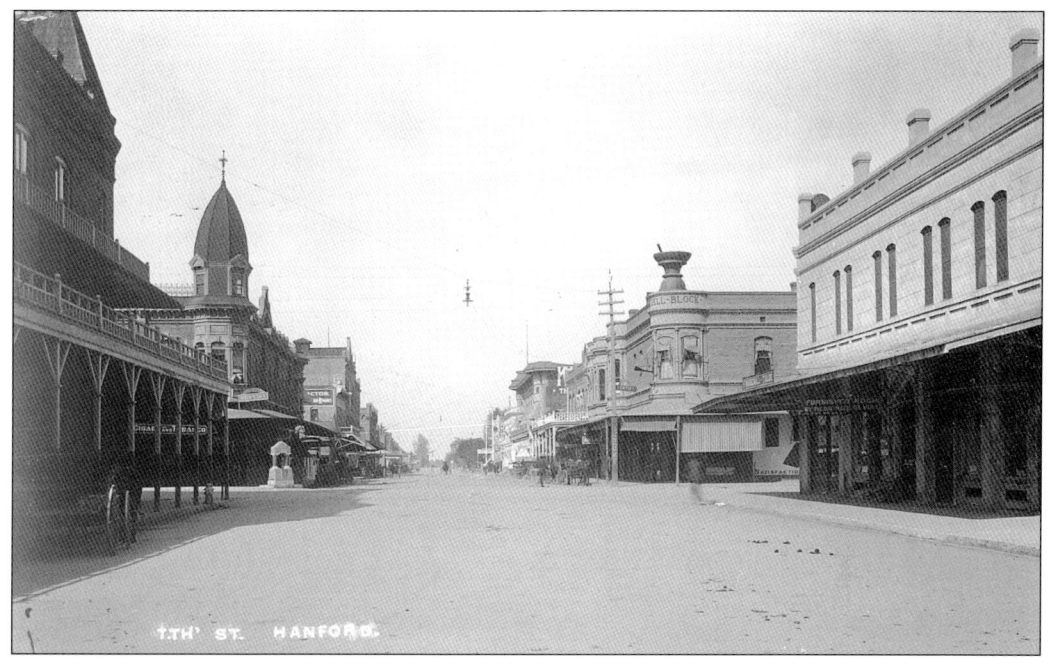

SEVENTH STREET LOOKING WEST ACROSS DOUTY STREET. This view shows the Aborn Hotel, left, and the Kate Jacobs Hotel on the right.

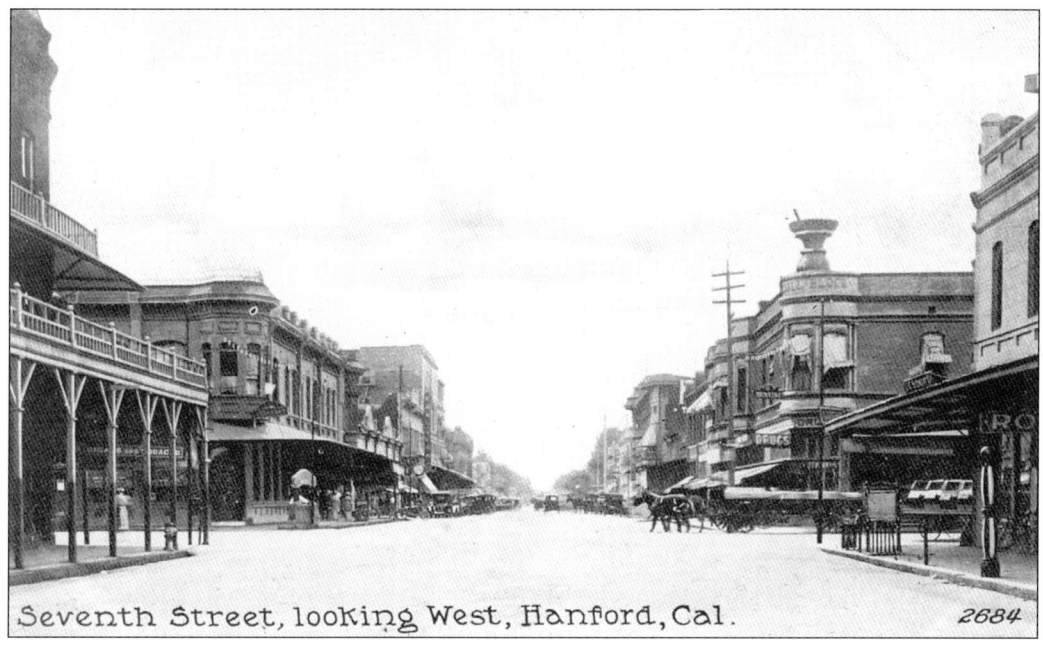

SEVENTH STREET LOOKING WEST ACROSS DOUTY STREET. Another view of the busy intersection of Douty and Seventh Streets shows the Aborn Hotel (left), a prominent hotel of the time that hosted many important occasions.

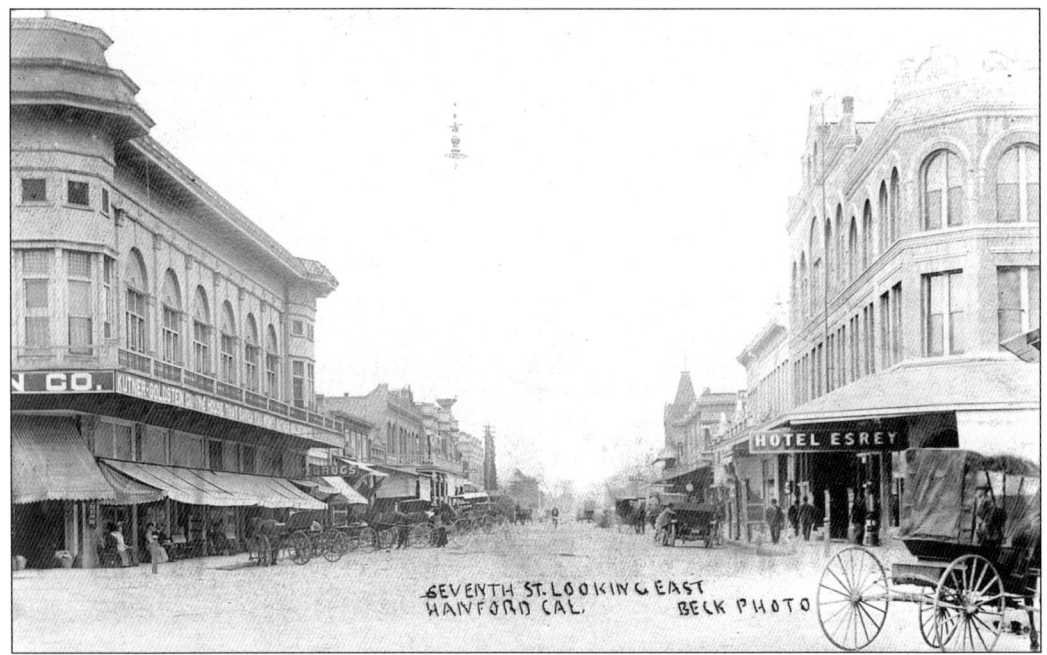

SEVENTH STREET LOOKING EAST. This 1911 postmarked card shows the Kutner-Goldstein building on the left and the Hotel Esrey on the right. This intersection was considered the heart of downtown Hanford.

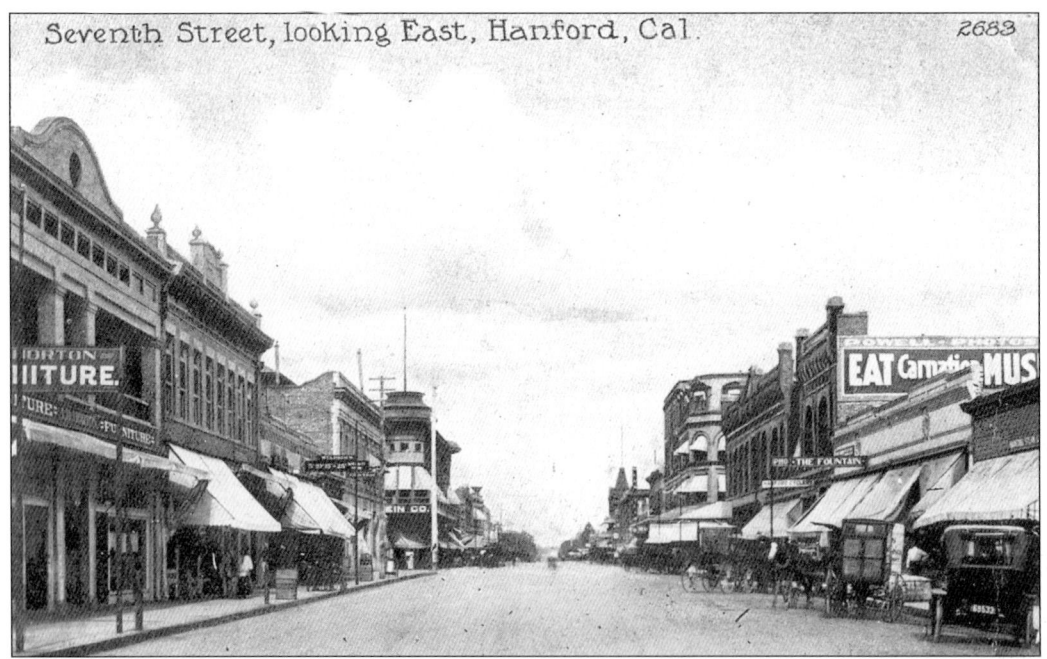

SEVENTH STREET LOOKING EAST. The view on this 1912 postcard shows the numerous businesses that lined both sides of Seventh Street. Since Hanford was the county seat, many businesses chose to locate here to trade with the local residents.

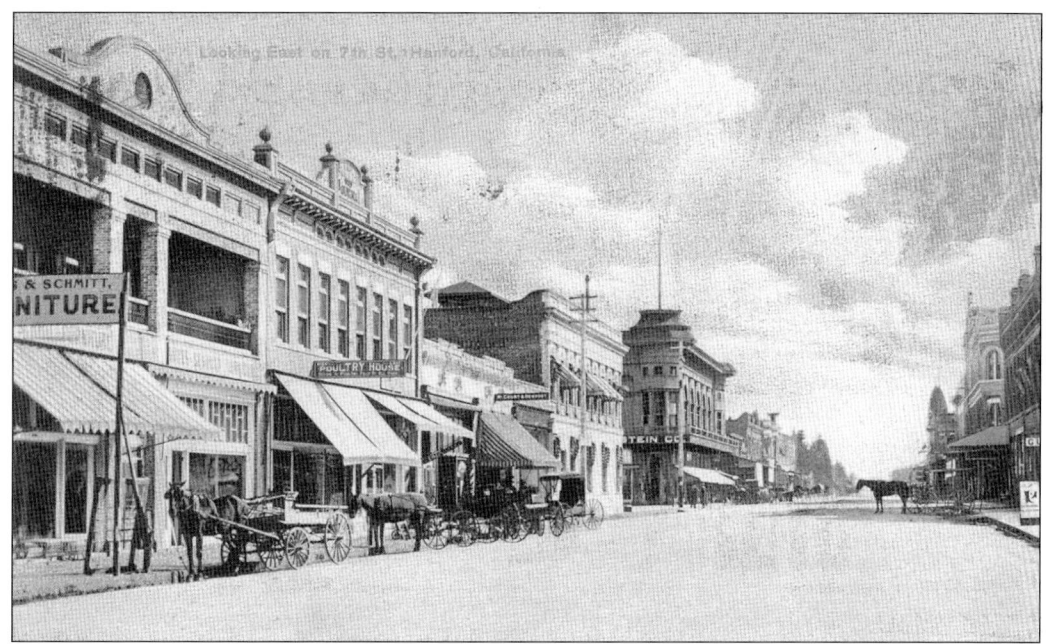

SEVENTH STREET LOOKING EAST. This 1911 postmarked card shows a thriving Hanford downtown. The businesses located on the left side of the street include the Hayes and Schmitt Furniture Store, High Lake Poultry House, and the *Hanford Daily Journal*. Horse power was the preferred mode of transportation at this time.

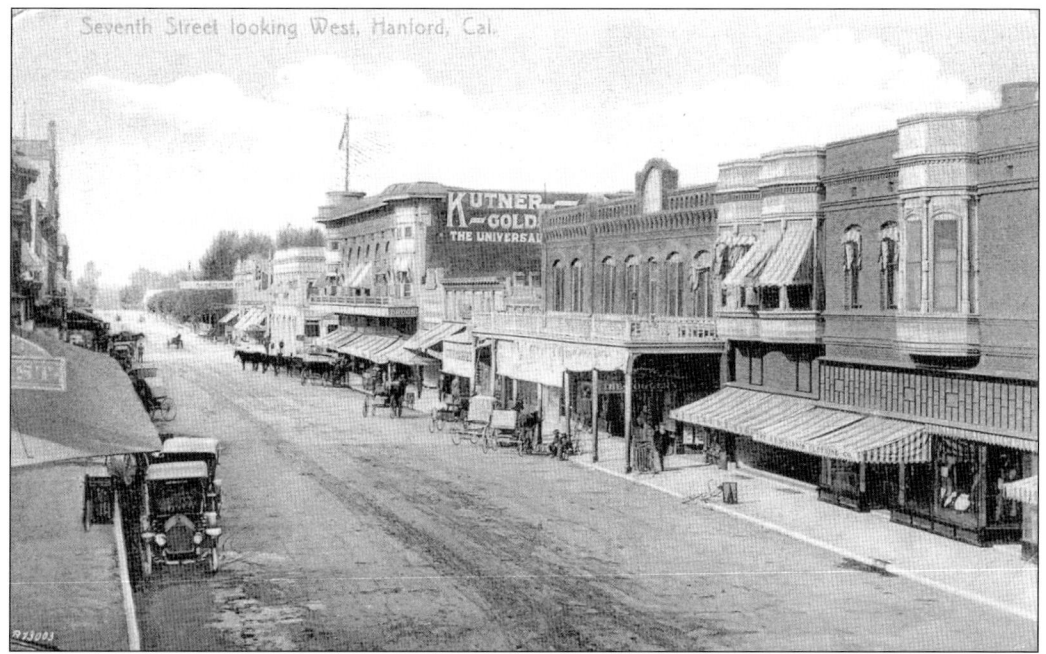

SEVENTH STREET LOOKING WEST. Pictured in this 1915 postmarked card are the businesses that lined the north side of Seventh Street. They included the Kutner-Goldstein Store, the Hefton Drug Store, City Market, and the B. B. McGinnis Clothing Store. Horse-drawn wagons were a common sight in Hanford until the mid-1920s.

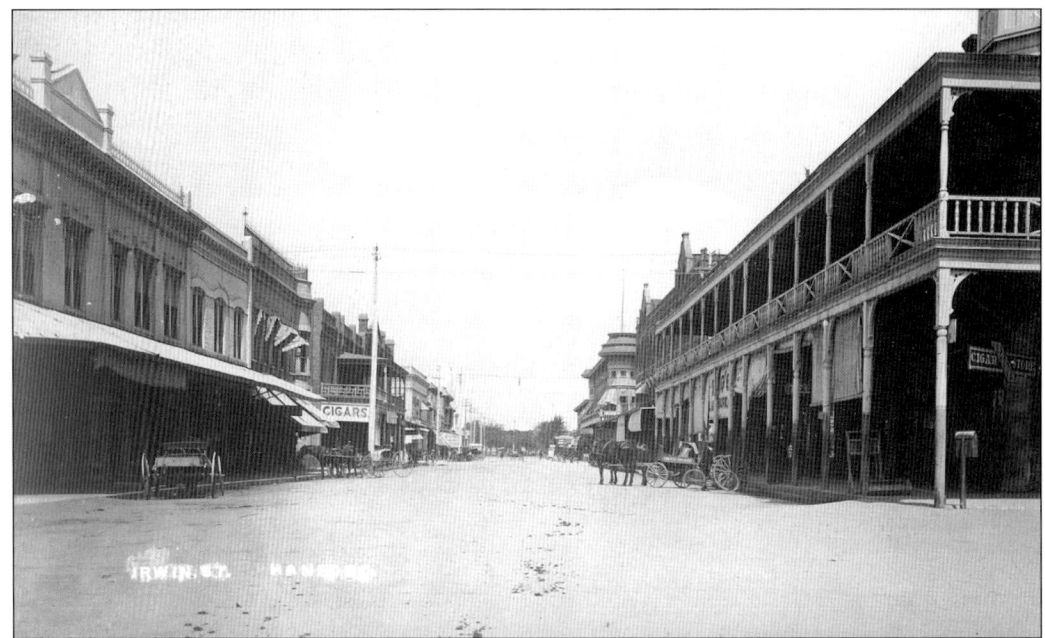

IRWIN STREET LOOKING NORTH FROM SIXTH STREET. This unused postcard, dated pre-1907, shows Irwin Street looking north. On the left side are the Bank of Hanford and the Sequoia Club Cigar Store. On the right side is the Artesia Hotel. The wagon parked in front of the hotel is an early taxi and has the name "Hanford Transfer" painted on it.

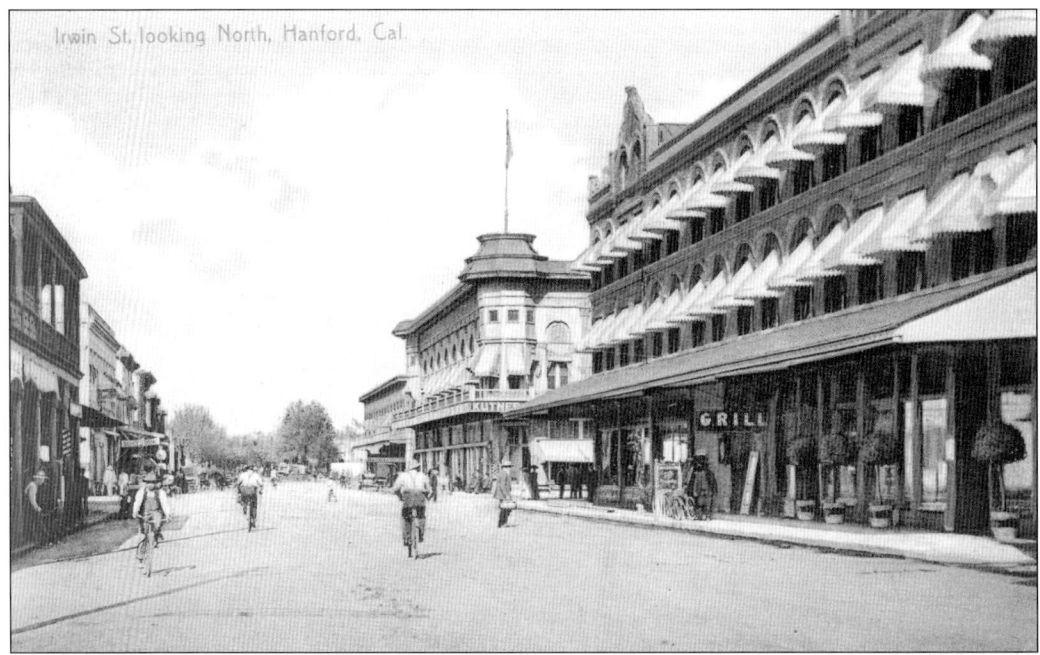

IRWIN STREET LOOKING NORTH FROM SIXTH STREET. This unused postcard shows the eastern side of Irwin Street. The building in the center is the Kutner-Goldstein Store and the building on the right is the Esrey Hotel. Located in the hotel was the Esrey Grill, a popular restaurant of the time.

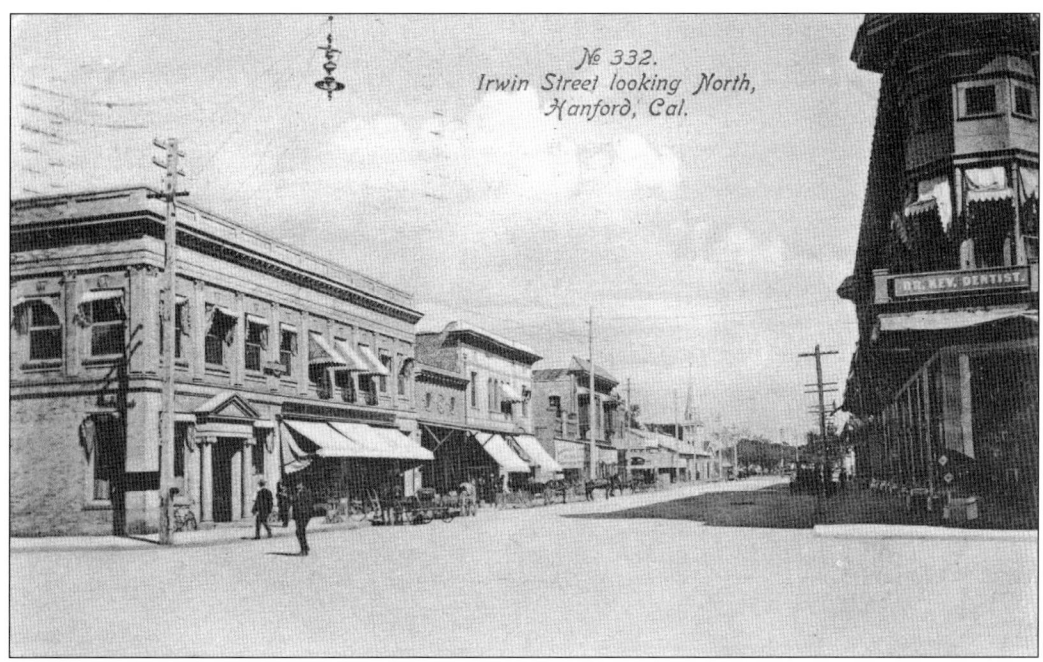

IRWIN STREET LOOKING NORTH. This postcard, published for Raney's Drug Store in Hanford, shows the Irwin Street business block between Seventh and Eight Streets. This block was considered one of the best business locations in Hanford.

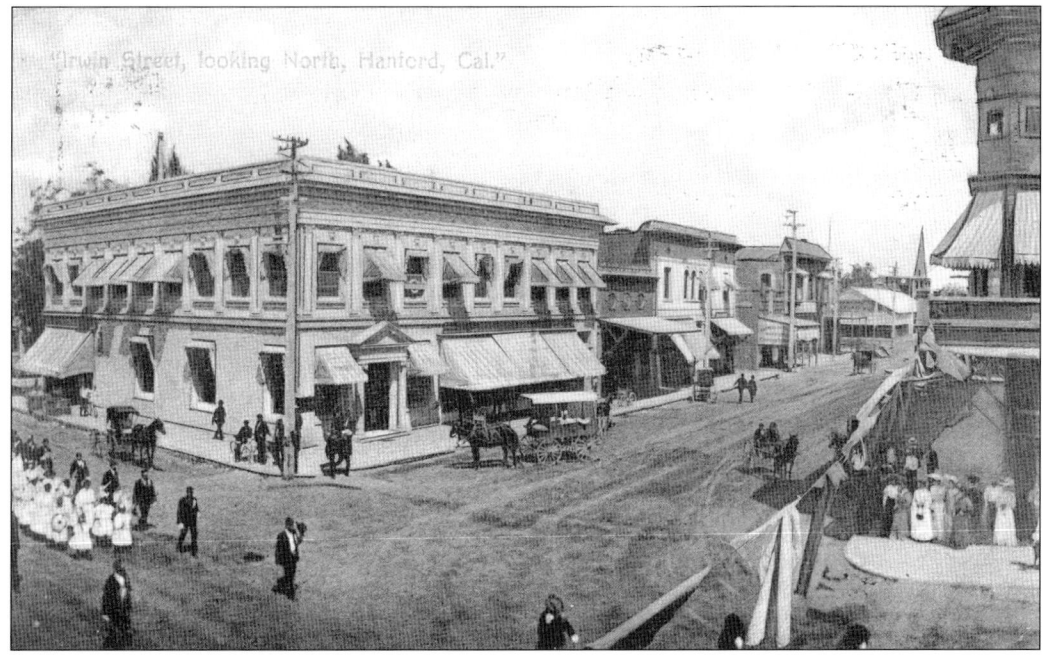

IRWIN STREET LOOKING NORTH. This card, postmarked in 1907, shows the First National Bank of Hanford that occupied the northwest corner of Seventh and Irwin Streets. A parade is pictured traveling east down Seventh Street.

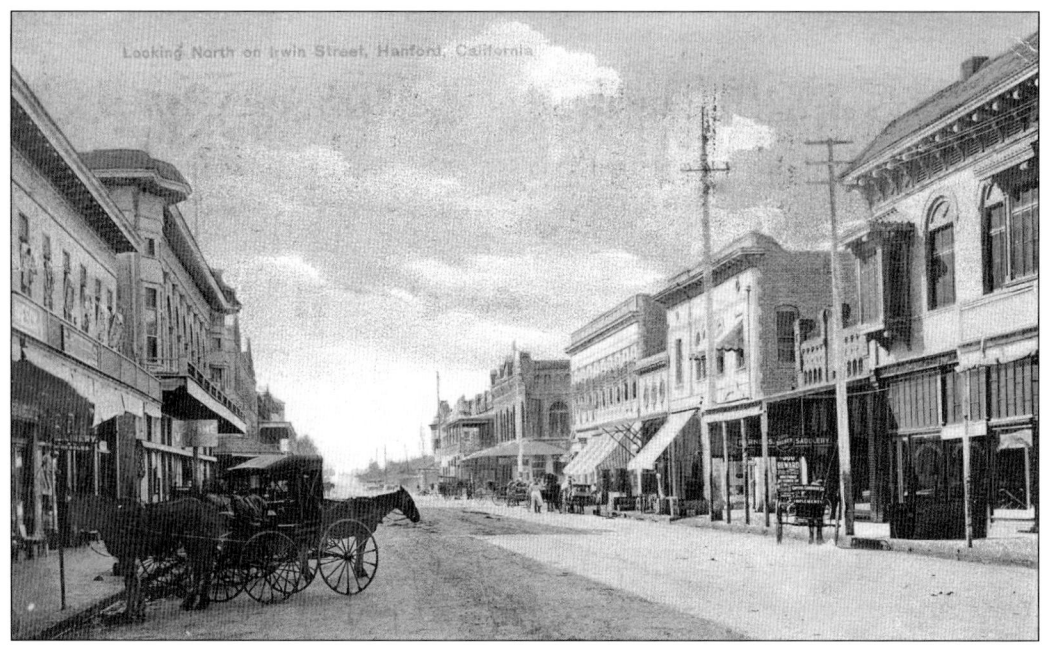

LOOKING SOUTH ON IRWIN STREET. This postcard is erroneously captioned. The view shows Irwin Street looking south from Eighth Street.

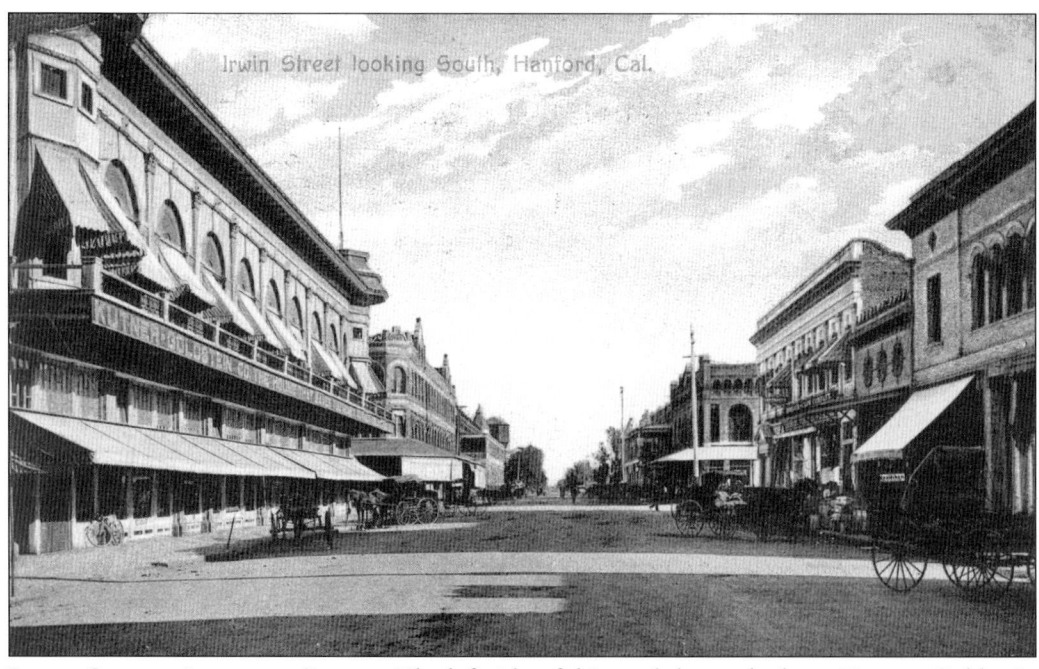

IRWIN STREET LOOKING SOUTH. The left side of this card shows the large Kutner-Goldstein Department Store. Kutner-Goldstein was a franchised variety store based in San Francisco, with locations throughout the Central San Joaquin Valley.

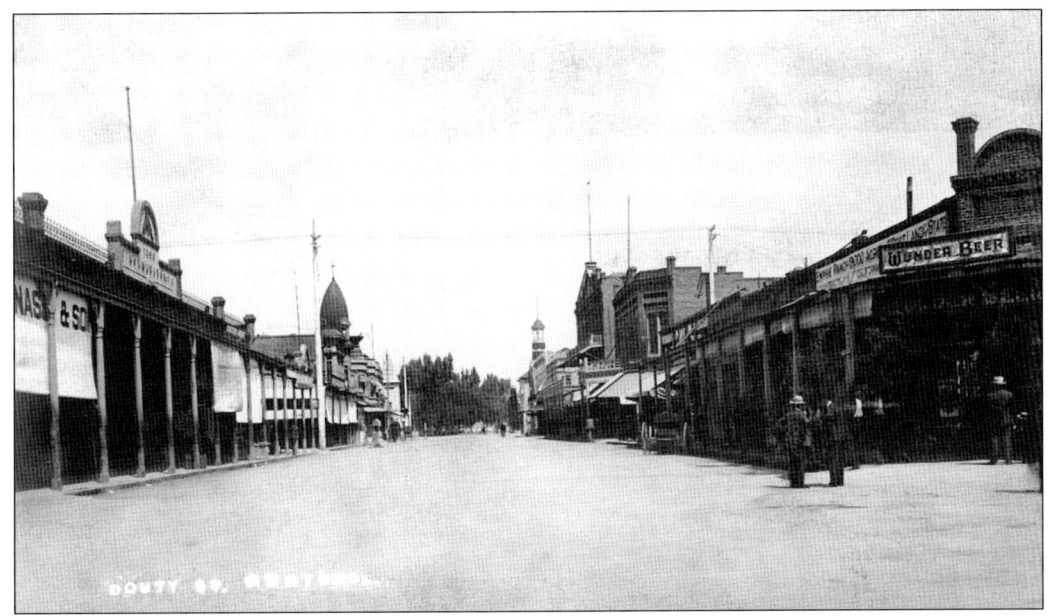

DOUTY STREET LOOKING NORTH FROM SIXTH STREET. This unused postcard has been dated to around 1906 and provides a view north on Douty Street. On the left is the Manasse and Sons Mercantile Store. On the right is a partial view of "Whiskey Row," a notorious area of Hanford where all the bars and pool halls were located. The building with the "Wunder Beer" sign was the Hughes Saloon. Next to that sign is an advertisement for "Empire Ranch, 18,000 acres of the best land in the state."

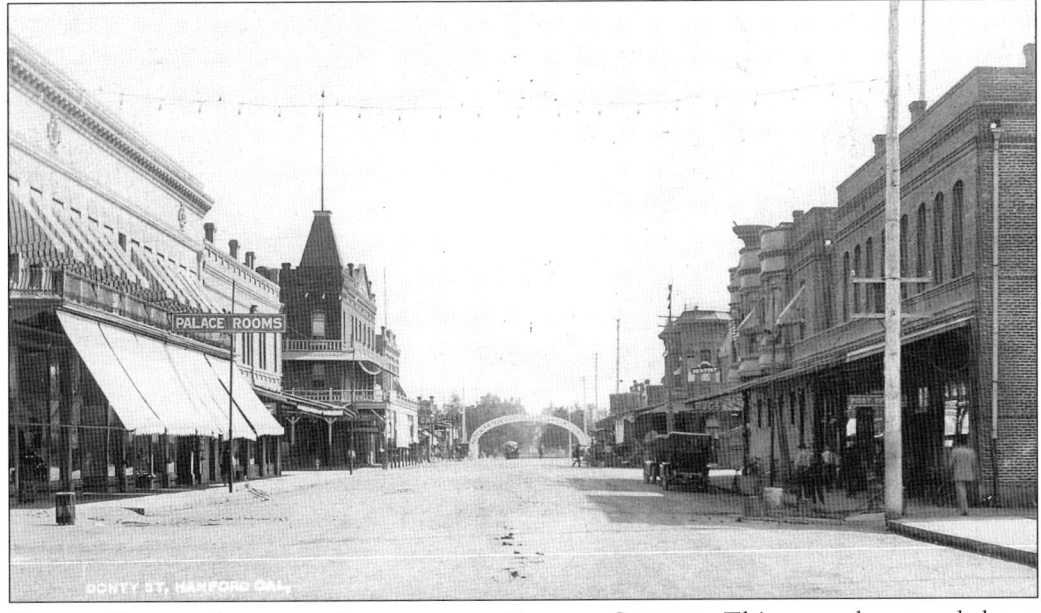

DOUTY STREET LOOKING SOUTH FROM EIGHTH STREET. This unused postcard shows Douty Street looking south past the Seventh Street intersection. Numerous businesses appear in this photograph including the Palace Apartments on the left and the post office on the right. Most of the buildings shown still exist today. The purpose of the arch across Douty Street is not known. (Courtesy Ron Burris.)

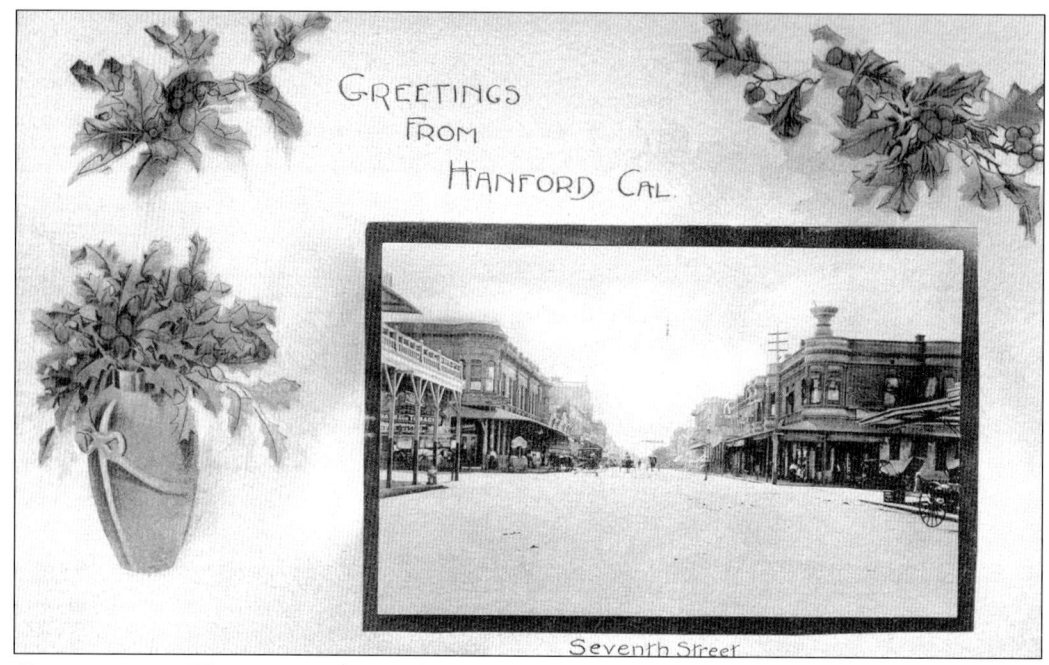

CHRISTMAS IN HANFORD. This card is captioned "Greetings from Hanford Cal" and shows a small view of Seventh Street looking west.

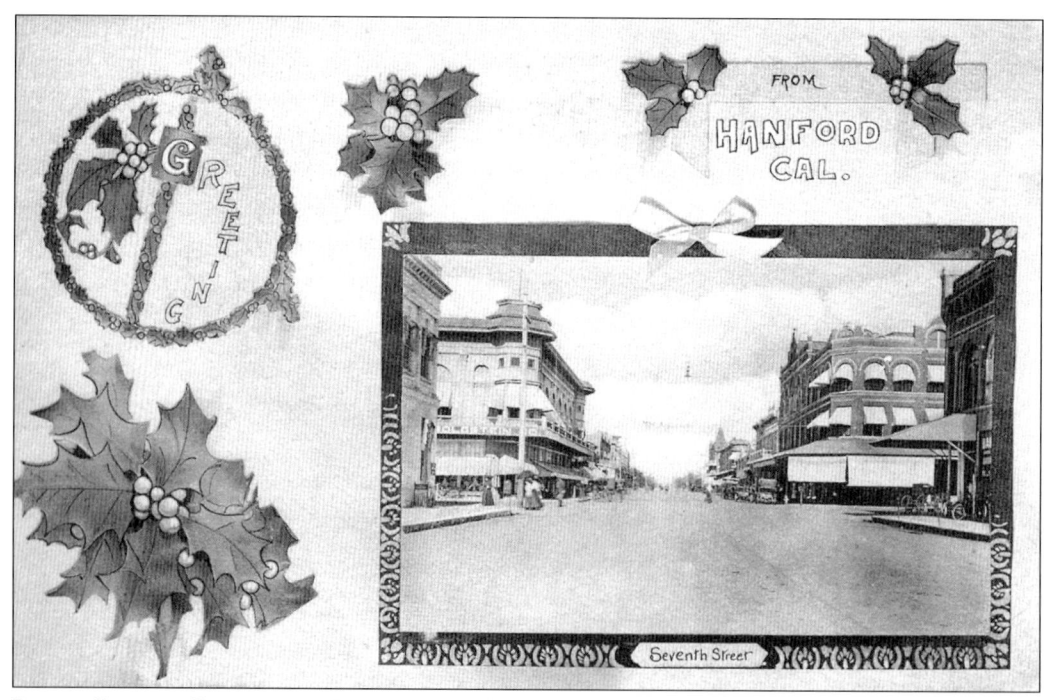

IRWIN STREET CHRISTMAS POSTCARD. This card has a small eastern view of the intersection of Irwin and Seventh Street.

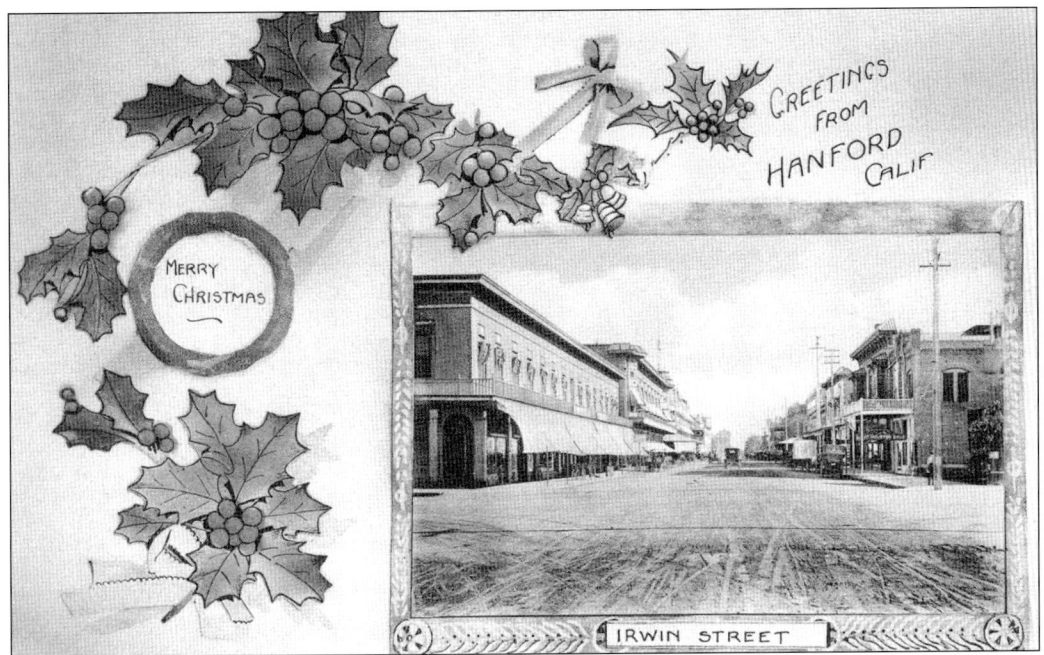

IRWIN AND EIGHTH AT CHRISTMAS. This postcard shows the intersection of Irwin and Eighth Streets.

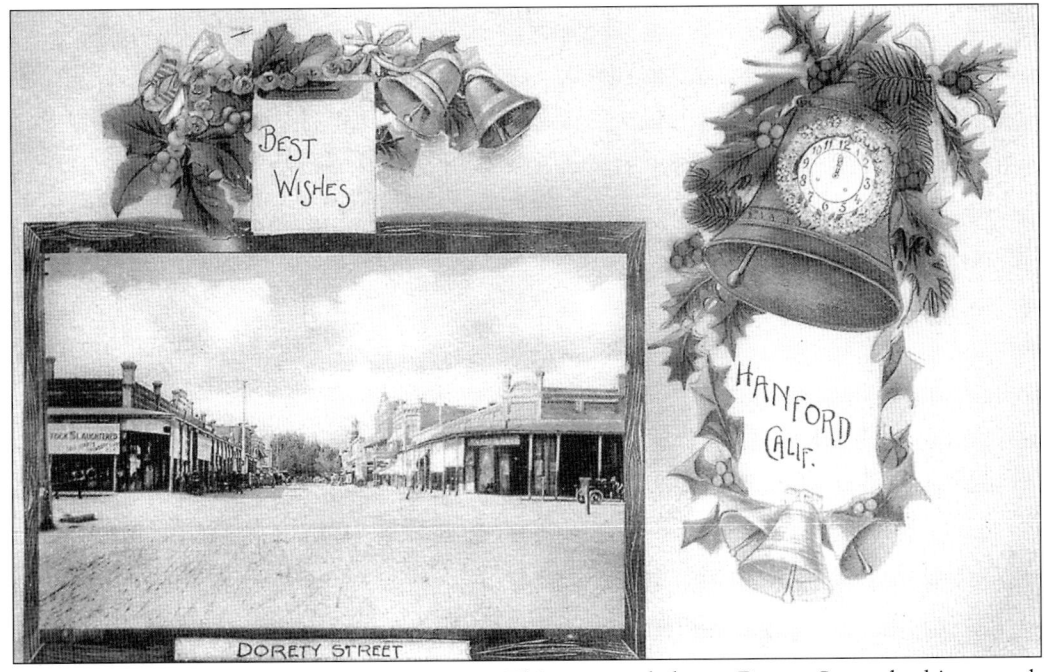

DOUTY STREET CHRISTMAS POSTCARD. This postcard shows Douty Street looking north from Sixth Street. It is erroneously identified as "Dorety Street."

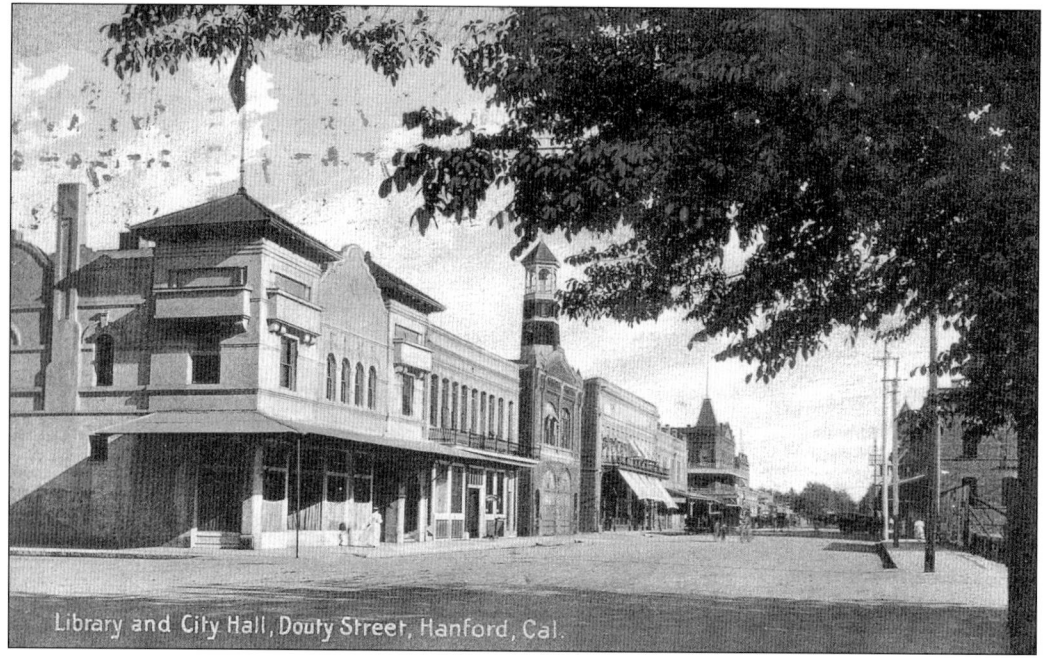

DOUTY STREET LOOKING SOUTH FROM EIGHTH STREET. This 1909 postmarked card depicts the southeast corner of Douty and Eighth Streets. The building on the left is the Hanford Masonic Hall. The building with the bell tower is the city hall/fire station.

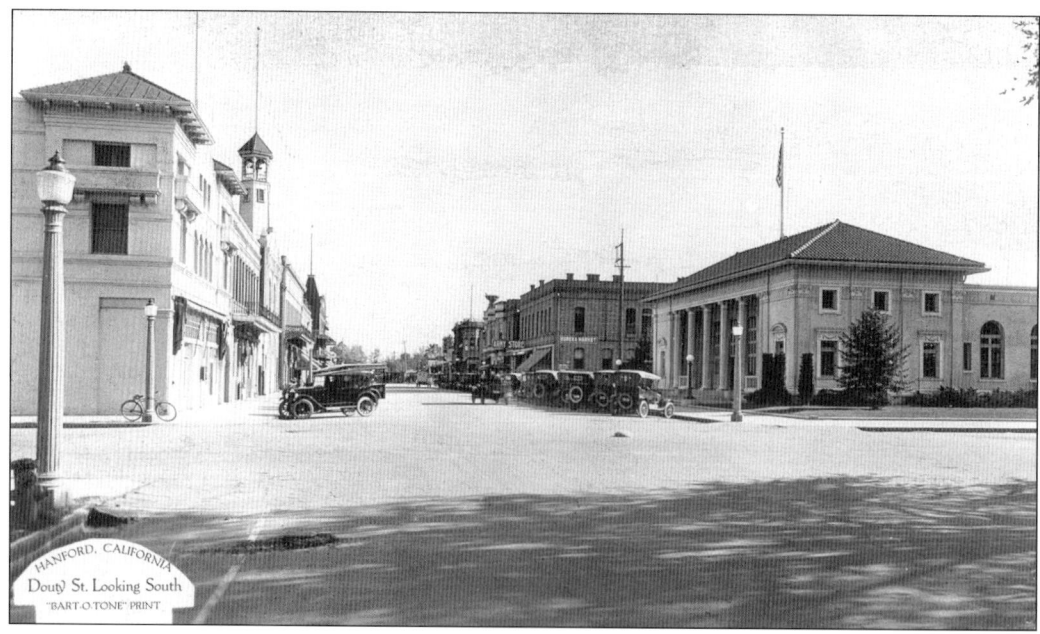

DOUTY STREET LOOKING SOUTH. This card, postmarked 1923, shows a southern view of Douty Street from Eighth Street. The building on the right is the Hanford Post Office.

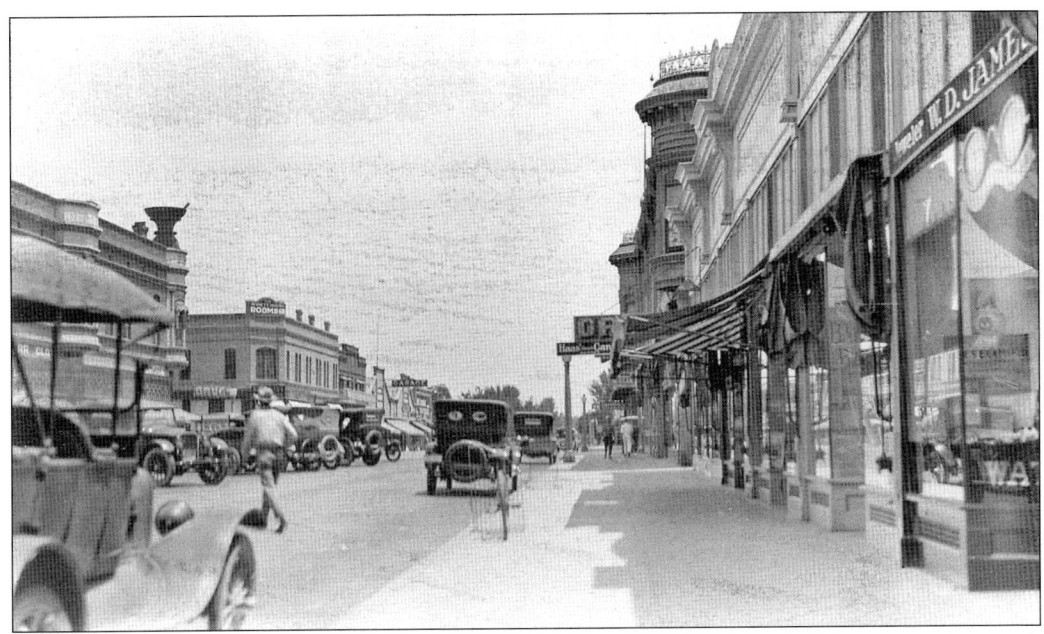

SEVENTH STREET LOOKING EAST. This rare postcard view shows the mid-block of Seventh Street. The W. D. James Jewelry Store is shown at right.

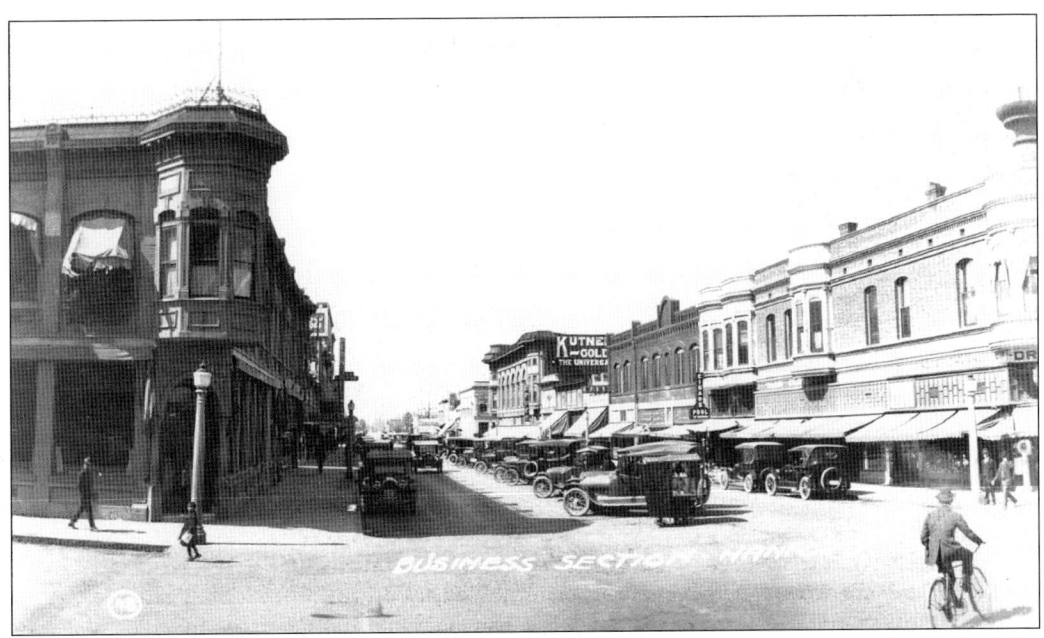

BUSINESS SECTION OF HANFORD. Seventh Street looks west during the early 1920s. The building on the left was the Farmers and Merchants Bank.

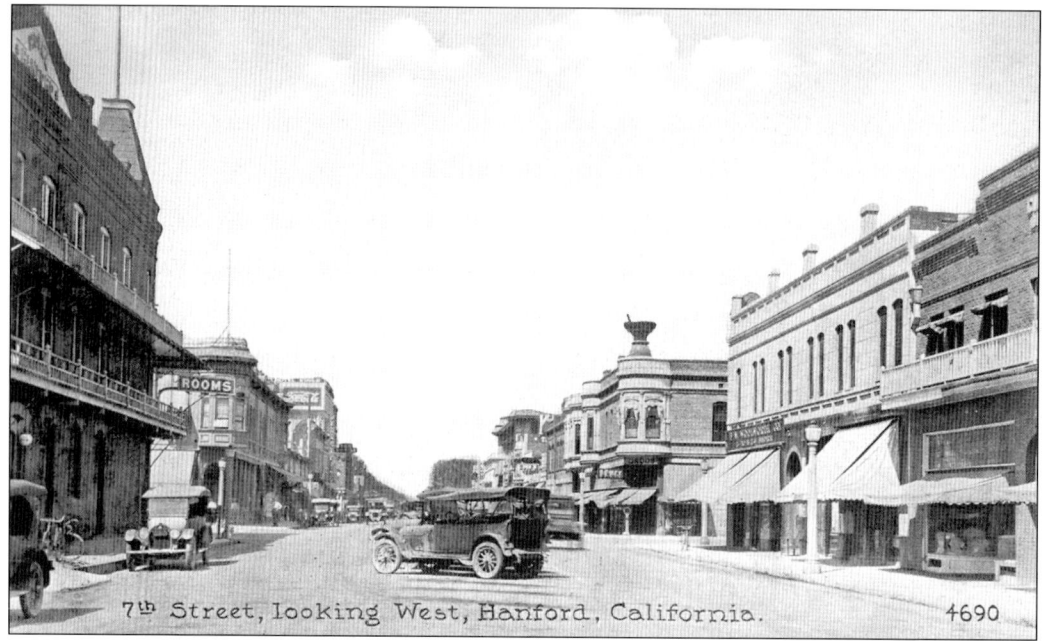

SEVENTH STREET LOOKING WEST. During the 1920s, the automobile became more prevalent in Hanford. To accommodate the increase in vehicular traffic, diagonal parking was allowed in the middle of the street.

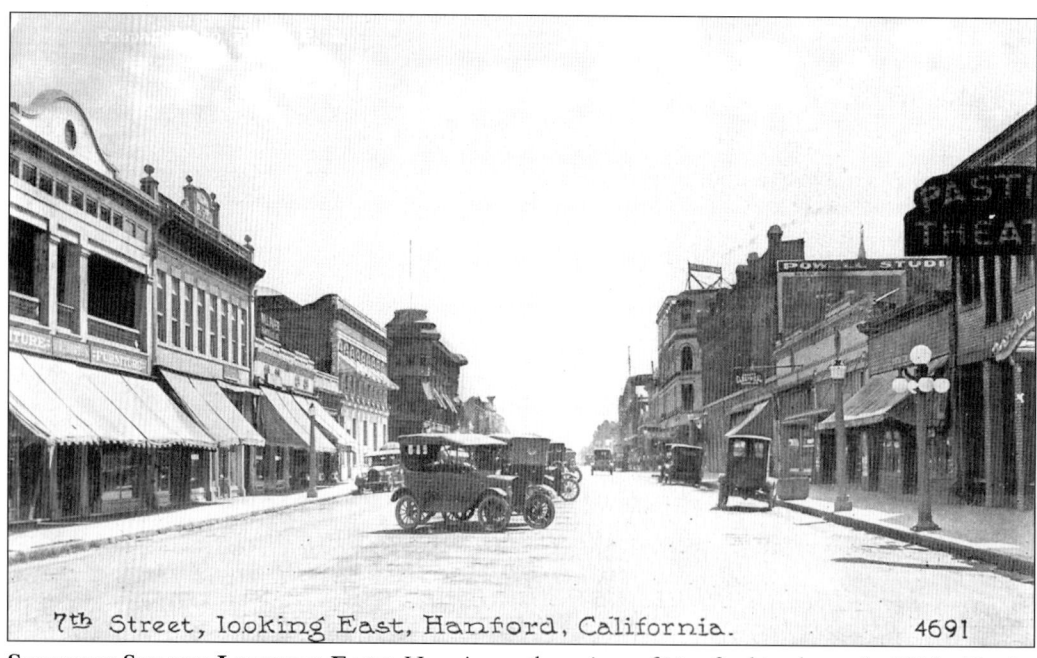

SEVENTH STREET LOOKING EAST. Here is another view of Hanford in the early 1920s. To the right and painted on the building is the sign "Powell Studio." L. W. Powell was an early Kings County photographer who established a photograph studio that existed until the early 1980s.

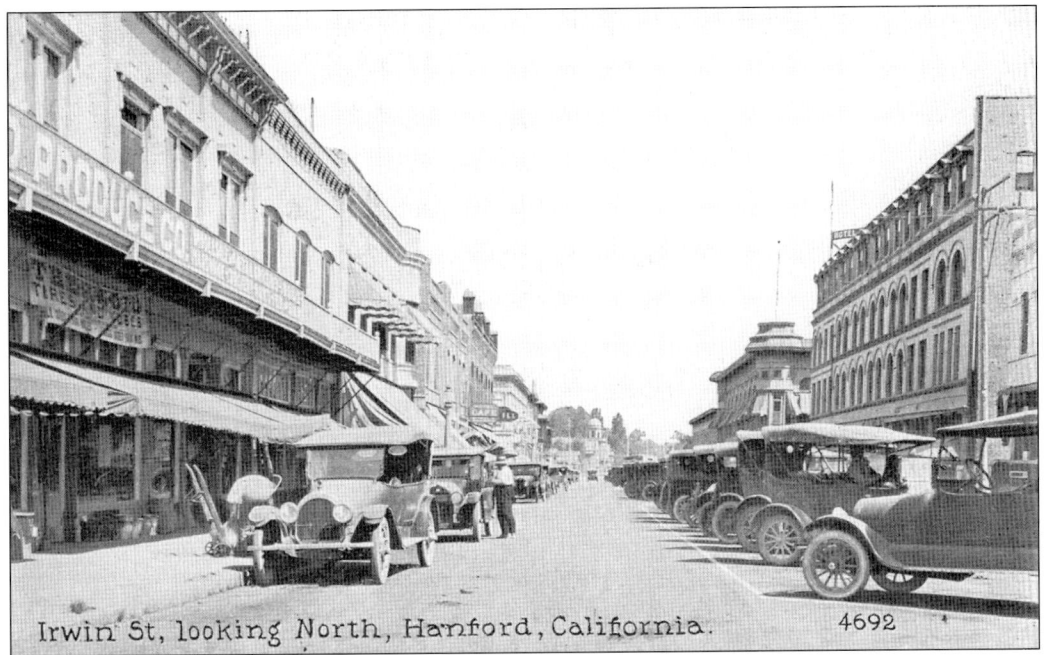

IRWIN STREET LOOKING NORTH. Irwin Street, between Sixth and Eighth Streets, was an extremely busy section of the downtown area. At the very end of the street is the Presbyterian church.

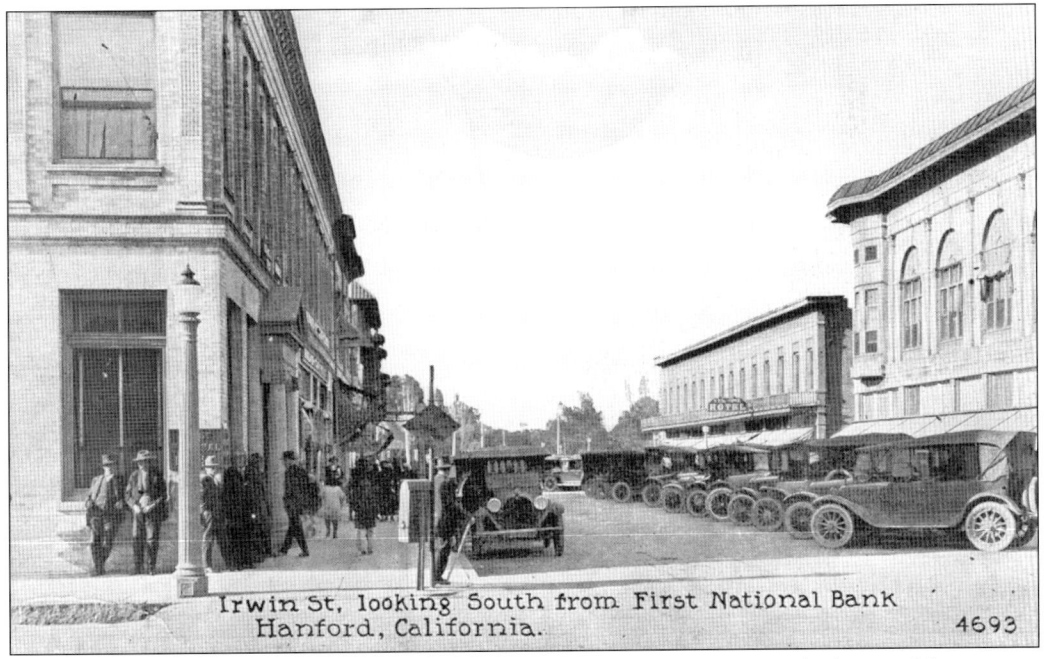

NORTH VIEW ON IRWIN. The corner of Seventh and Irwin Streets was the heart of downtown Hanford. The building on the left was the First National Bank of Hanford. The caption on this card is erroneous.

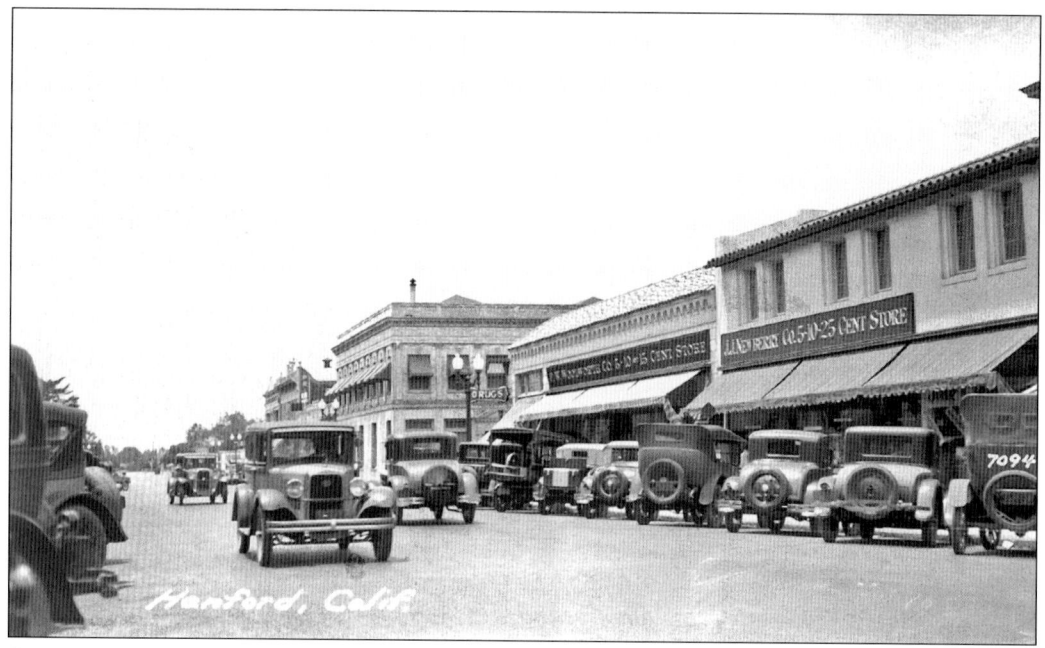

SEVENTH STREET LOOKING WEST. This unused 1930s postcard shows downtown Hanford during a busy afternoon. The building in the middle is the First National Bank of Hanford. In the middle is F. W. Woolworth and to the right is J. J. Newberry Company 5-10-25 Cent Store.

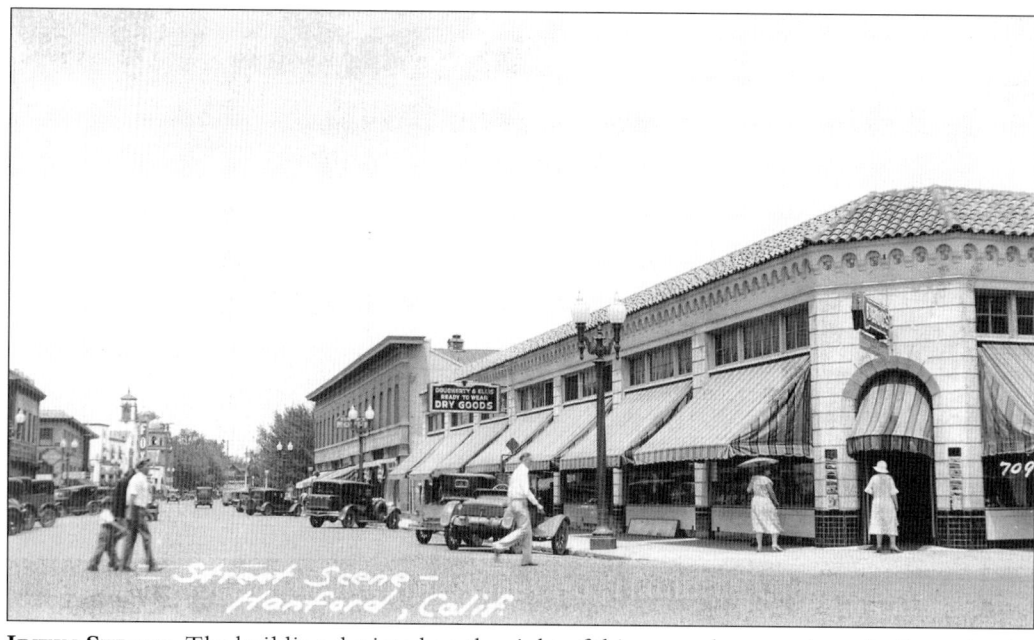

IRWIN STREET. The building depicted on the right of this unused postcard was built on the site of the old Kutner-Goldstein Store in 1930. In 1928, the Kutner-Goldstein Store burned down in a spectacular fire that almost leveled the entire city block.

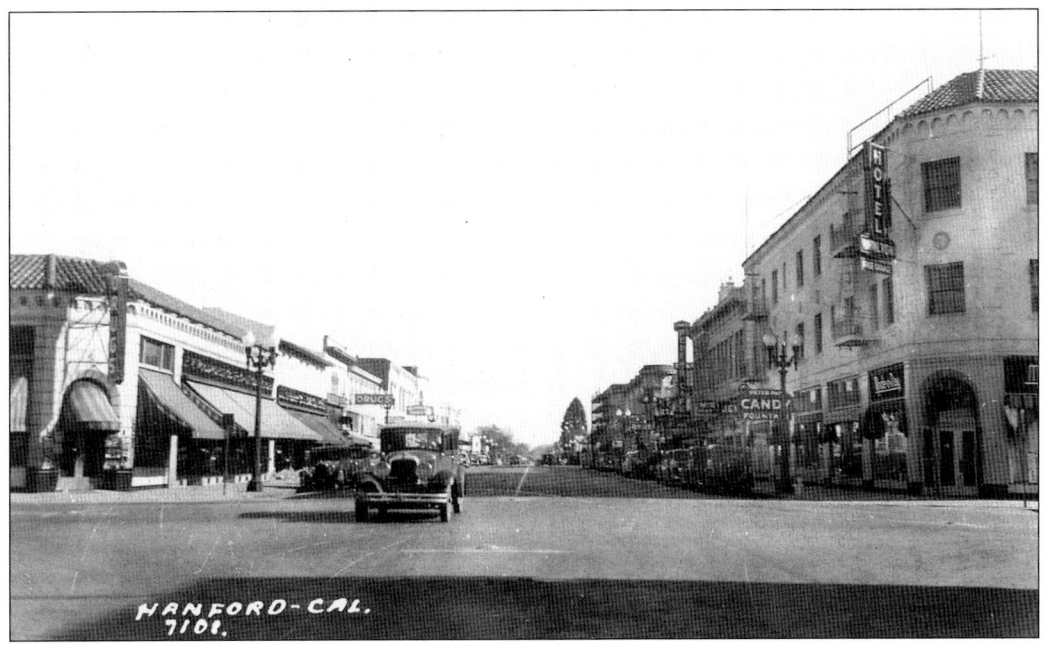

SEVENTH STREET LOOKING EAST. This unused postcard provides a 1930s glimpse of Seventh Street. The building on the left is the LaMoine Drug Store, on the site of the old Kutner-Goldstein Store. The building on the right is the Hotel Whilton, previously the Esrey Hotel.

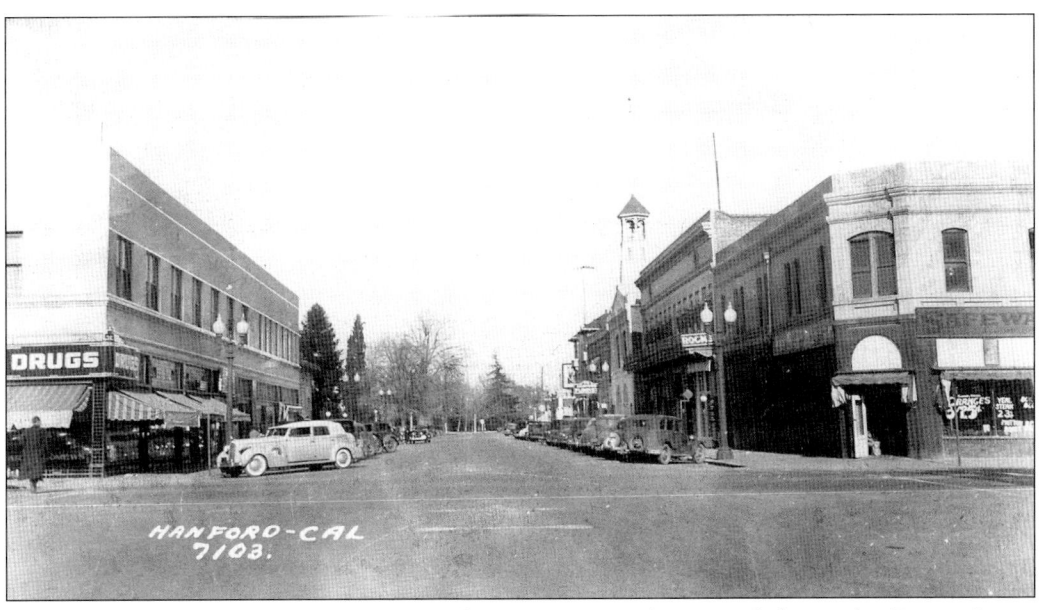

DOUTY STREET LOOKING NORTH. This 1930s unused postcard shows the Douty Street intersection looking north past Seventh Street. To the left is the Rexall Drug Store and to the right is the Safeway Grocery Store.

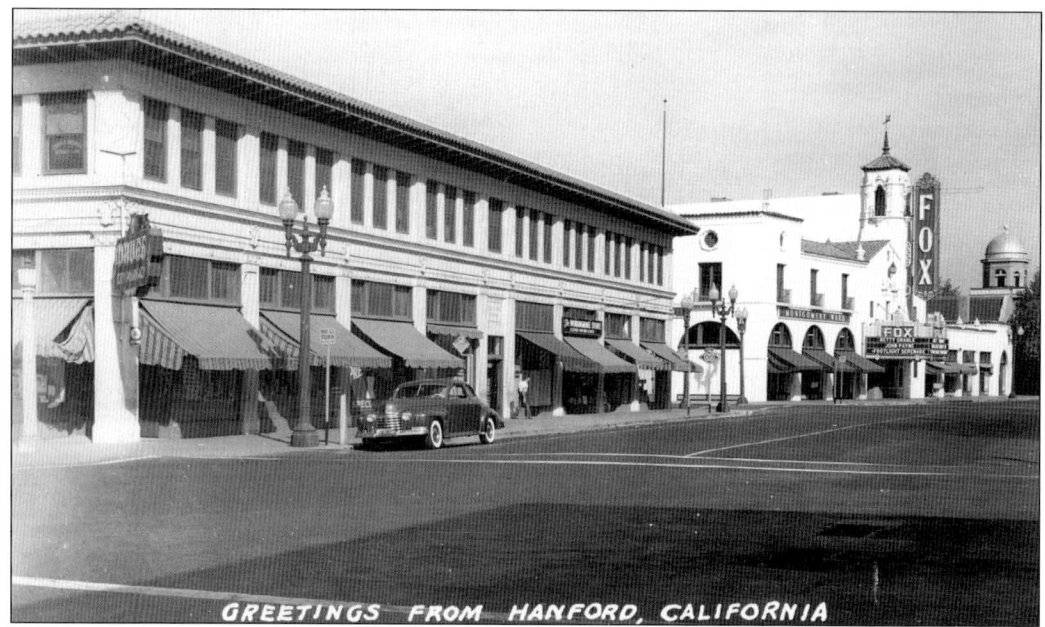

IRWIN STREET LOOKING NORTH. Irwin Street looks north toward Lacey Boulevard in this 1942 postcard. The building in the foreground is the Wealth Center Building. Next to it is the Fox Theatre, while the building with the dome on the right is the First Presbyterian Church. Showing at the theatre is *Moonlight Serenade*, which was released in 1942.

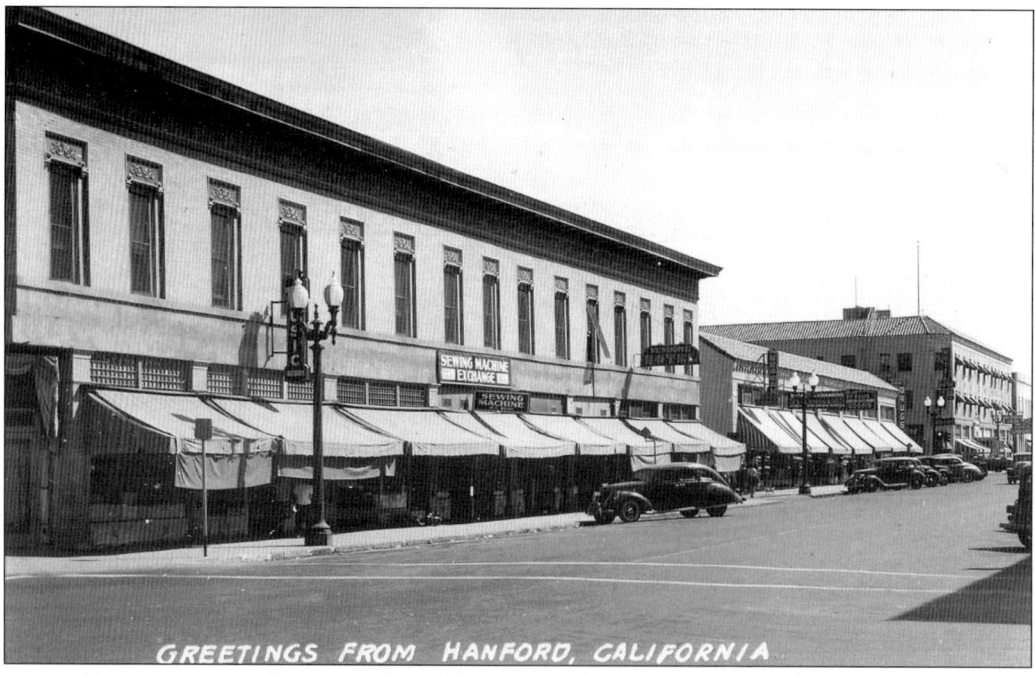

IRWIN STREET TO THE SOUTH. This 1942 postcard shows three separate buildings that line the east side of Irwin Street. The businesses shown include the Sewing Machine Exchange, Seamans Shoe Repair, and Branch and Chambers Stationery Store. The Hotel Whilton is on the right.

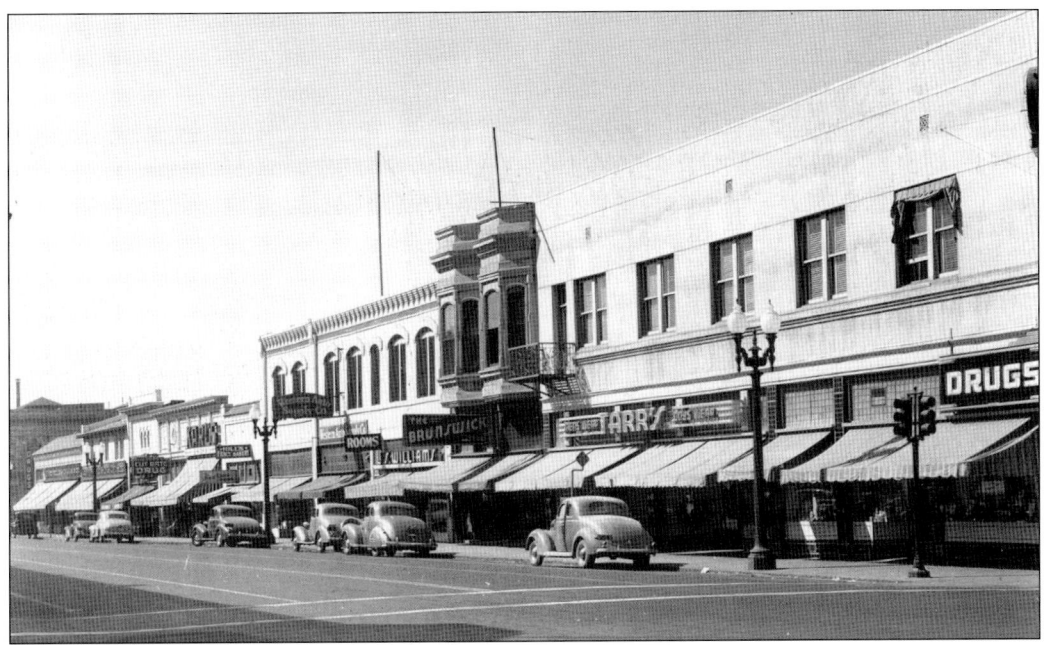

SEVENTH STREET, HANFORD. This 1942 postcard view shows the north side of Seventh Street between Douty and Irwin Streets. The businesses shown are the Econo Cut Rate Drug, Karl's Shoes, Hill's Bakery, Smart Dress Shop, Western Auto Supply, L. S. Williams, The Brunswick, Tarr's Men's Wear, and Rexall Drug Store.

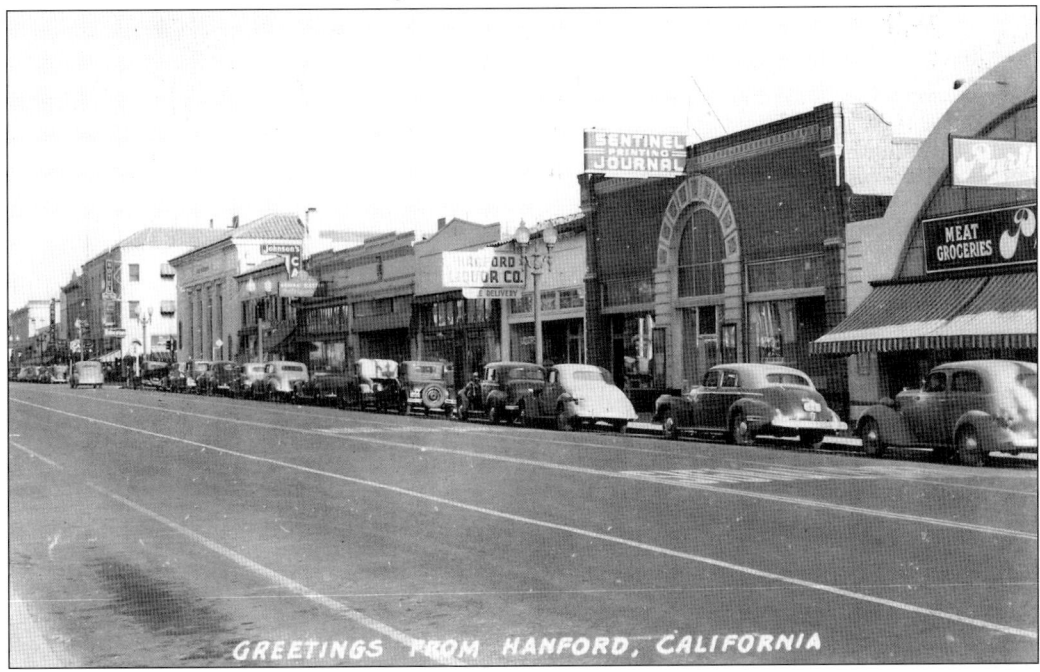

SEVENTH STREET, SOUTH SIDE. This rare 1942 view of the south side of Seventh Street provides a glimpse of the businesses that existed at that time. The buildings shown include the Hotel Whilton, the Bank of America Building, the Hanford Liquor Company, the Hanford Sentinel Building, and the Purity Grocery Store.

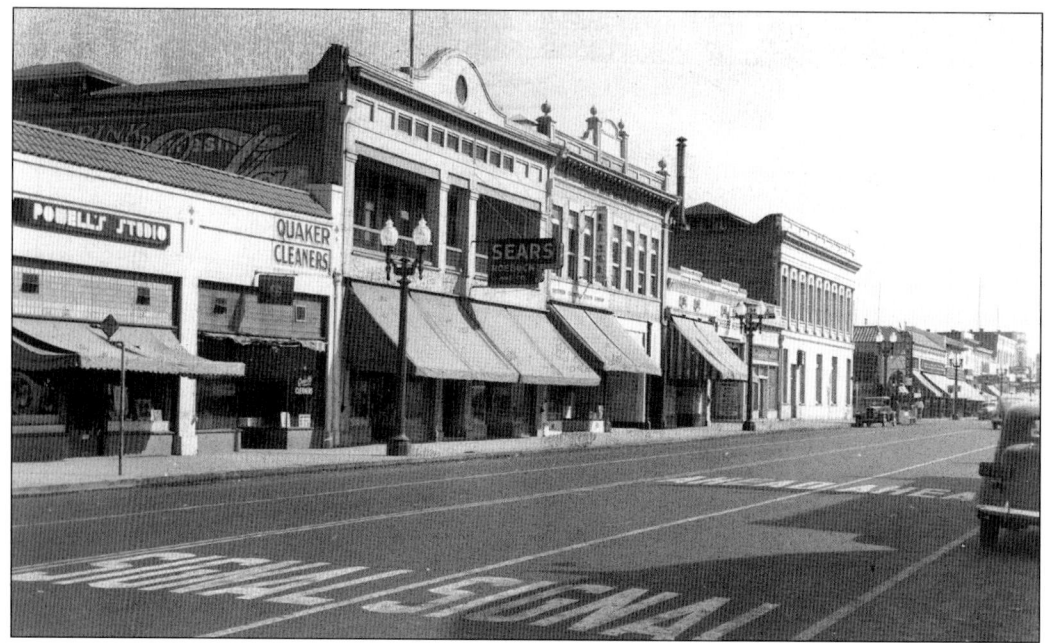

SEVENTH STREET, NORTH SIDE. This 1942 view of Seventh Street shows a variety of businesses that were located in the downtown area. Occupying the buildings shown were Powell's Studio, Quaker Cleaners, Sears, Southern California Edison, Driskell's Appliances, and the First National Bank of Hanford.

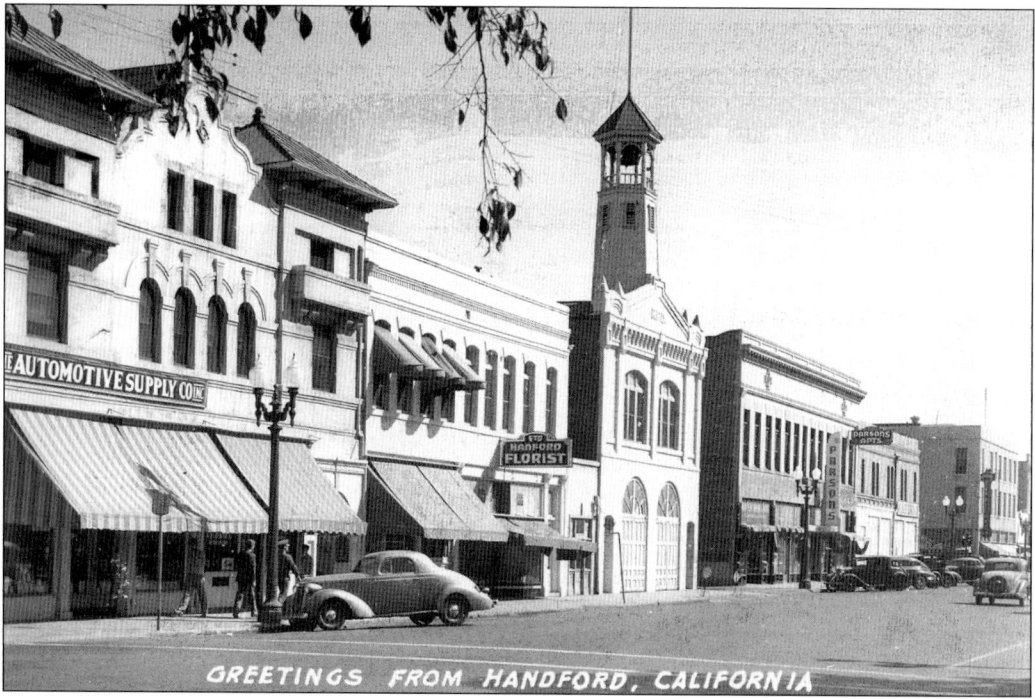

DOUTY STREET, EAST SIDE. The Masonic Lodge, the Phone Building, Hanford Fire Department, the Parson's Apartments, and the Safeway Grocery Store line the east side of the street in this 1942 postcard.

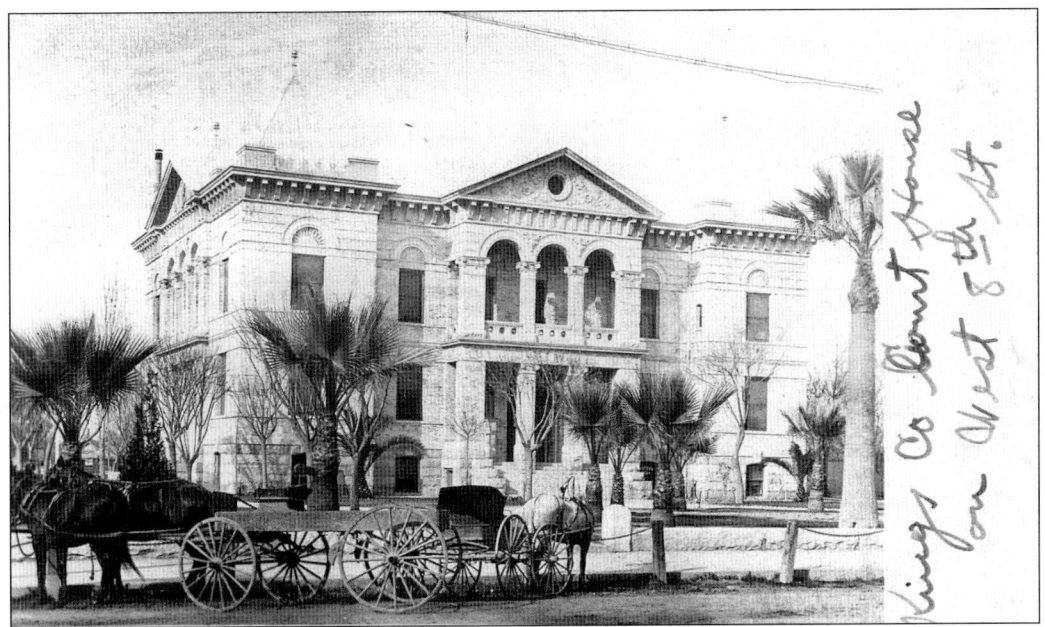

KINGS COUNTY COURTHOUSE. The courthouse building was designed by W. H. Wilcox and built in 1897 by John Hagerty at a cost of $26,364. Neoclassical in design, it was the center of government for Kings County until 1977. Shown in this pre-1905 postcard are wagons parked on the south side of the building. (Courtesy Ron Burris.)

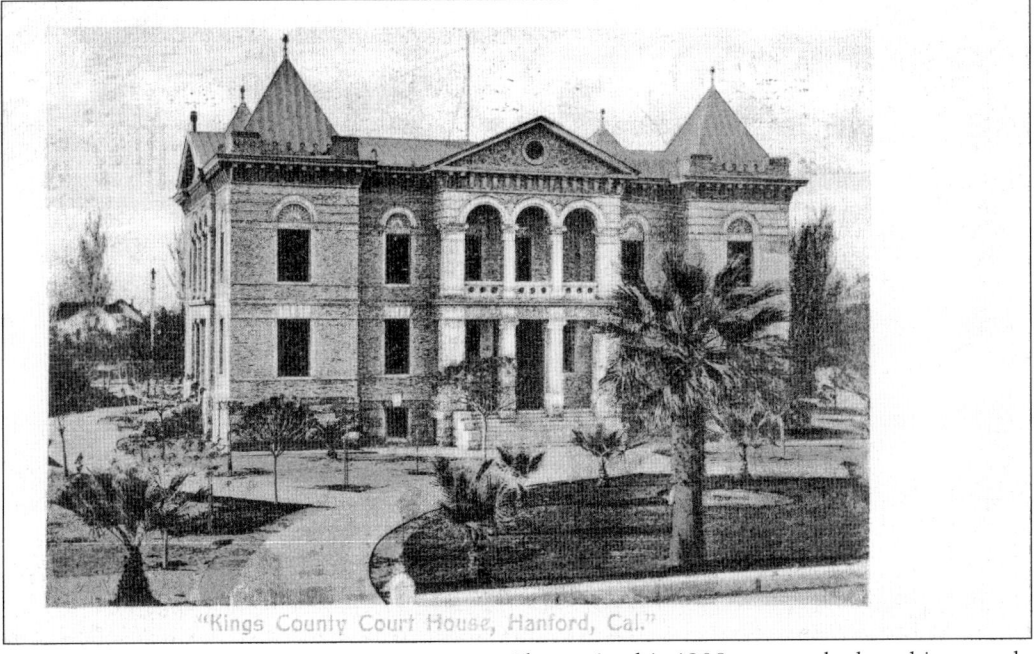

KINGS COUNTY COURTHOUSE, HANFORD. Shown in this 1908 postmarked card is an early view of the courthouse. The original plan for the building called for a dome to be built in the center, but it became cost prohibitive.

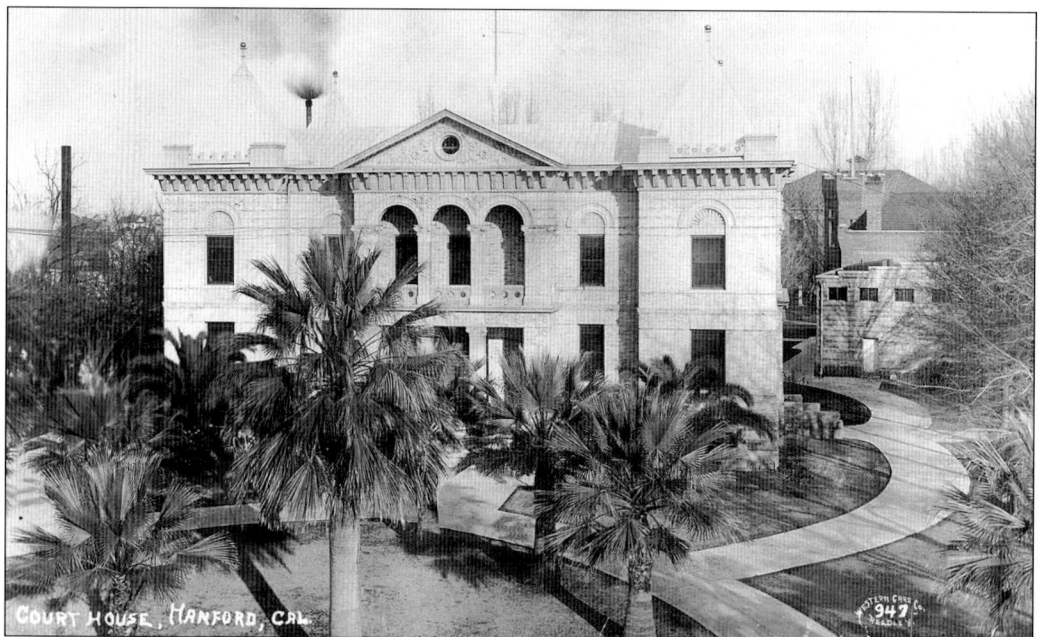

COURTHOUSE, HANFORD. The site of this building was originally occupied by the residence of Dr. Davidson, who planted the taller palm trees shown in this 1913 postmarked card. The castle turret on the right is the Kings County Jail.

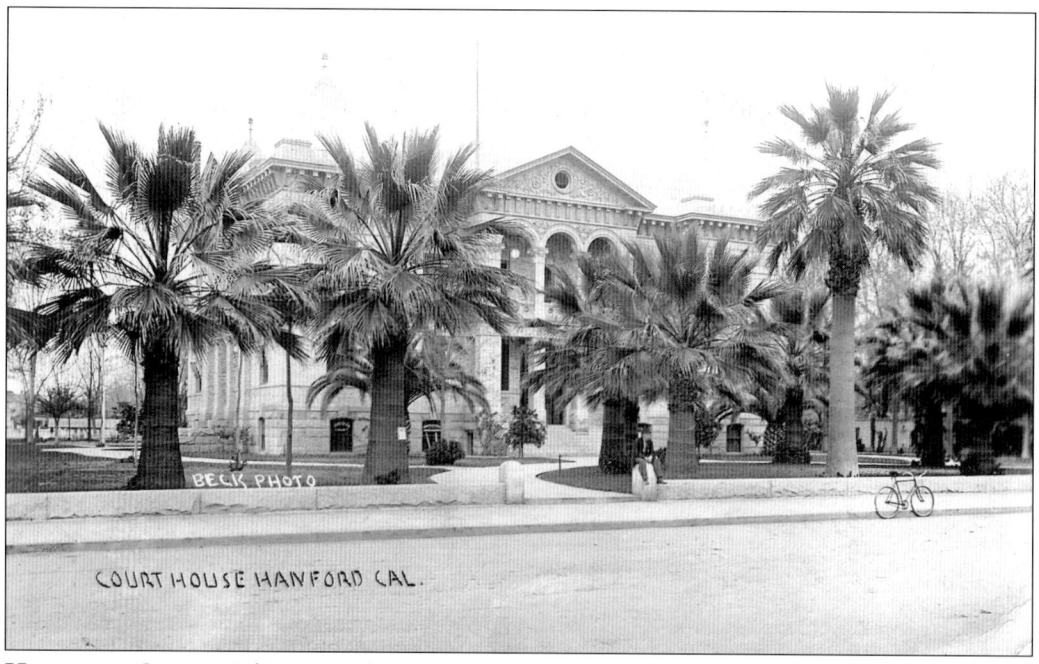

HANFORD COURT. This unused 1910s postcard shows larger palm trees on the courthouse grounds and a local individual taking a break next to the courthouse gate.

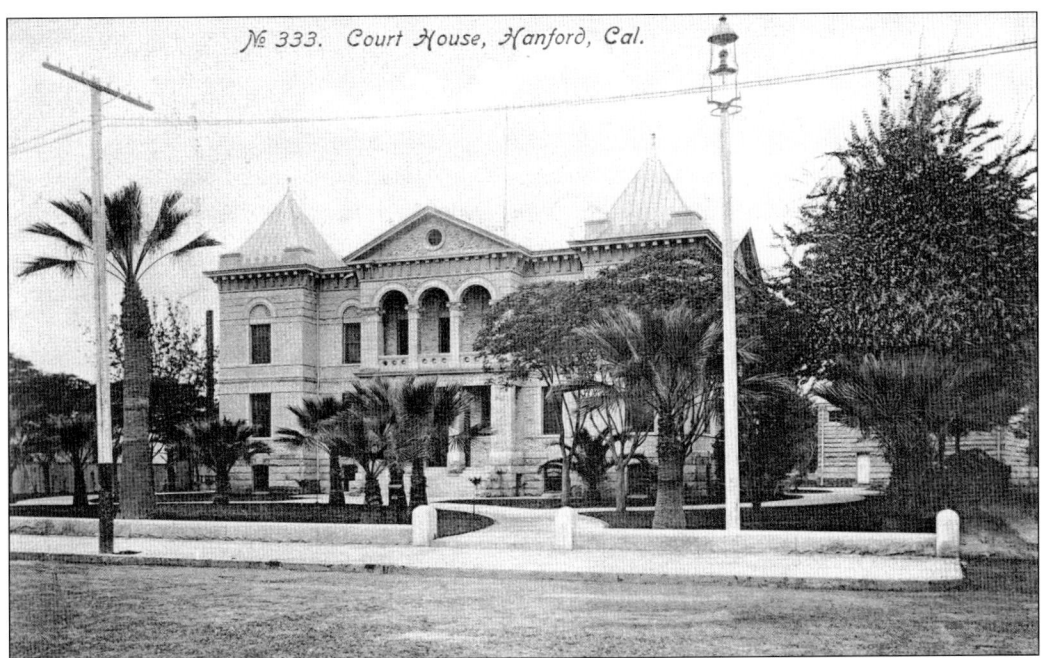

SEE YOU IN COURT. Here is another view of the courthouse on a 1907 postcard. The Kings County Courthouse was widely depicted in many different postcards. This card was published for Raney's Drug Store in Hanford.

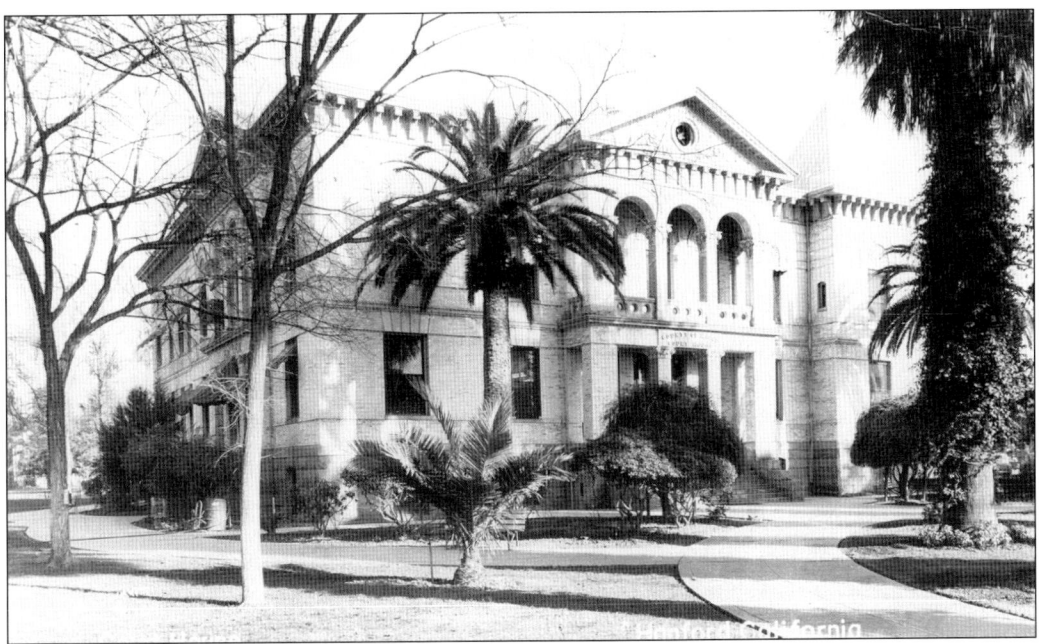

KINGS COUNTY COURTHOUSE, HANFORD. This 1940s postcard shows a more modern view of the courthouse. In 1914, the courthouse was expanded (the addition can be seen on the left side of the building). In 1977, the county government abandoned this building in favor of a new government complex that was built one mile to the west. After being remodeled in the early 1980s, it is currently home to various businesses.

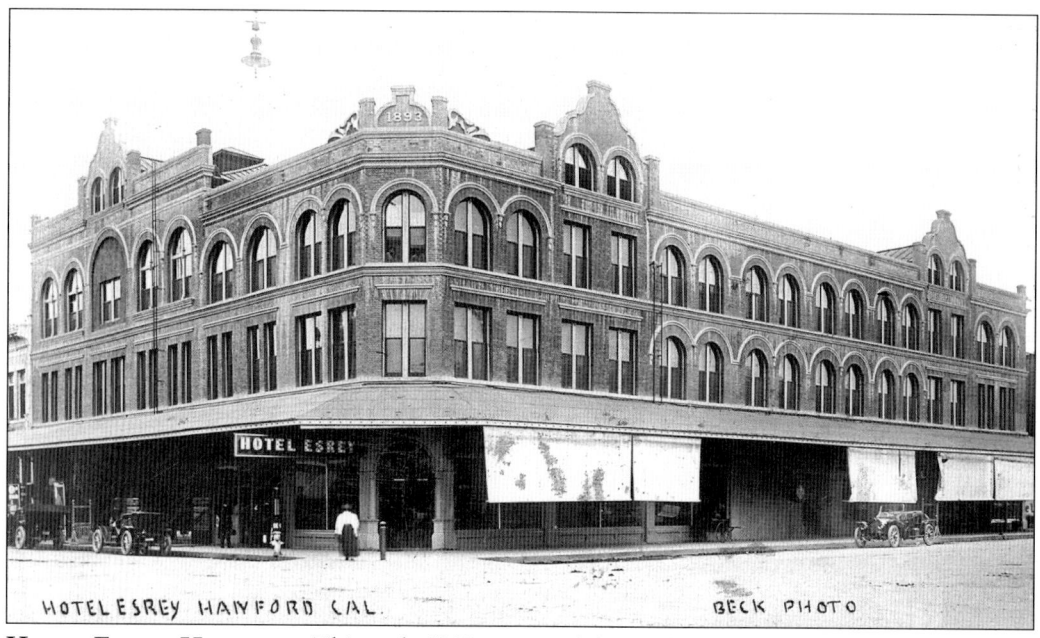

Hotel Esrey, Hanford. This early 1910s postcard shows the Hotel Esrey, which was located in the Opera House on the southeast corner of Irwin and Seventh Streets.

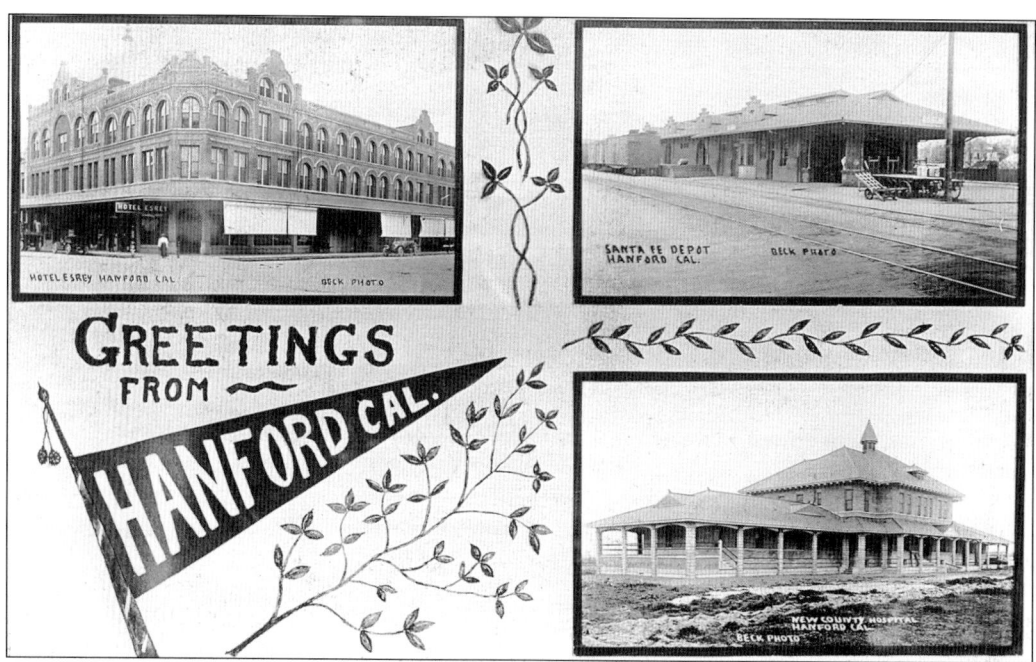

Multi-View Postcard, Hanford. This unused postcard was printed to depict various prominent buildings located in the city of Hanford. Also shown on these two pages are the actual postcards.

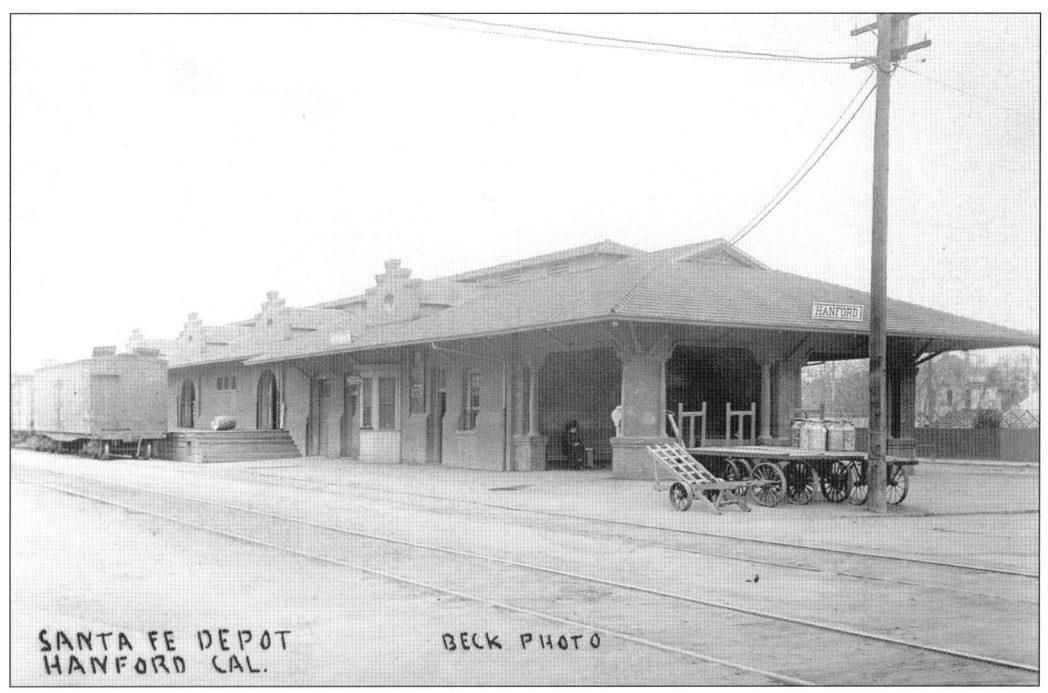

SANTA FE TRAIN DEPOT, HANFORD. This postcard shows the Santa Fe Train Depot as it appeared in 1910. It was originally built in 1897 for the San Francisco & San Joaquin Valley Railroad.

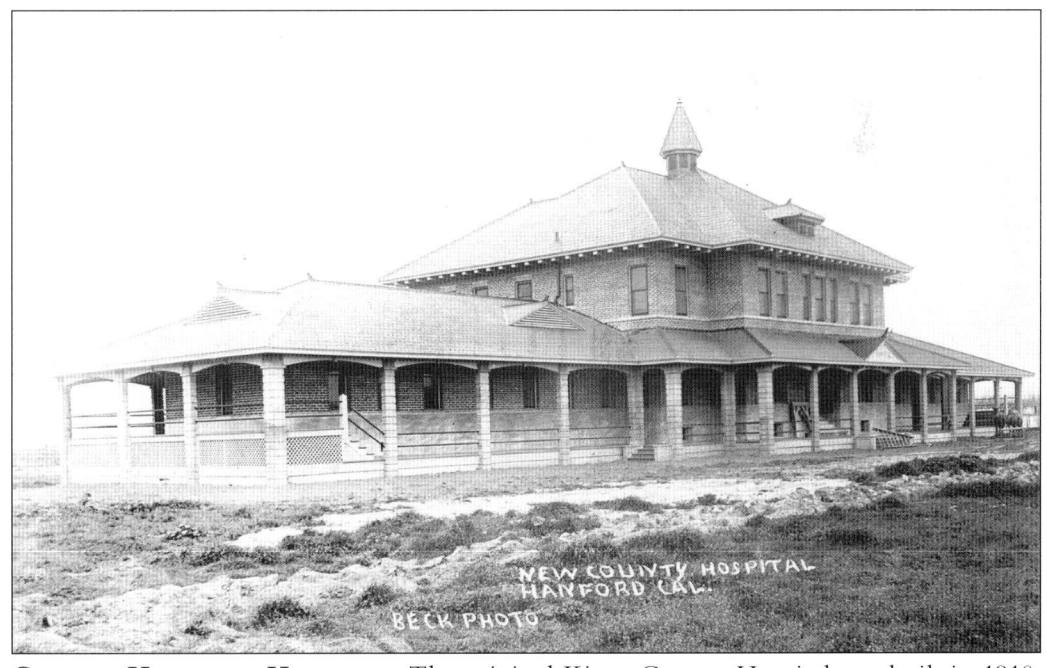

COUNTY HOSPITAL, HANFORD. The original Kings County Hospital was built in 1910. Originally it had 33 rooms and a small surgery suite. Later it was greatly expanded and served as the county hospital until 1973. It is currently occupied by various Kings County departments.

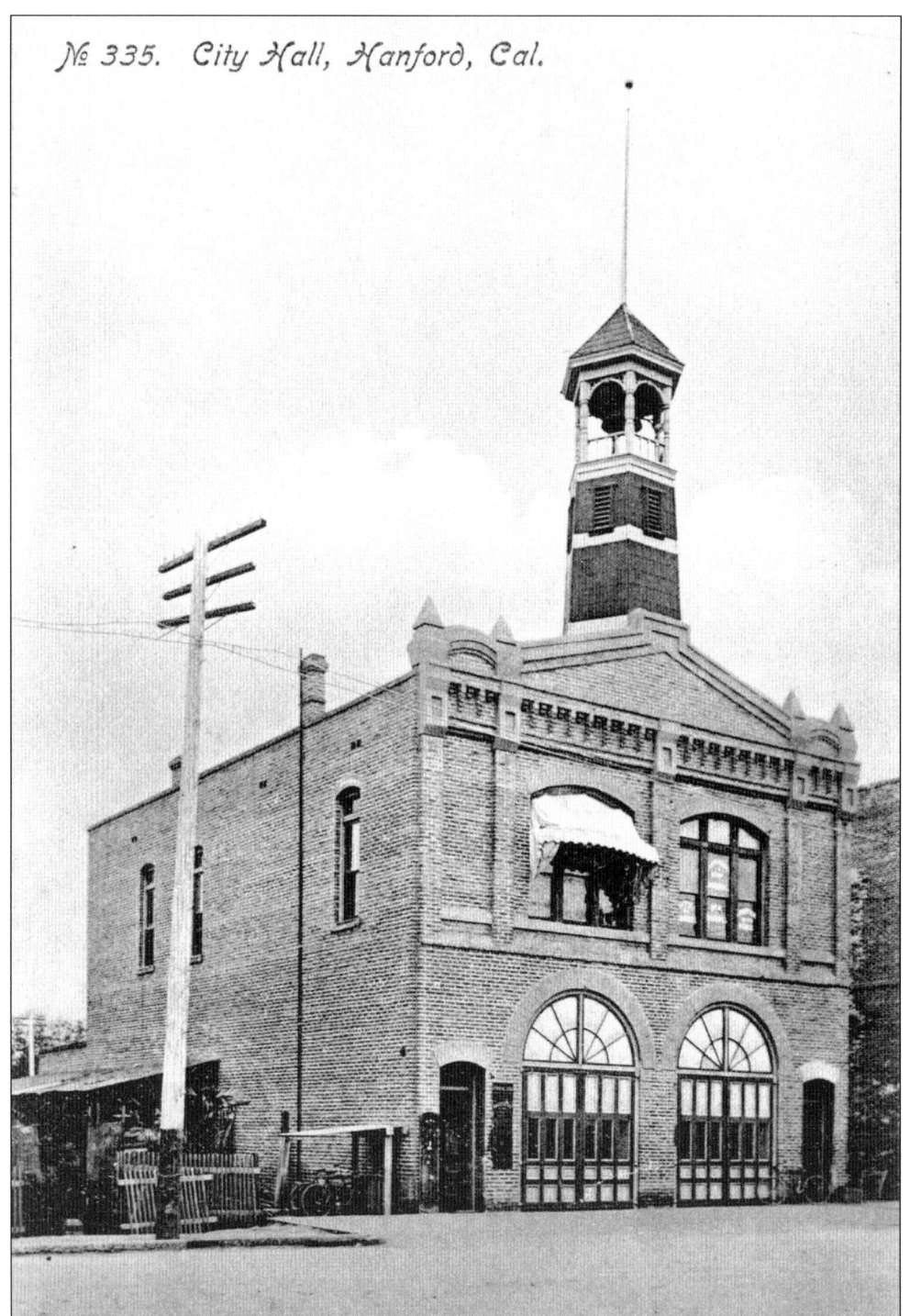

HANFORD FIRE. This building housed the Hanford City offices and the Hanford Fire Department. The building was designed by the architectural firm of Little and French and was built in 1894 by J. M. Robertson of Hanford. It was used by the city until the Lacey Boulevard station was built in 1939.

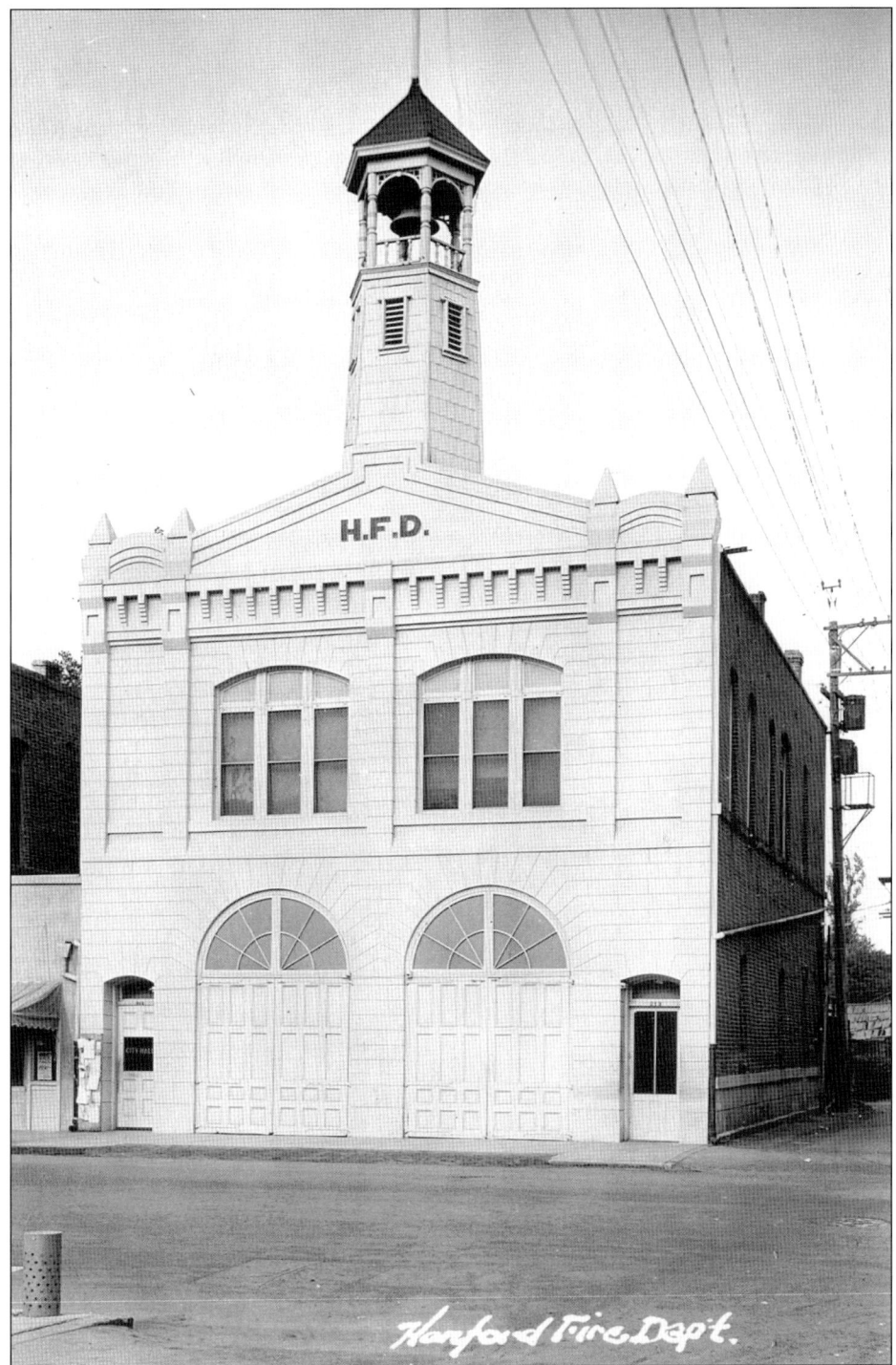

HANFORD FIRE DEPARTMENT. This late 1910s unused postcard depicts the west side of the Hanford Fire Department. During the Second World War, the bell was destined for the scrap bin, but it was saved and hidden by local citizens until after 1945. The bell is now displayed in front of the new fire station located on Grangeville Boulevard.

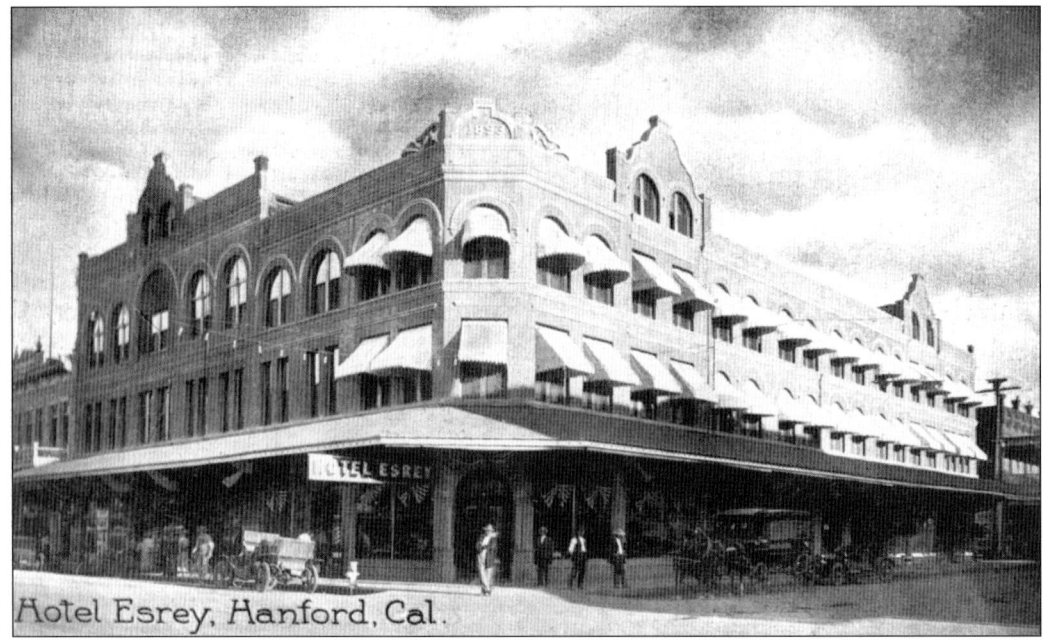

HOTEL ESREY, HANFORD. The Hotel Esrey was considered one of the finer establishments in Hanford. The building was constructed in 1893 at a cost of $65,000 by the English firm of Robinson and Rawlins. The building temporarily housed the offices of Kings County from 1893 until 1896, when the new courthouse was built.

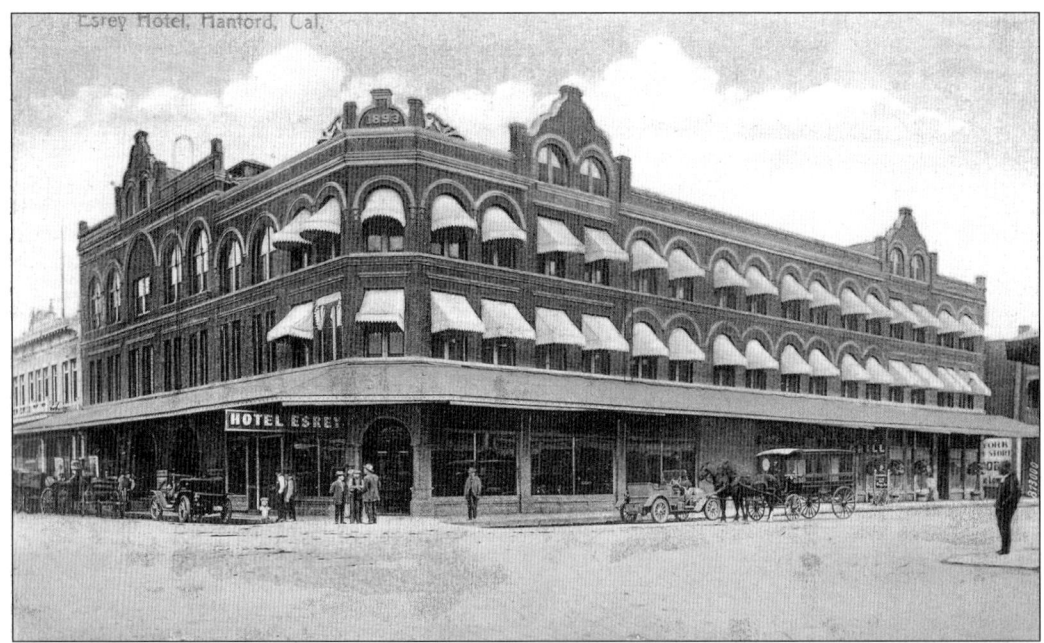

THE HOTEL ESREY. This postcard, mailed in 1911, shows the Hotel Esrey, which operated in the Opera House located on the southeast corner of Seventh and Irwin Streets. The left side of the building housed a theatre that had a seating capacity of 700. Below the hotel sign was the Esrey Liquor Store.

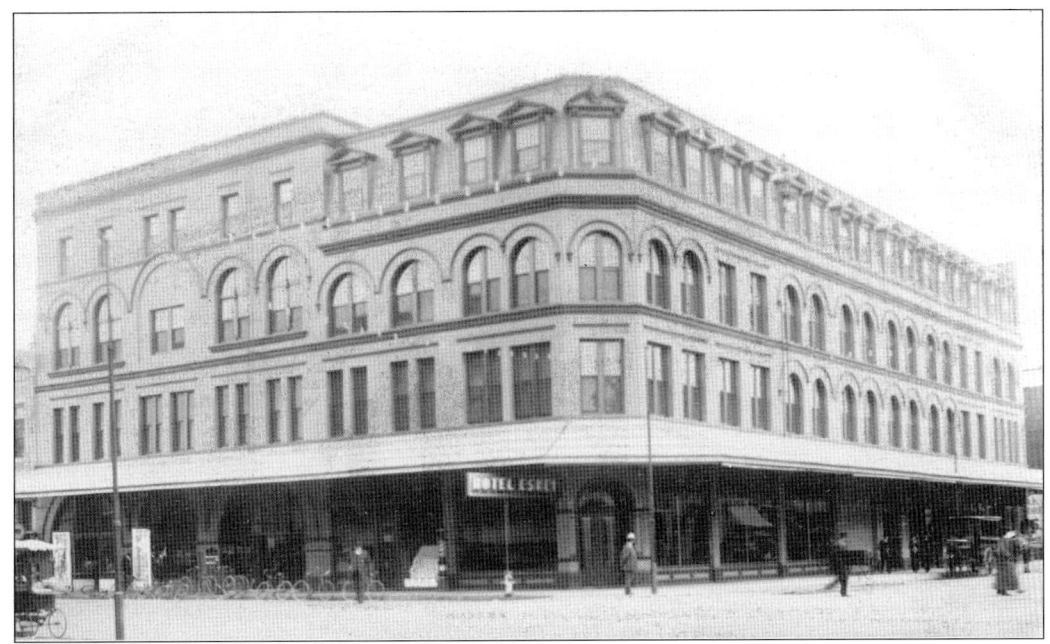

OPERA HOUSE, HANFORD. This postcard was dated January 1, 1913, and shows the Opera House after the fourth floor was added. (Courtesy James Hickman.)

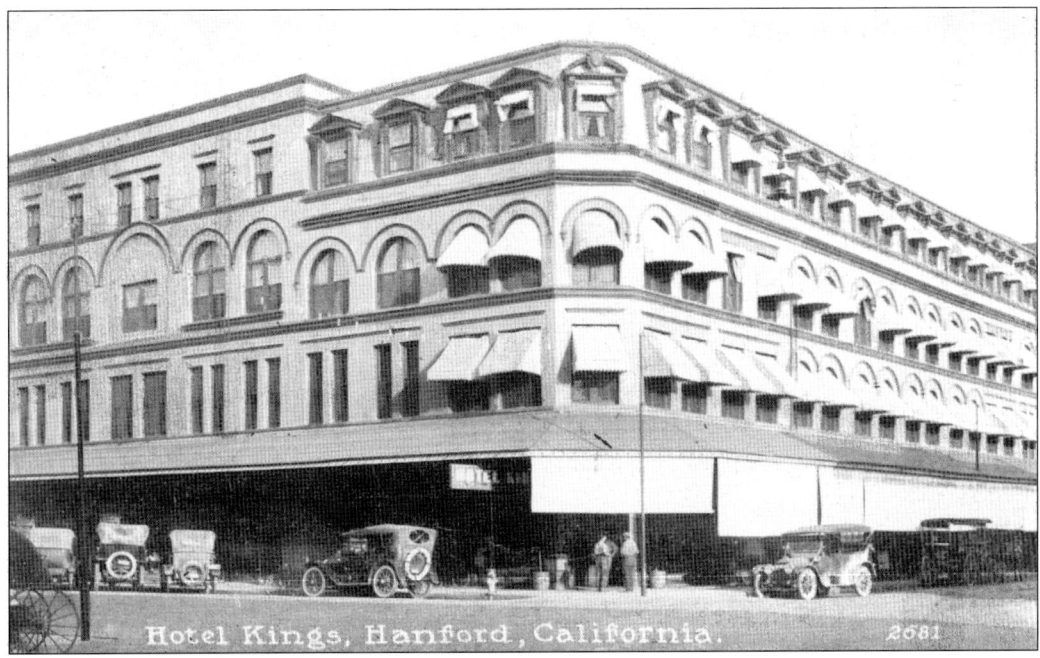

THE OPERA HOUSE. In 1912, a fourth floor was added to the structure. Since the building was not designed to have a fourth floor made out of brick, the level was added using wood. In 1928, flames licked across Seventh Street from the Kutner-Goldstein fire and burnt the fourth floor off the building.

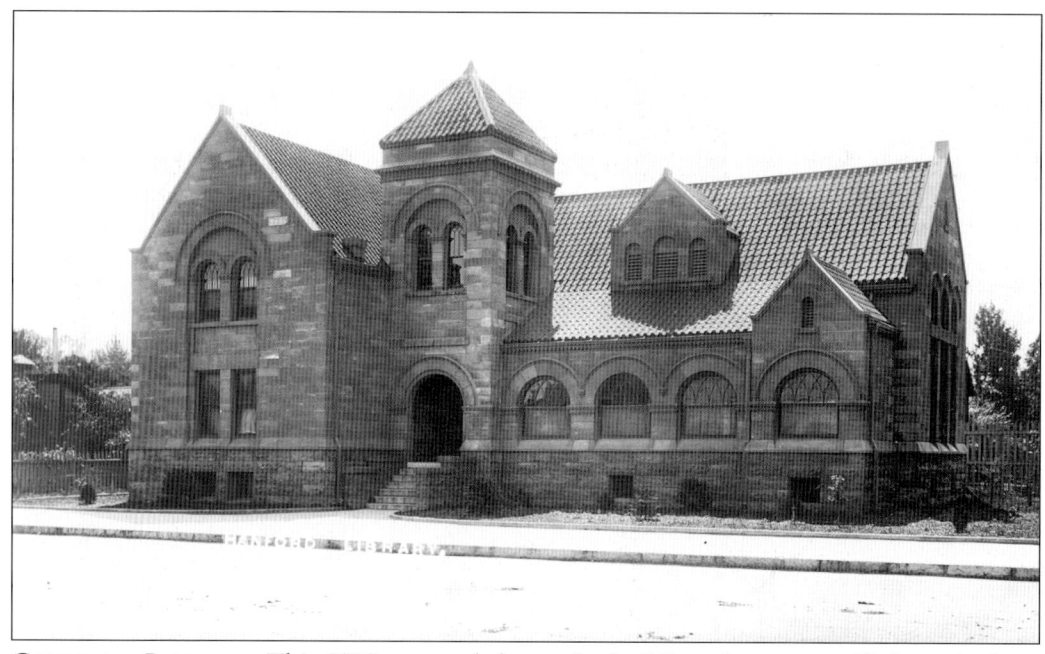

CARNEGIE LIBRARY. This 1910 postcard shows the building that was a gift from Andrew Carnegie to the citizens of Hanford. It was built in 1905 and 1906 by David Gamble at a cost $12,500. It was designed by the McDougal Brothers, prominent architects of the time. The building is constructed of cement block and has a pressed metal roof.

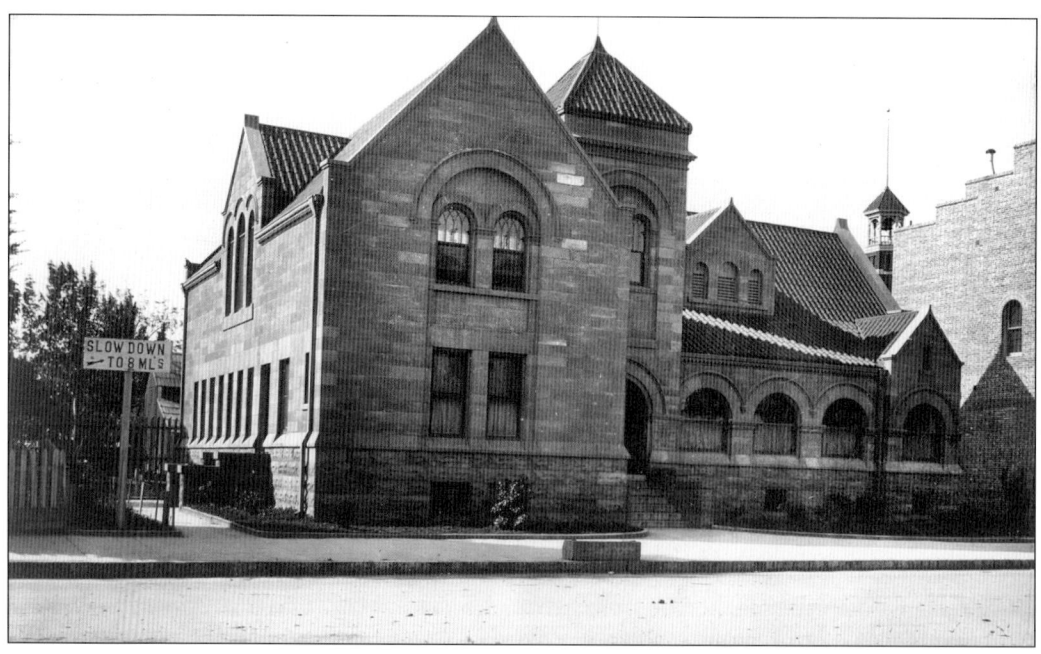

HANFORD CARNEGIE LIBRARY. This unused postcard shows the library from the east side. It was used as the main library until 1968, when a new structure was built. Today the building houses the Hanford Carnegie Museum. Note the speed limit sign. (Courtesy Ron Burris.)

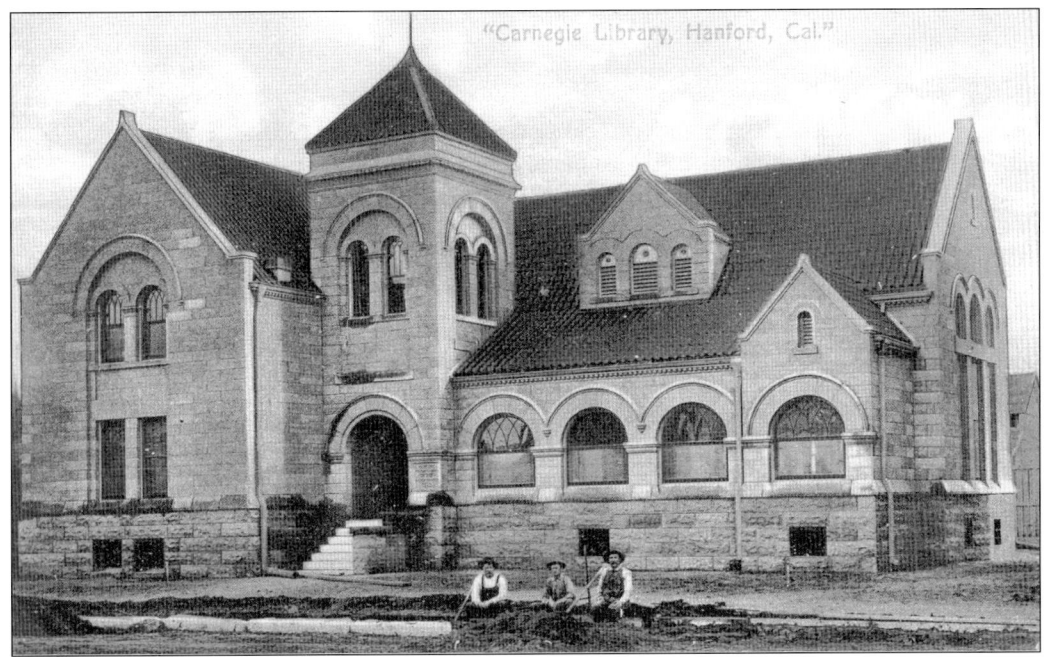

CARNEGIE LIBRARY, HANFORD. This postcard shows workers installing the granite curbs that lined the street in front of the library. This photograph appears to have been taken right after the building was completed.

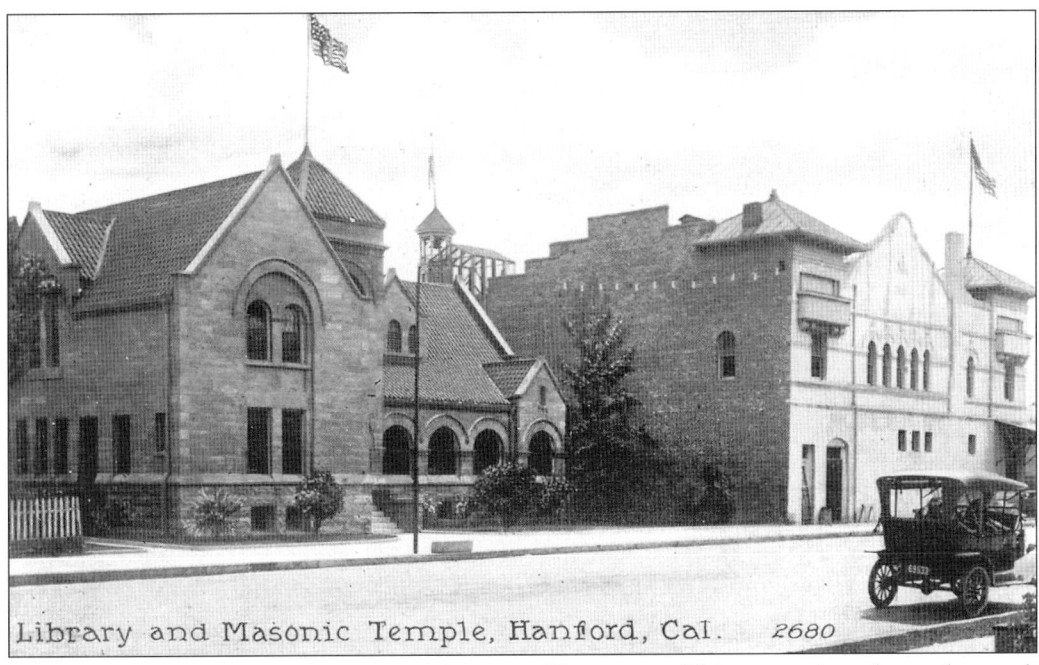

CARNEGIE LIBRARY AND MASONIC TEMPLE, HANFORD. This street view shows the south side of Eighth Street looking west toward Douty. The bell tower in the middle belongs to the fire station. Both buildings pictured are in current use today.

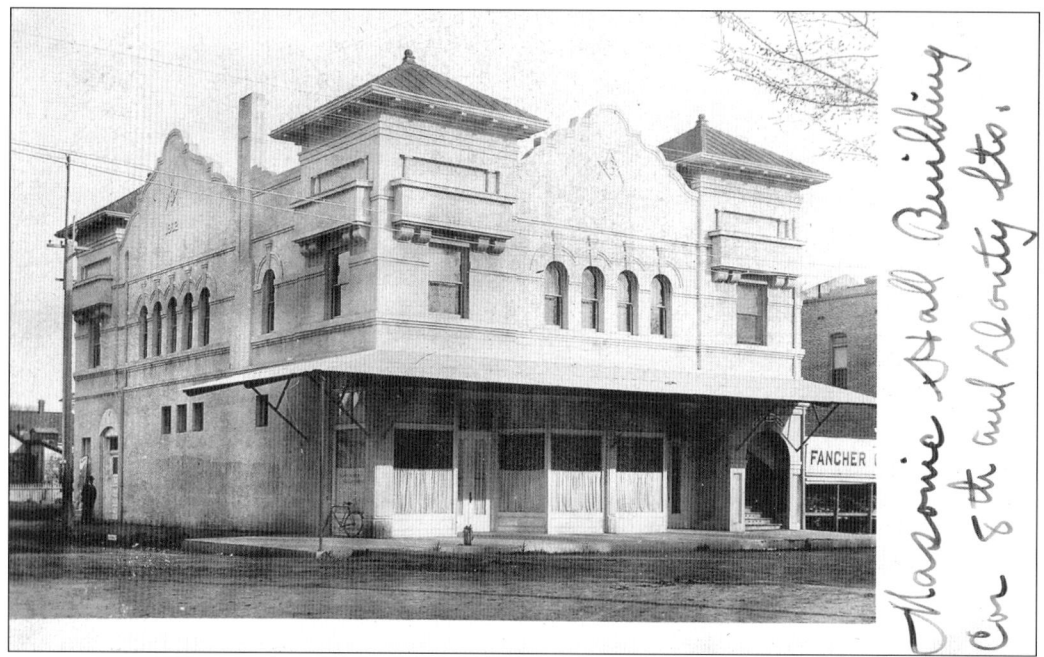

Masonic Hall Building on 8th and Douty Sts.

MASONIC TEMPLE, HANFORD. This pre-1905 postcard shows an early view of the Hanford Masonic Temple. The Hanford Masonic Lodge's charter was issued on October 16, 1885, after the Lemoore Lodge petitioned the Grand Lodge for a dispensation to form and open a lodge in Hanford. There were 28 original charter members. (Courtesy Ron Burris.)

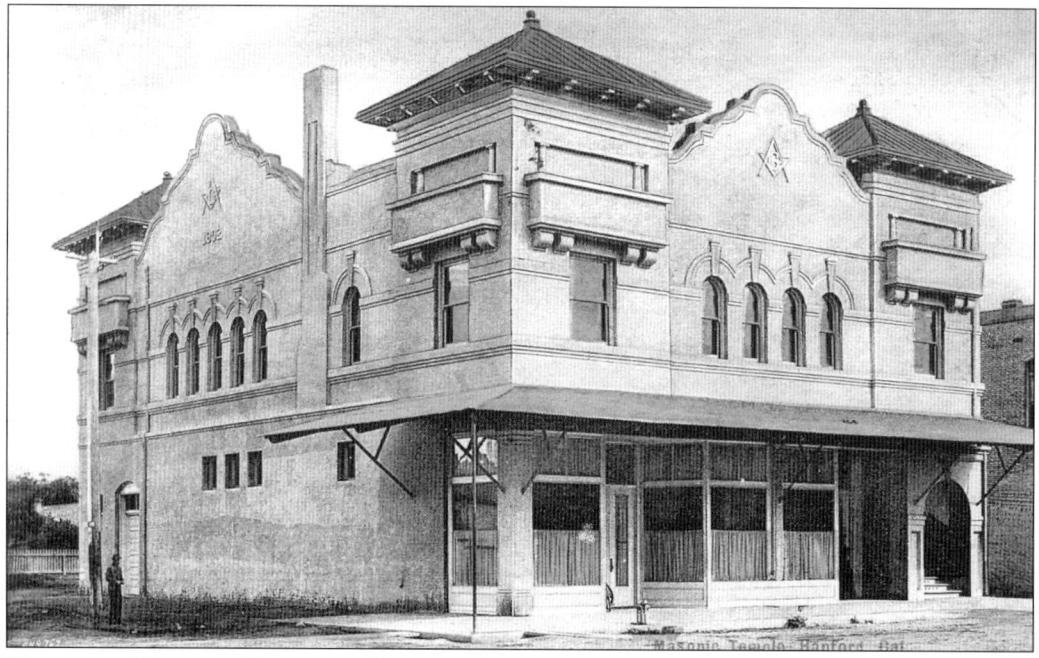

HANFORD MASONIC TEMPLE. This printed postcard's image dates to before 1906. In 1891, the lodge purchased the entire east side of Douty Street, from Eighth Street to the alley, from the Methodist church for $6,400 in gold coin. Subsequently they sold the lots south of the temple site for $7,493.75.

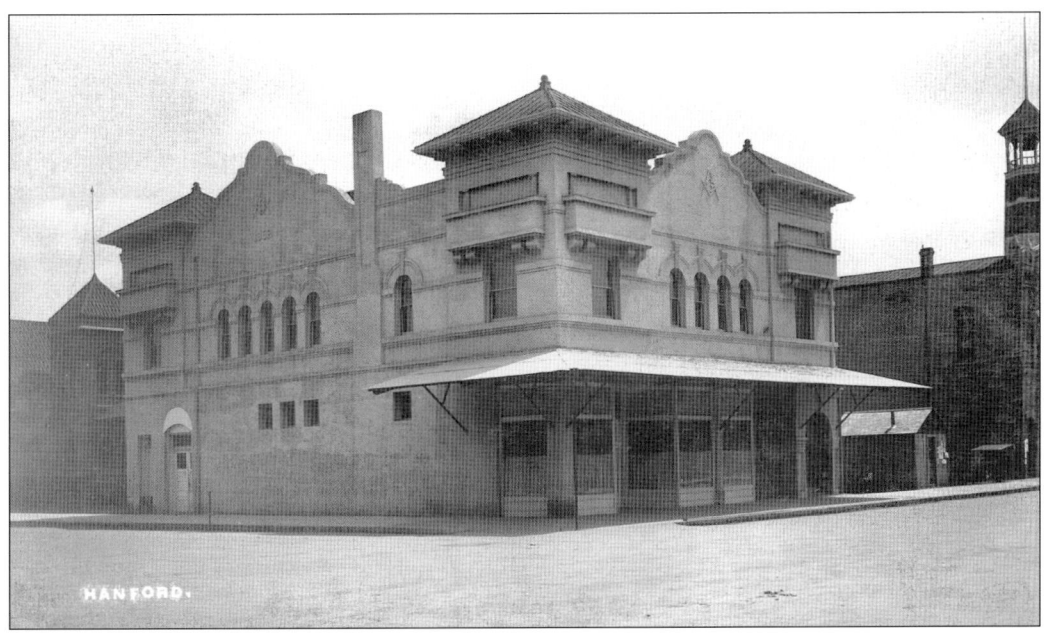

HANFORD MASONS. This 1907 postmarked card shows the home of the Hanford Masonic Lodge F&AM 279. On September 25, 1901, the cornerstone was laid and on May 23, 1902, the building was dedicated. The total cost for constructing the building was $10,997.49.

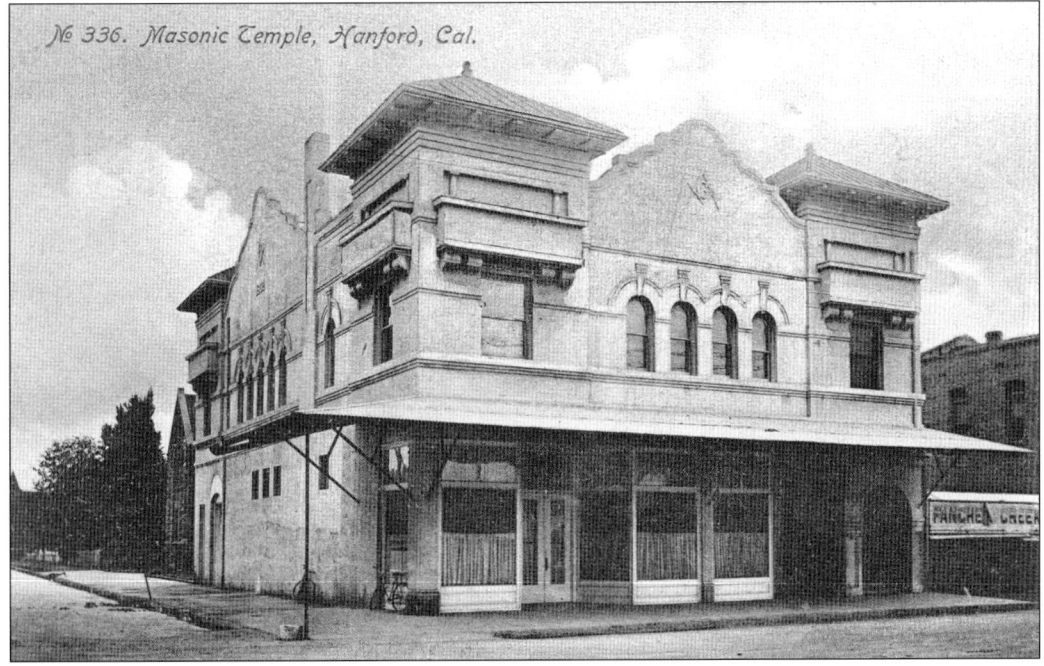

MASONIC TEMPLE. This post-1910 postcard provides a frontal view of the first floor shops. The second story houses the meeting room for the lodge while the street level is devoted for rentable storefront space. One of the first tenants was J. C. Rice Mortuary. The Masons currently hold regular meetings in the building.

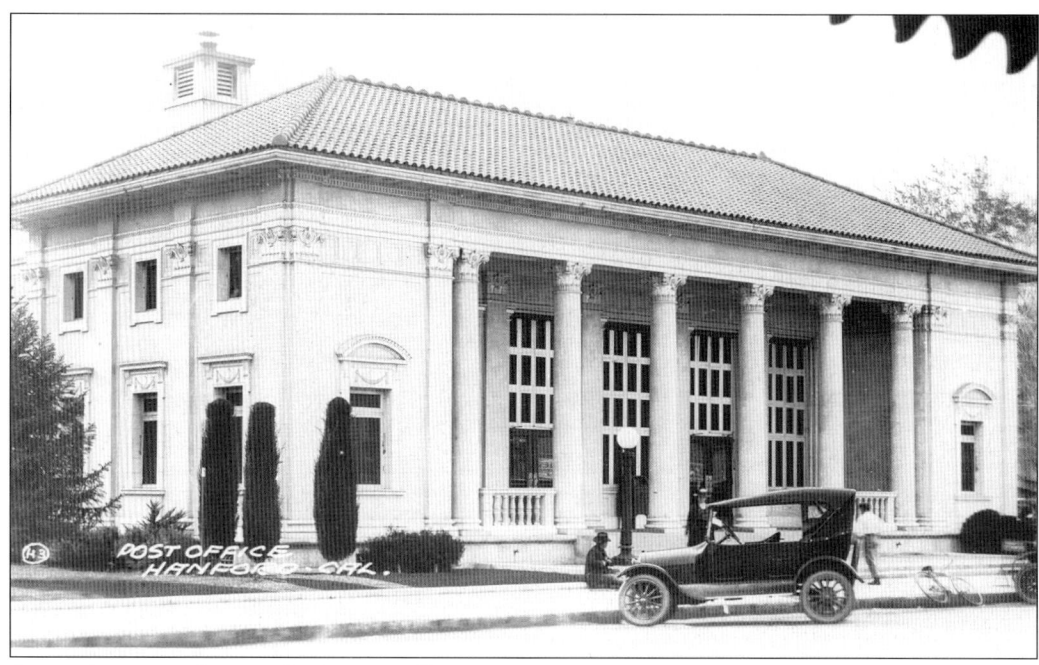

POST OFFICE. The Hanford Post Office opened on January 1, 1916, and was located on the southeast corner of Eight and Douty Streets. Until the early 1960s, the building served as the main post office. It later housed the Kings County Justice Court until 1977. It is now occupied by a bank.

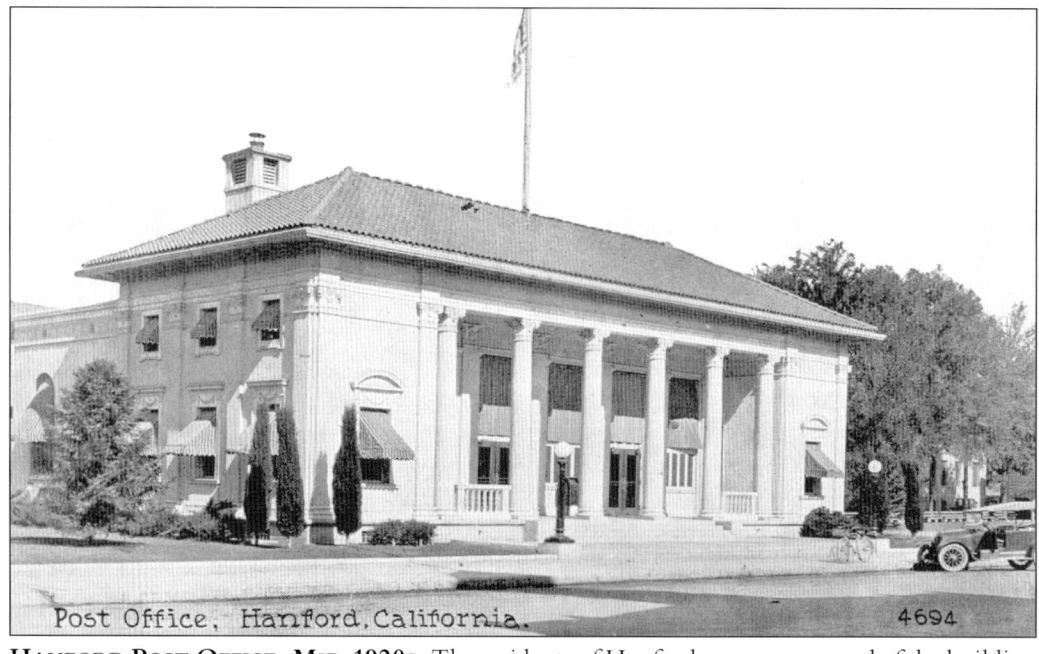

HANFORD POST OFFICE, MID-1920S. The residents of Hanford were very proud of the building as this postcard is one of the most common ones available of Hanford.

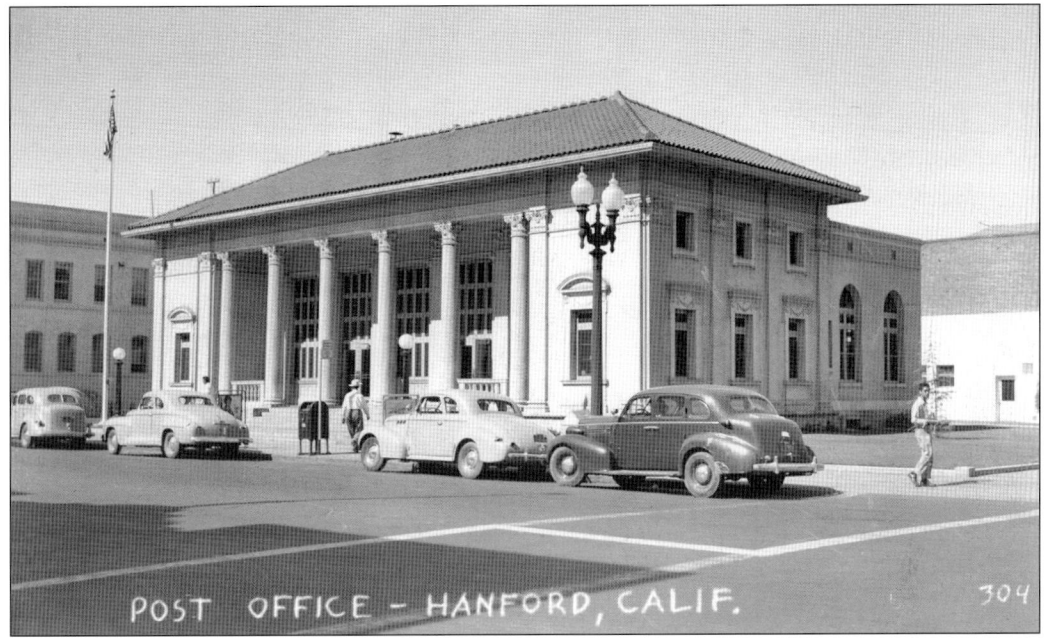

Post Office. This image of the post office was used in a 1943 Hanford City directory.

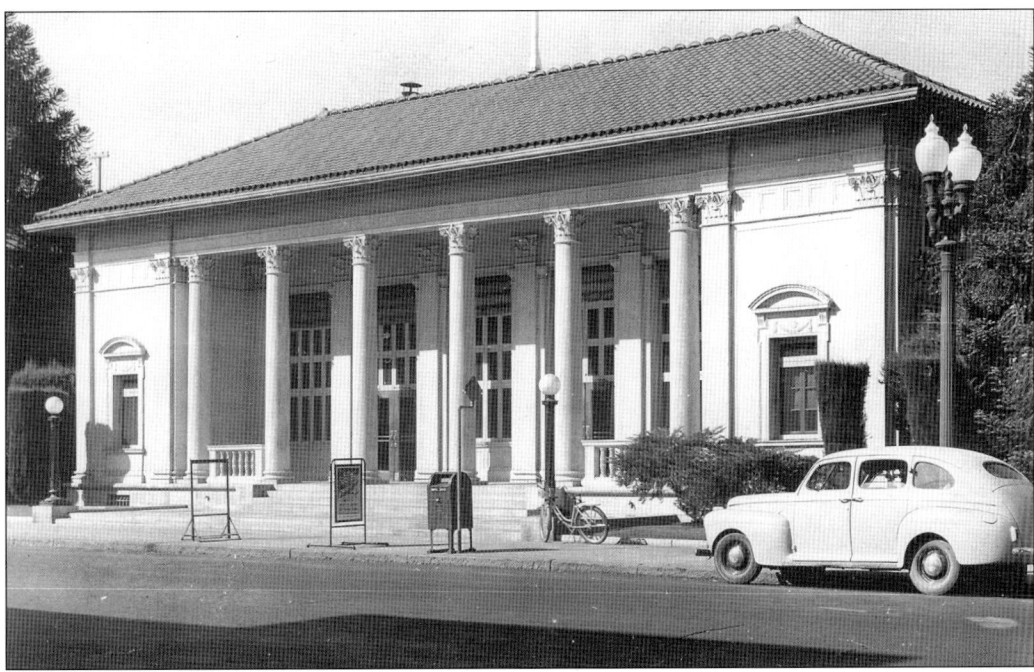

Hanford Post Office. In a more innocent time, banks would mail their cash transfers through the U.S. mail. The postmaster would have to deliver the cash transfers to the local railroad station using a contracted delivery service. To protect the shipment, he was armed with a World War I, .45 caliber pistol.

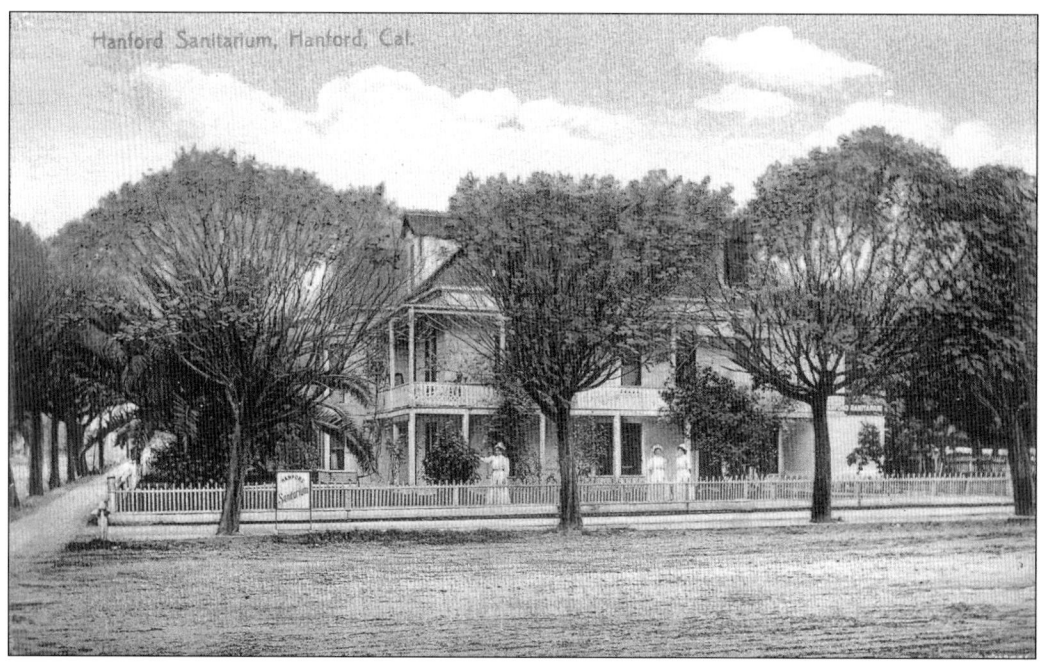

HANFORD SANITARIUM. In 1907, the Hanford Sanitarium was opened by Dr. C. T. Rosson and others. It occupied a three-story building located on the southeast corner of Irwin and Ivy Streets.

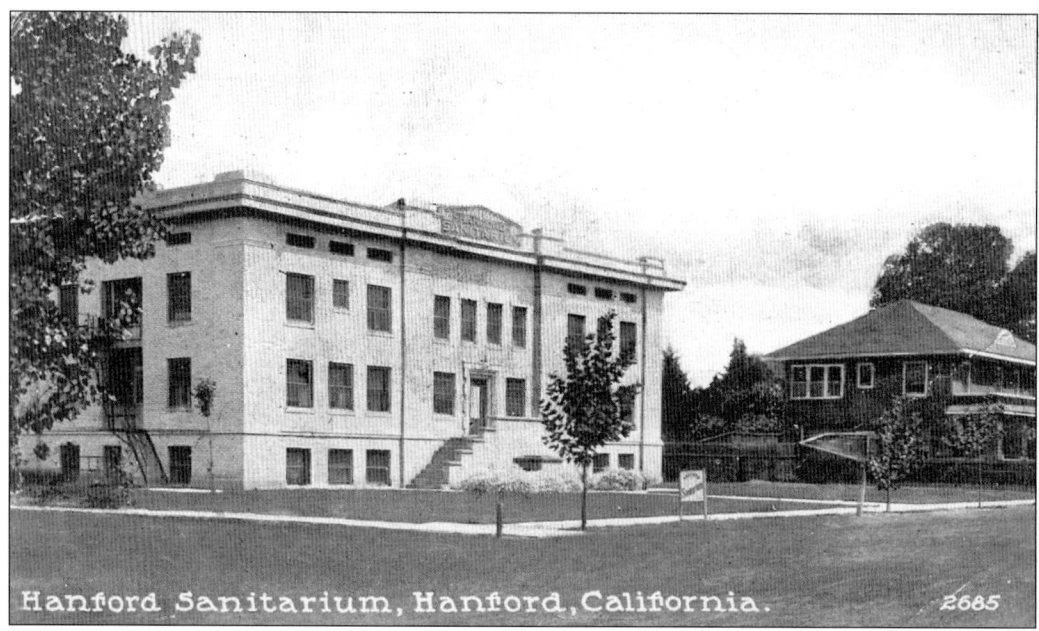

SANITARIUM, HANFORD. In April 1913, the sanitarium was moved into a newly completed building on the southeast corner of Keith and Irwin Streets. The hospital remained at this location until January 1965, when it was replaced by the newly opened Community Hospital. The building was demolished in the 1970s. The building on the right was the original Catholic hospital.

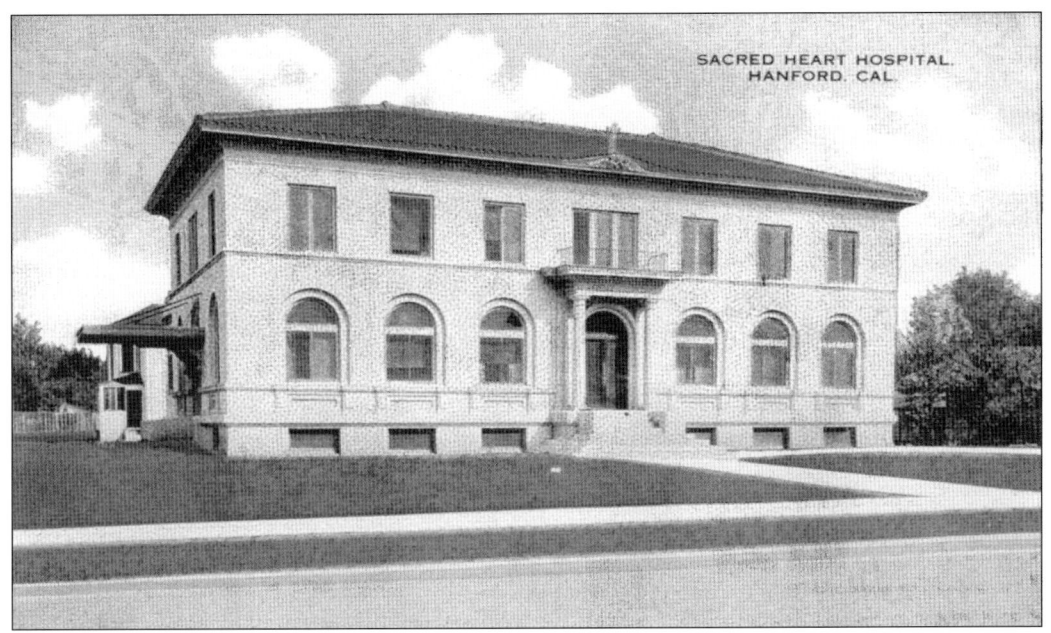

SACRED HEART HOSPITAL, HANFORD. In 1914, the Dominican Sisters established a Catholic hospital next to the Hanford Sanitarium. (See previous card.) In 1915, the facility was moved to the new Sacred Heart Hospital shown above.

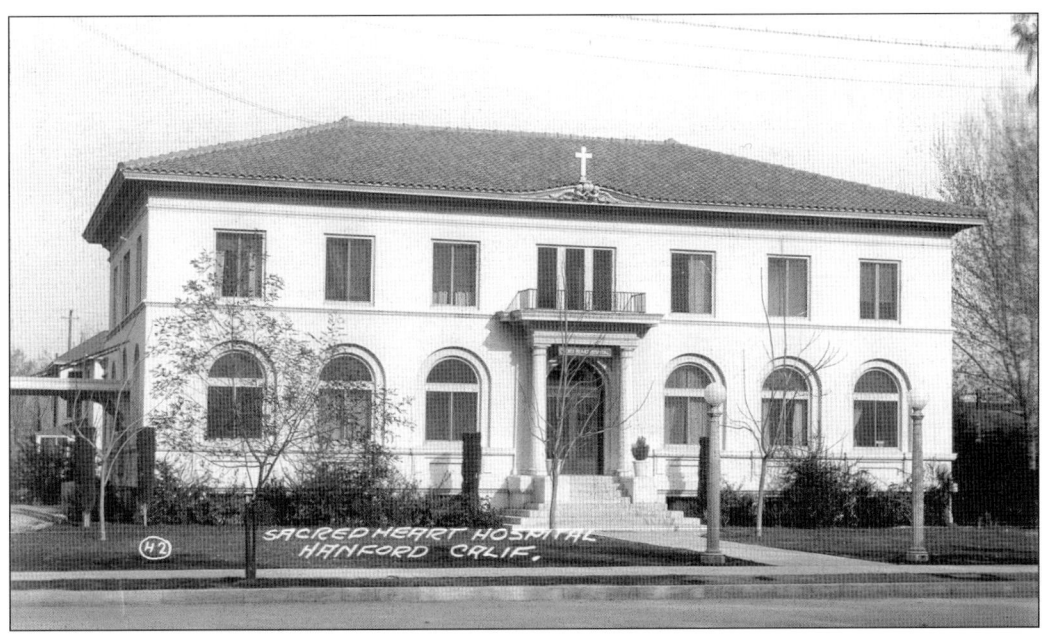

DOMINCAN SISTERS AT SACRED HEART, HANFORD. The Dominican Sisters operated a 20-bed facility located on North Douty Street. Built in 1915, it was used as a hospital until 1962 when a newer facility was built. In 1963, it was demolished.

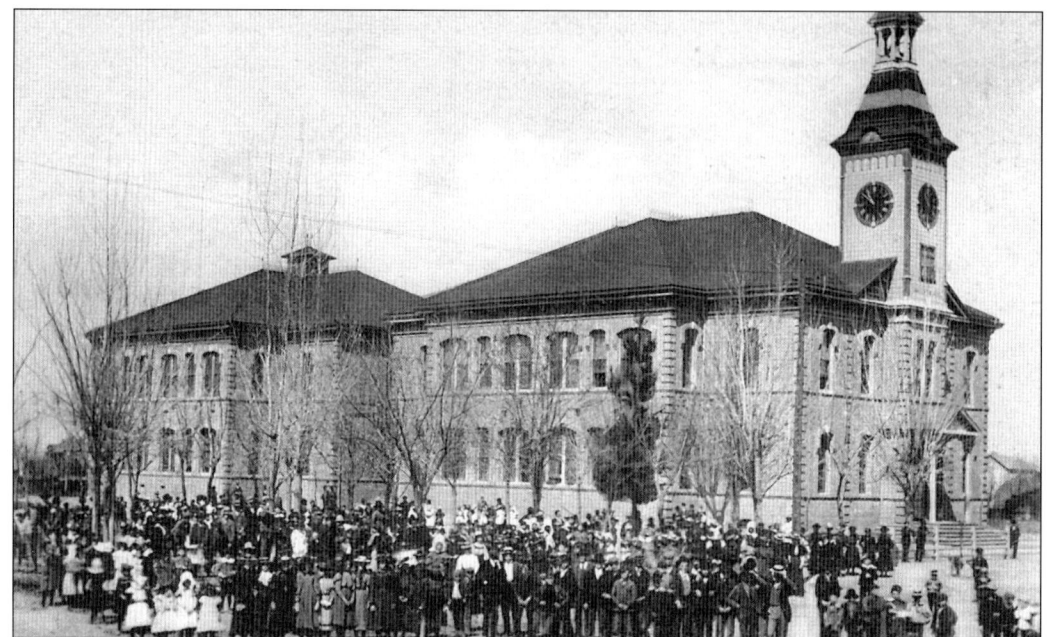

HANFORD GRAMMAR SCHOOL. This unused 1907 postcard shows the entire school population standing on the south lawn posing for a photograph. The building was designed by the firm of McDougal and Son and was built in 1887 by Carl, Croby, and Abernathy of Stockton and Sacramento for $20,000.

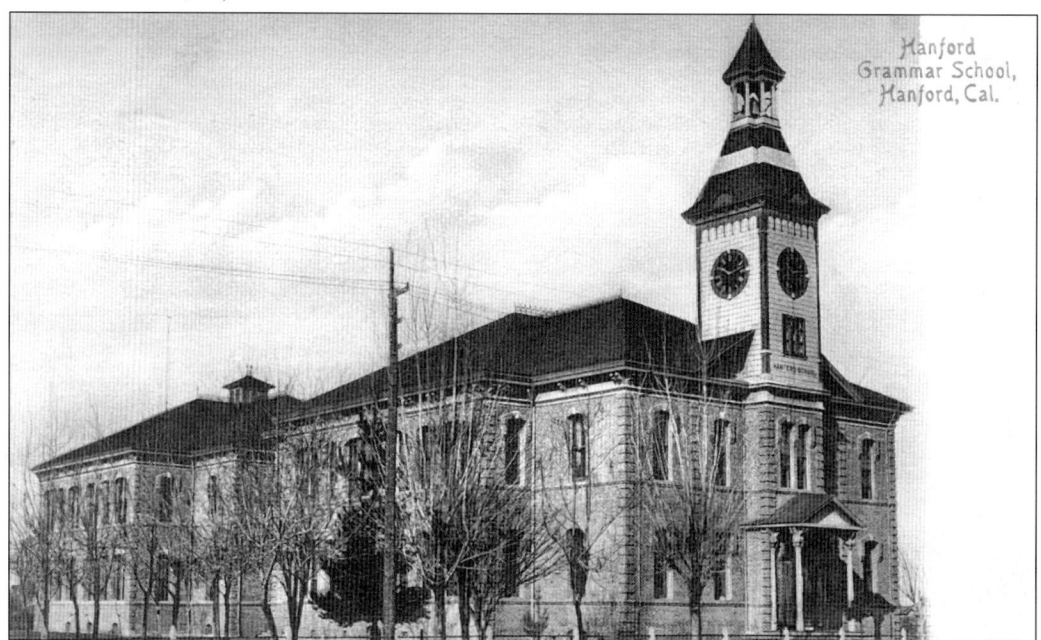

GRAMMAR SCHOOL FROM DOUTY STREET. This 1909 postmarked postcard depicts the Hanford Grammar School as it appeared from Douty Street. The clock in the tower, which weighed over 900 pounds, was purchased in 1886 for $412 from the Seth Thomas Clock Company. It was salvaged from the building before demolition and was installed in the facade of the Hanford Civic Auditorium.

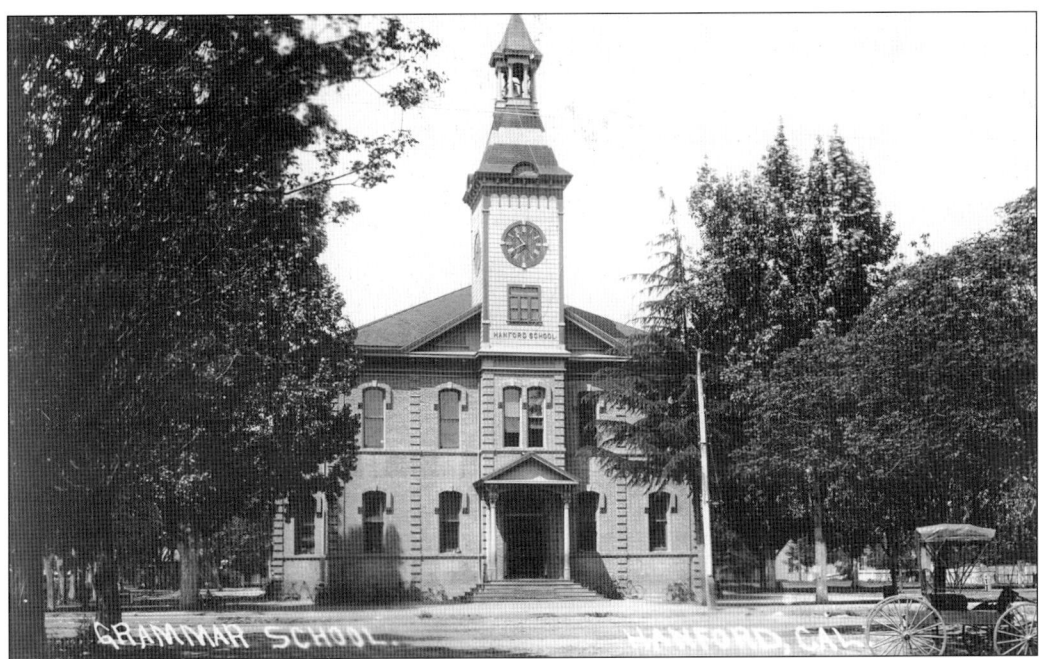

CENTRAL GRAMMAR SCHOOL. This 1906 postmarked card shows the Central Grammar School that was located at Ninth and Douty Streets. At the time, it was considered one of the finest grammar schools in the entire state. When the school was demolished in 1924, the clock was saved and is now installed in the Civic Auditorium Building that was built on the site.

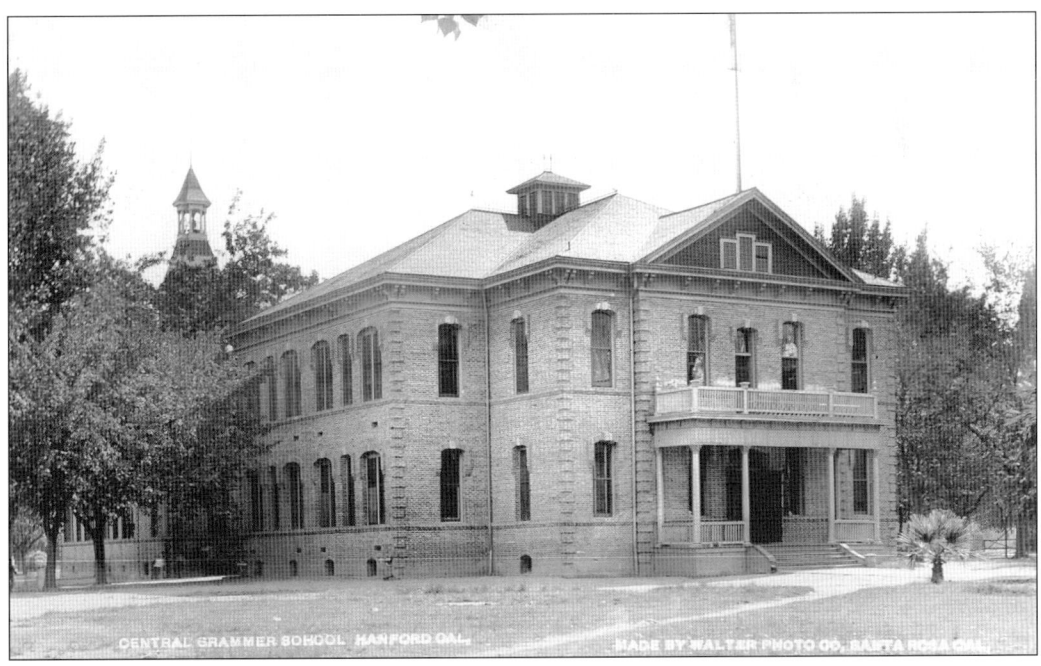

GRAMMAR SCHOOL, REAR VIEW. This rare postcard shows the back of Central Grammar School. This portion of the building was built in 1897 as an answer to the growing school population of Hanford. It was also designed by McDougal and Son.

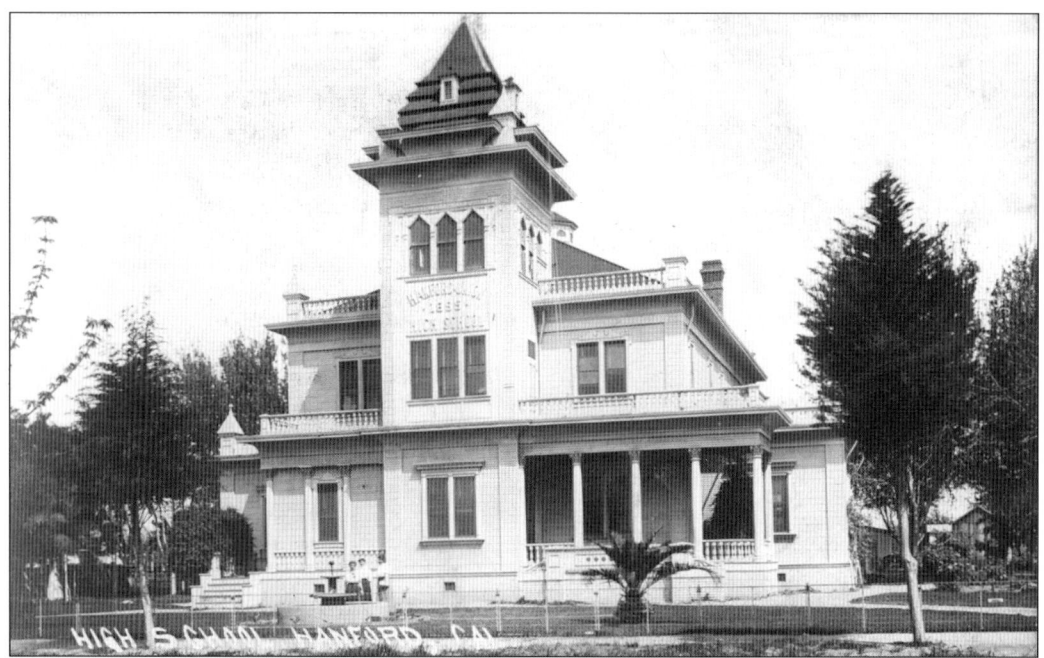

HANFORD HIGH SCHOOL. The original Hanford High School building was built in 1895 by David Gamble for $6,867. The structure sat on the northwest corner of Harris and Elm Street. In 1922, a new high school was built and a portion of this structure was moved to the Kings Country Club where it serves as the clubhouse today.

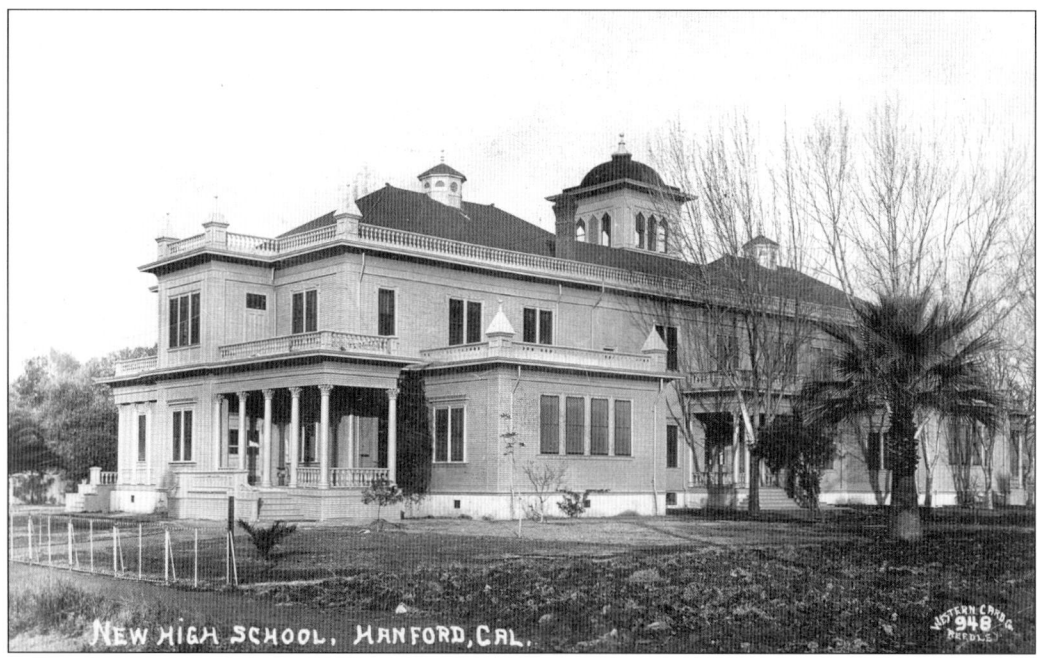

HIGH SCHOOL, 1912. This postmarked card from 1912 shows Hanford High School after it was expanded in 1909. The bell tower was removed from the front of the school and moved to the middle. More class space was added to accommodate the growing population of the city.

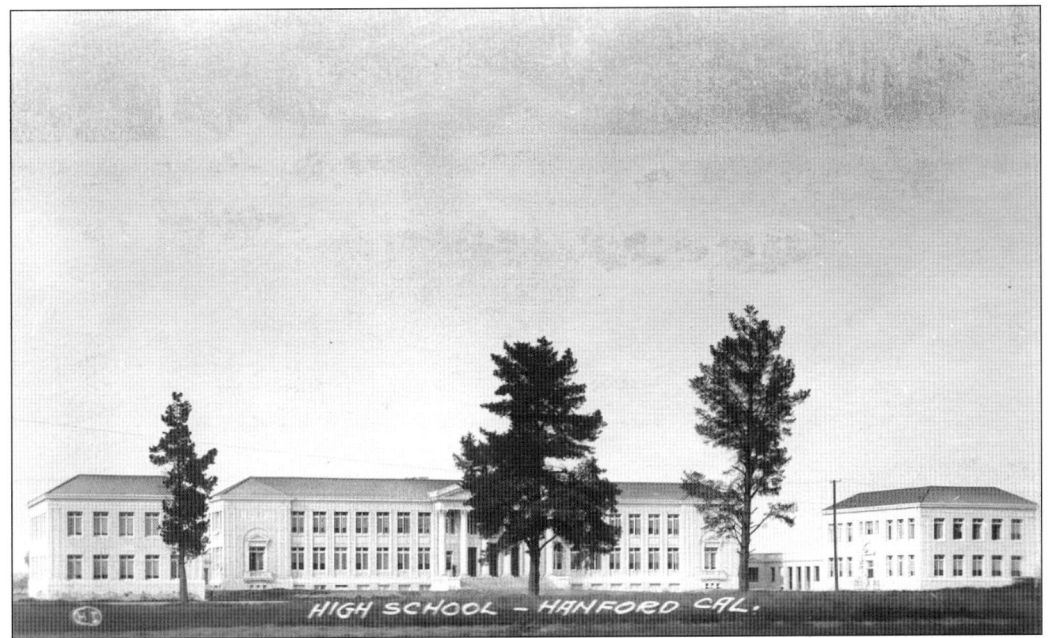

HANFORD HIGH SCHOOL, 1922. A new location for Hanford High was secured in 1919 when a 30-acre parcel was purchased on the northeast corner of Douty Street and Grangeville Boulevard. The land was purchased for $10 in gold coin.

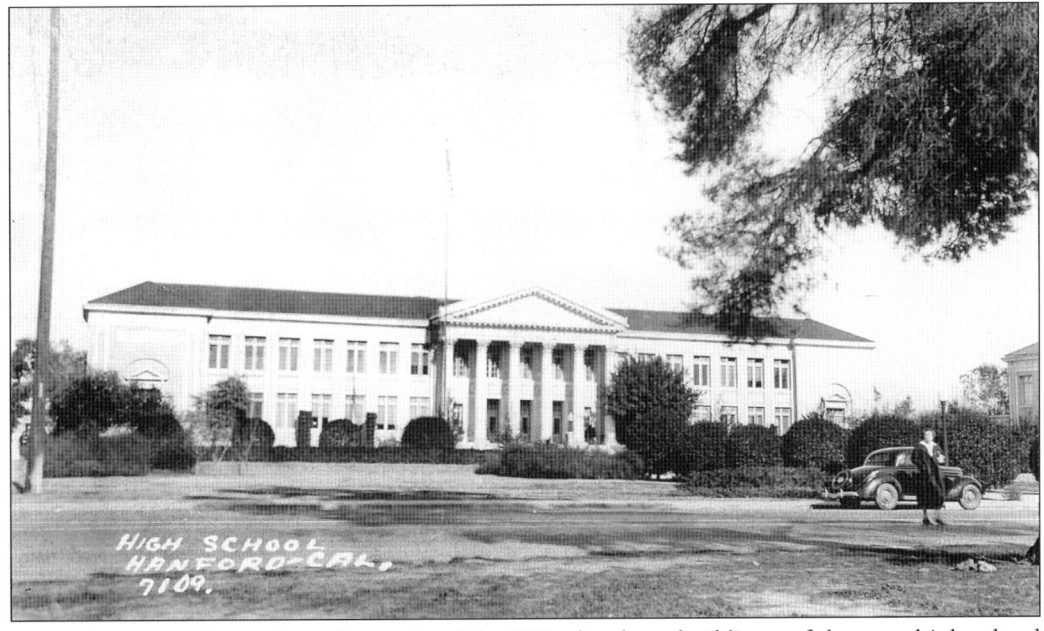

HIGH SCHOOL. Opened on September 26, 1921, the three buildings of the new high school were designed by the architect W. V. Coates of Coates and Traver of Fresno. It was built at a cost of $500,000.

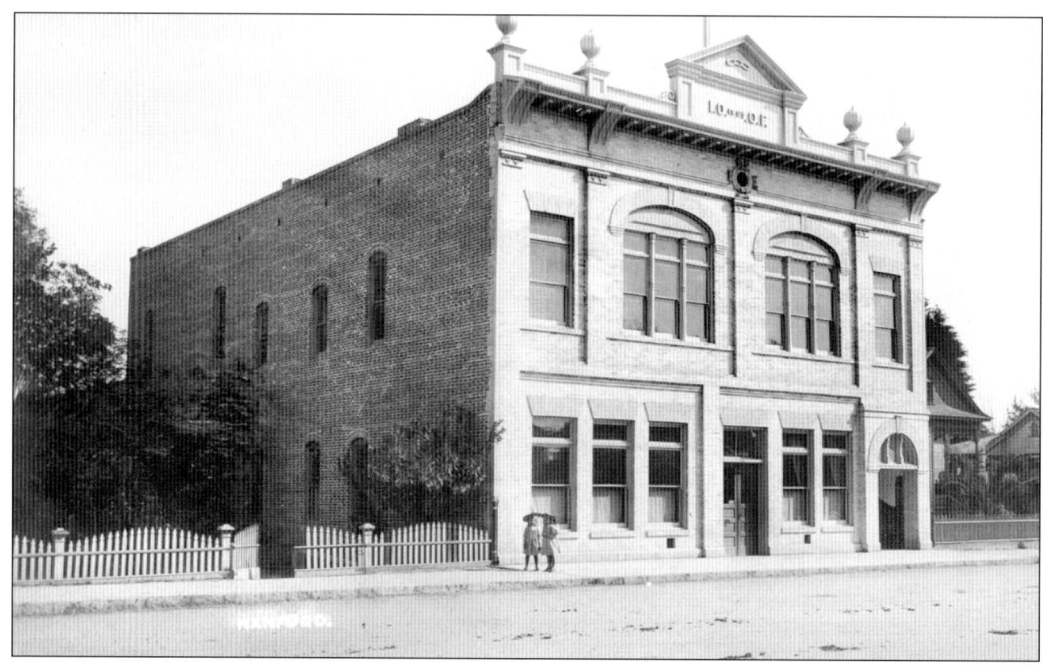

INTERNATIONAL ORDER OF ODD FELLOWS HALL. This unused postcard shows the IOOF Hall in 1910. The building was built in 1905 by Andrew J. Moates of Grangeville for a cost of $12,017. The architect was S. E. French.

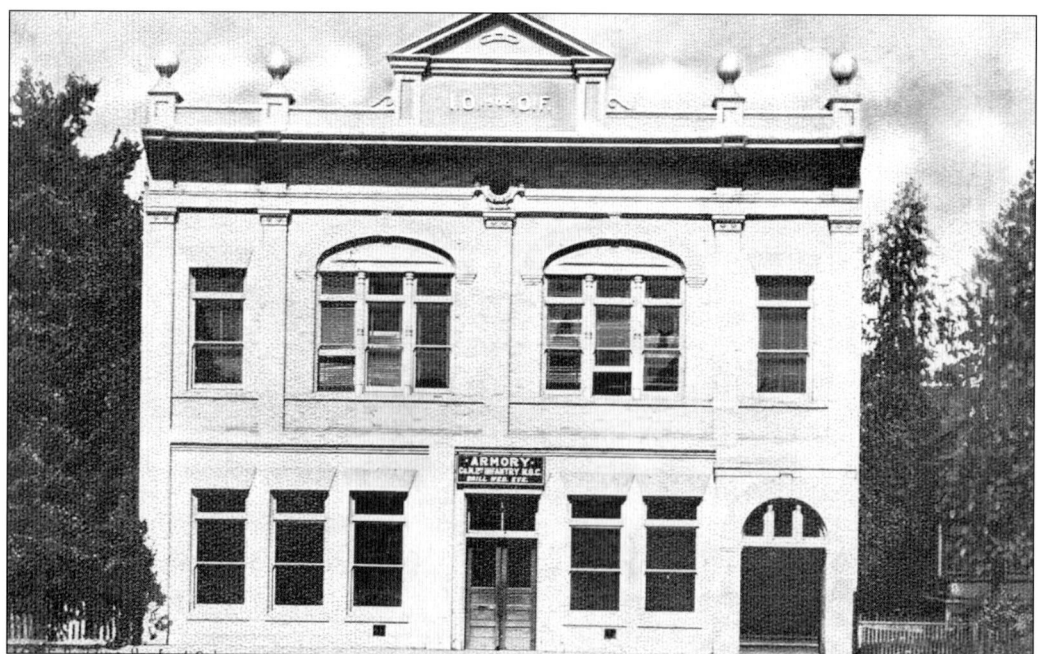

ODD FELLOWS. This mid-1910s postcard shows the IOOF Hall as the location for the local armory. The building has had minor remodeling and still has the second floor meeting room and armory.

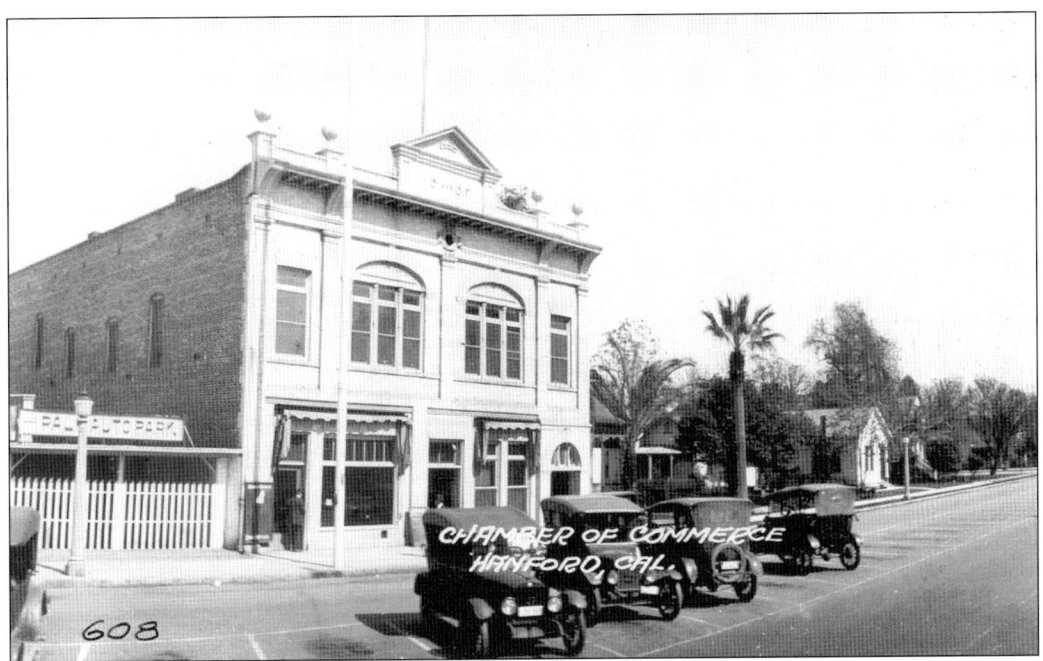

ODD FELLOWS HALL. This proof postcard shows the IOOF Hall as it appeared in 1918. The first floor was rented to many different organizations, including the Kings County Chamber of Commerce, the National Guard, and Kings County Welfare and Employment Department. Today the building houses an antique store.

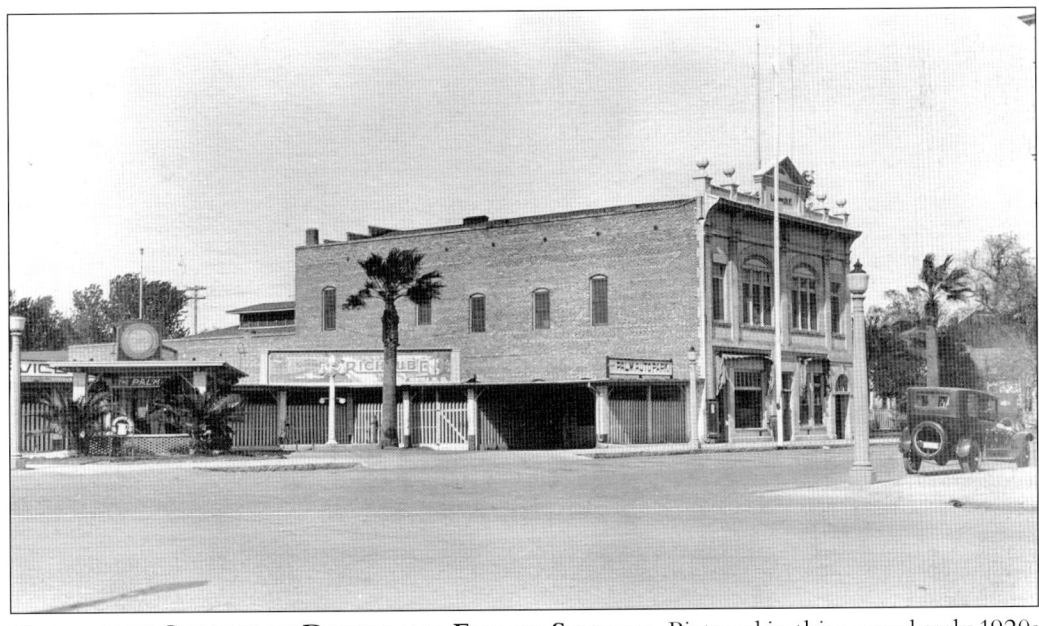

NORTHEAST CORNER OF DOUTY AND EIGHTH STREETS. Pictured in this unused early 1920s postcard is a rare view of the Palms Auto Court located next to the IOOF. The large flagpole was subsequently moved to the front of the American Legion Hall. (Courtesy Juliann Faulkner.)

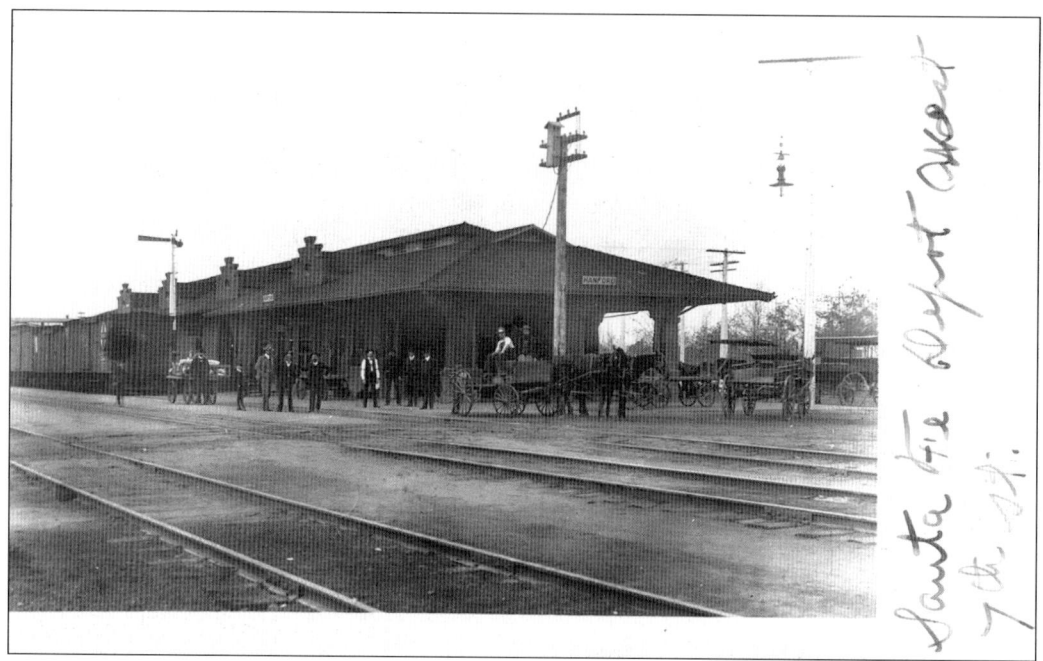

SANTA FE TRAIN DEPOT, HANFORD. This rare pre-1907 postcard shows depot employees lined up for the photographer. The wagon on the far right is the Artesia Hotel transport wagon.

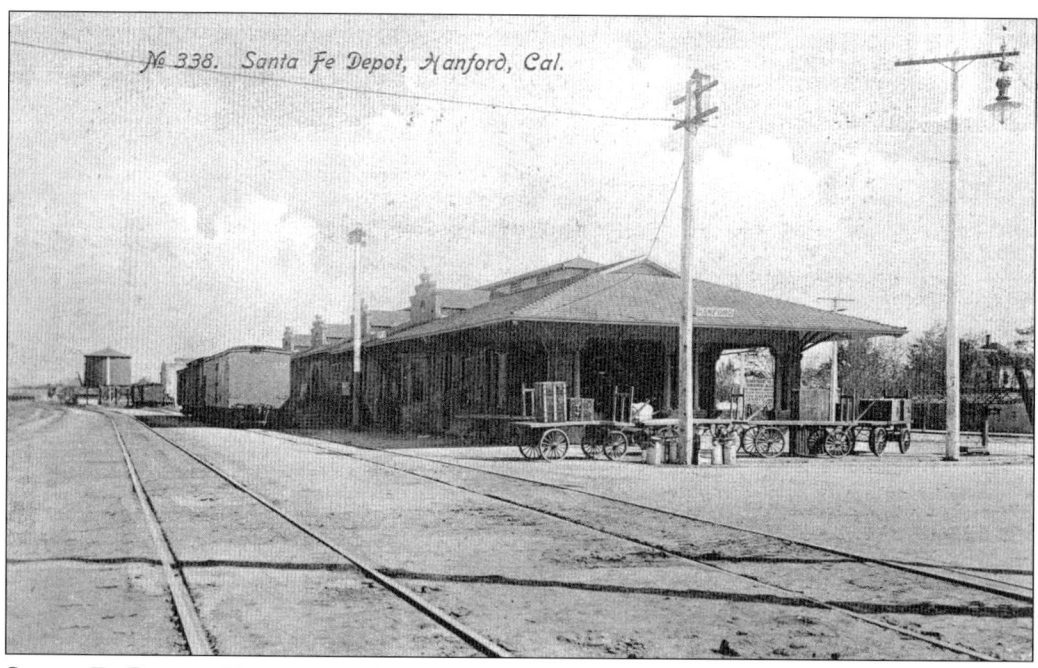

SANTA FE DEPOT, HANFORD. This wider view of the depot shows the area north and west of the main building. The water tank in the background was used to provide water to the steam locomotive engines.

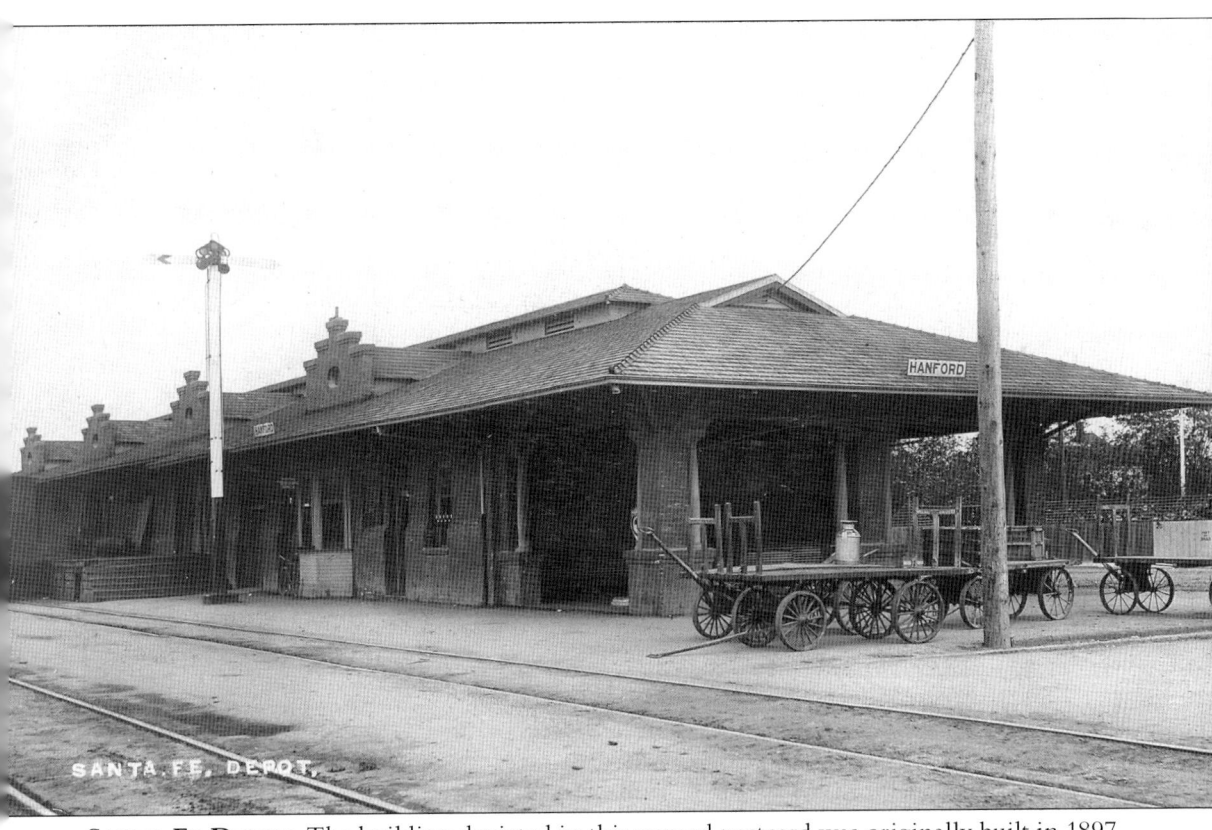

SANTA FE DEPOT. The building depicted in this unused postcard was originally built in 1897 by the San Francisco & San Joaquin Valley Railroad. The railroad, warmly welcomed by the citizens of Kings County when the line reached Hanford in 1897, was the first major competition to the Southern Pacific. The line was later sold to the Santa Fe Railroad and the station has become a major transportation hub for the county. Today the depot houses the Amtrak station, the Hanford Chamber of Commerce, and the Hanford Visitor Agency.

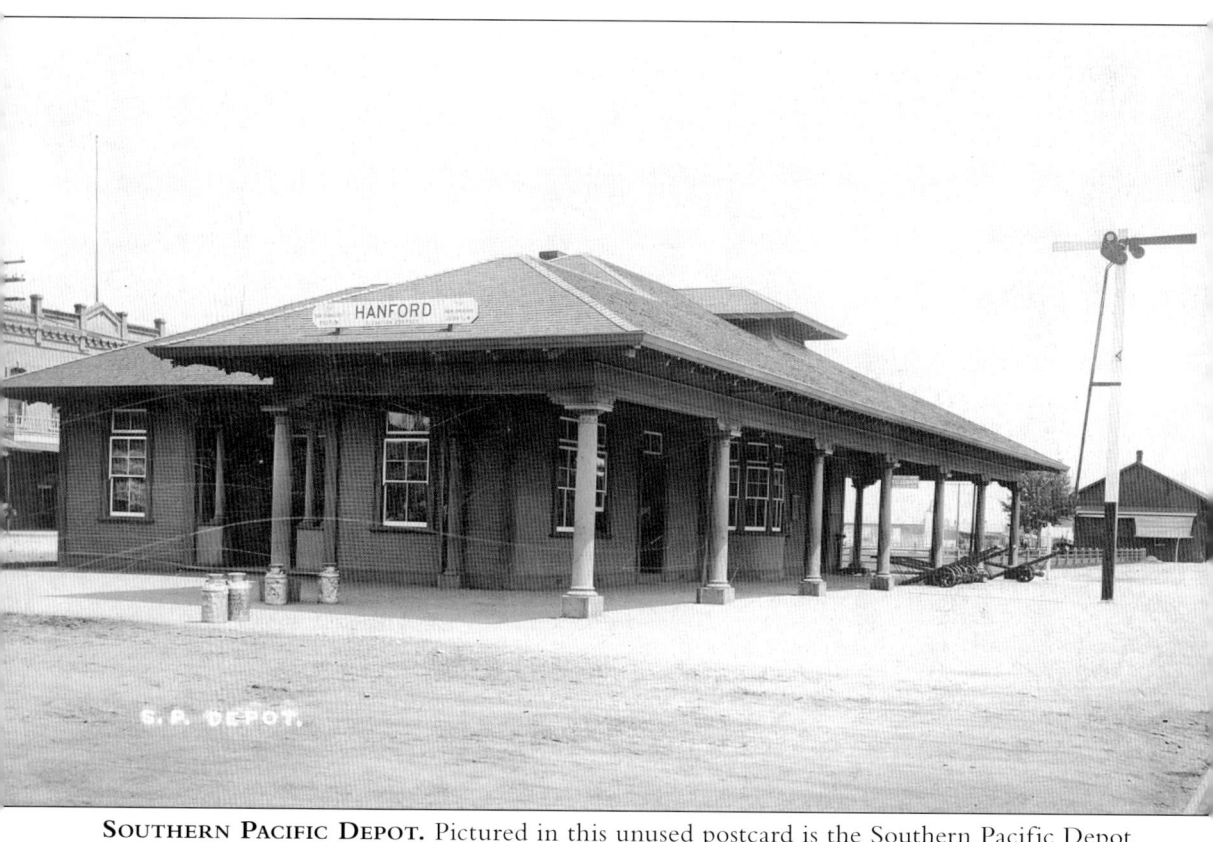

SOUTHERN PACIFIC DEPOT. Pictured in this unused postcard is the Southern Pacific Depot as it appeared before 1910. The Southern Pacific Railroad established the town site of Hanford in 1877, naming it after the railroad paymaster James Madison Hanford. The SP Railroad was despised by the local population since the company was known for exacting high tolls from the local agricultural shippers.

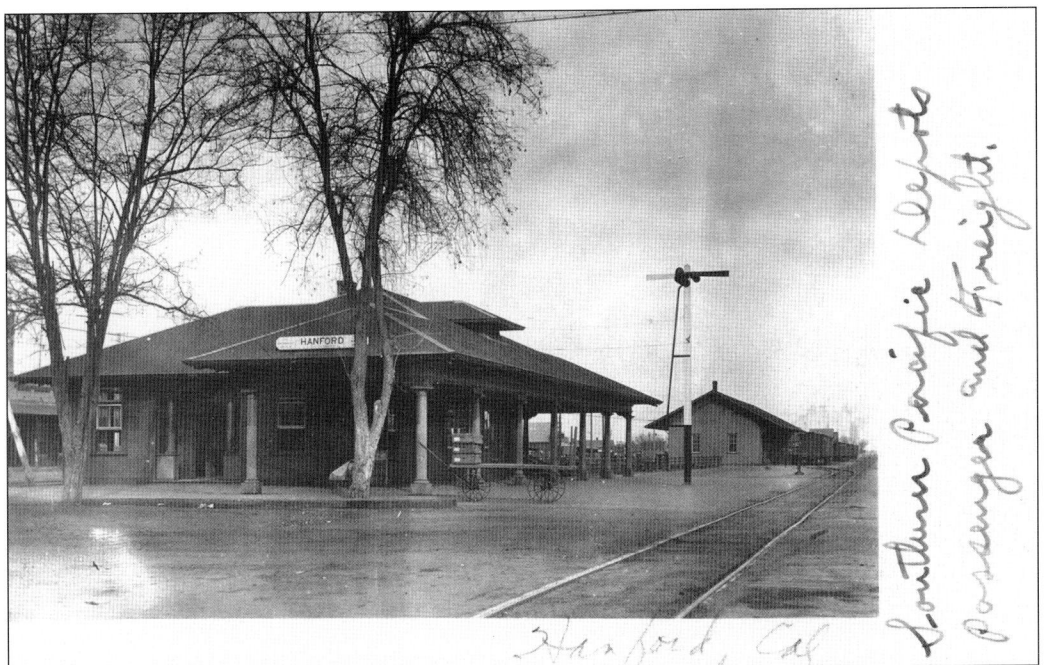

HANFORD SOUTHERN PACIFIC. This extremely rare view shows the depot with trees growing on the west side. In the background is the freight depot, which was moved to Roosevelt School in the 1970s.

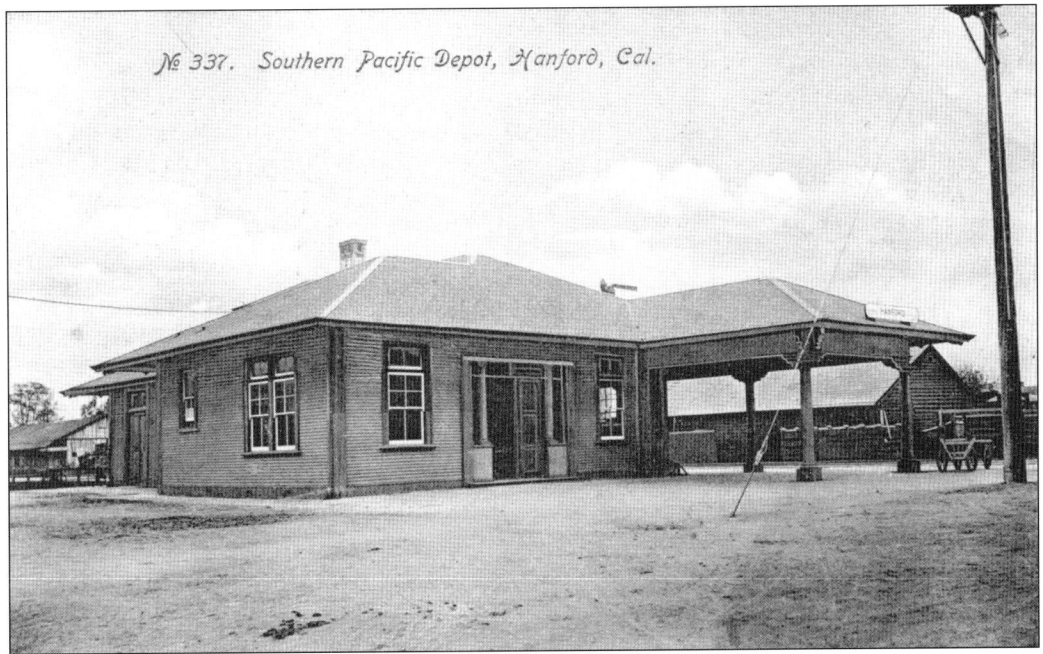

ANOTHER VIEW OF SP DEPOT. Shown in this 1907 postmarked card is another rare view of the north side of the depot building. Across the tracks is the Central Lumber building. Central Lumber was established in Hanford around 1877 and was one of the oldest businesses in Kings County. The lumber company closed in the 1960s. (Courtesy Ron Burris.)

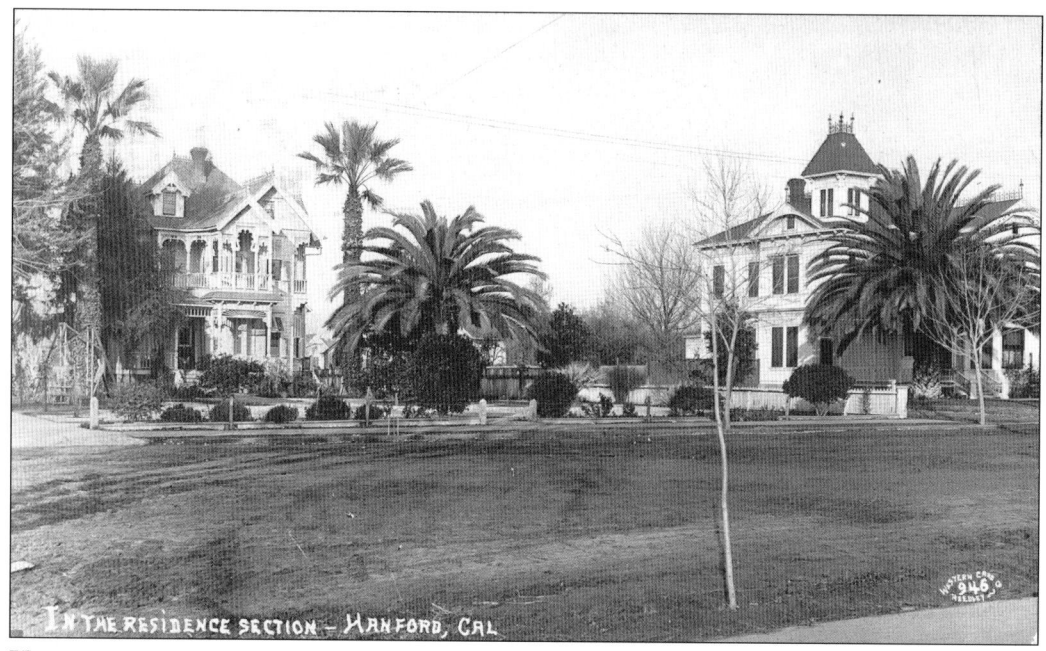

HOMES OF HANFORD. Two large residences were located on North Douty Street between Tenth and Eleventh Streets. The home on the left was built by *Hanford Journal* newspaper publisher Frank Dodge. The home on the right was built by J. T. McJunkin. Both homes have since been demolished.

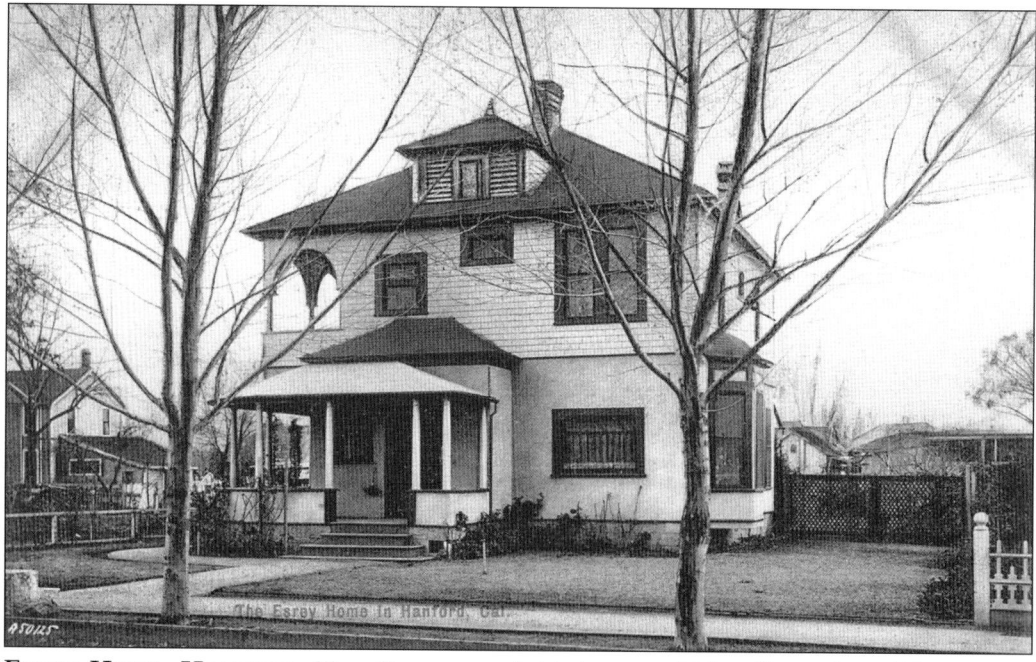

ESREY HOME, HANFORD. Tom Esrey owned this home, which still stands at 119 West Ivy Street. Esrey operated the local hotel and owned a liquor wholesale business.

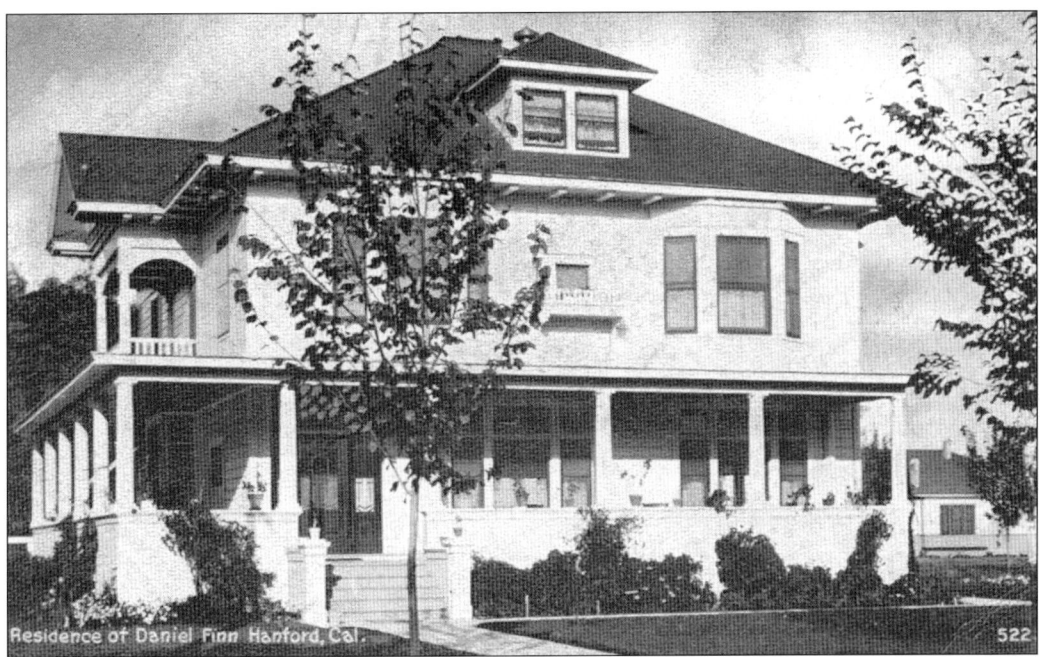

STATELY HANFORD HOME. The caption on this card states that this home was the residence of Daniel Finn, a farmer and the world's largest grower of prunes.

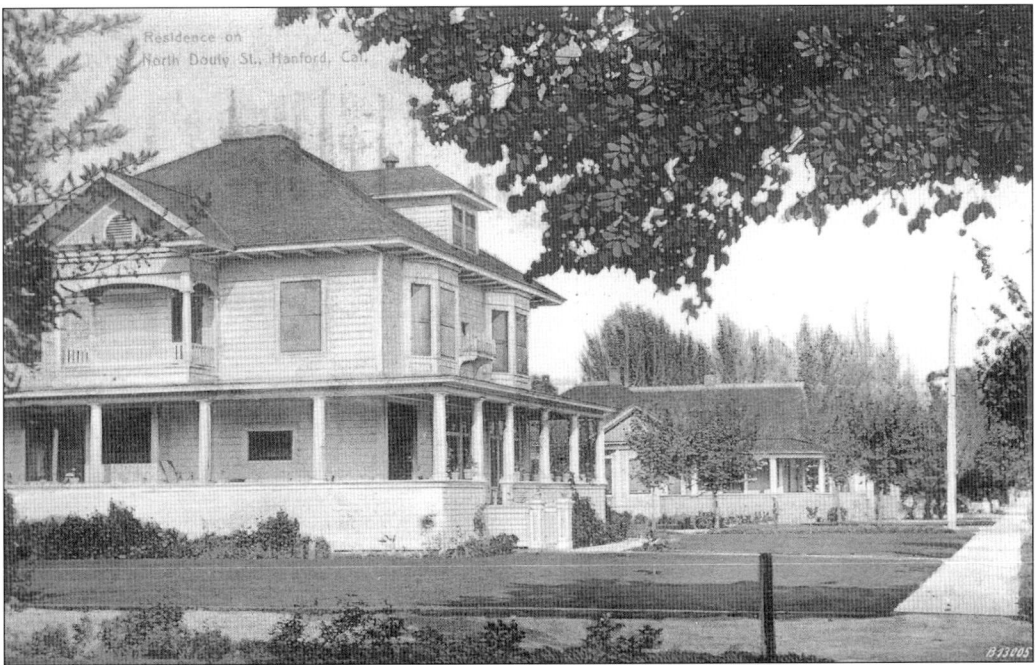

RESIDENCE, HANFORD. This is another view of the Daniel Finn home located at 772 North Douty Street. The building was used as a private residence until 2005, when it was remodeled into office space.

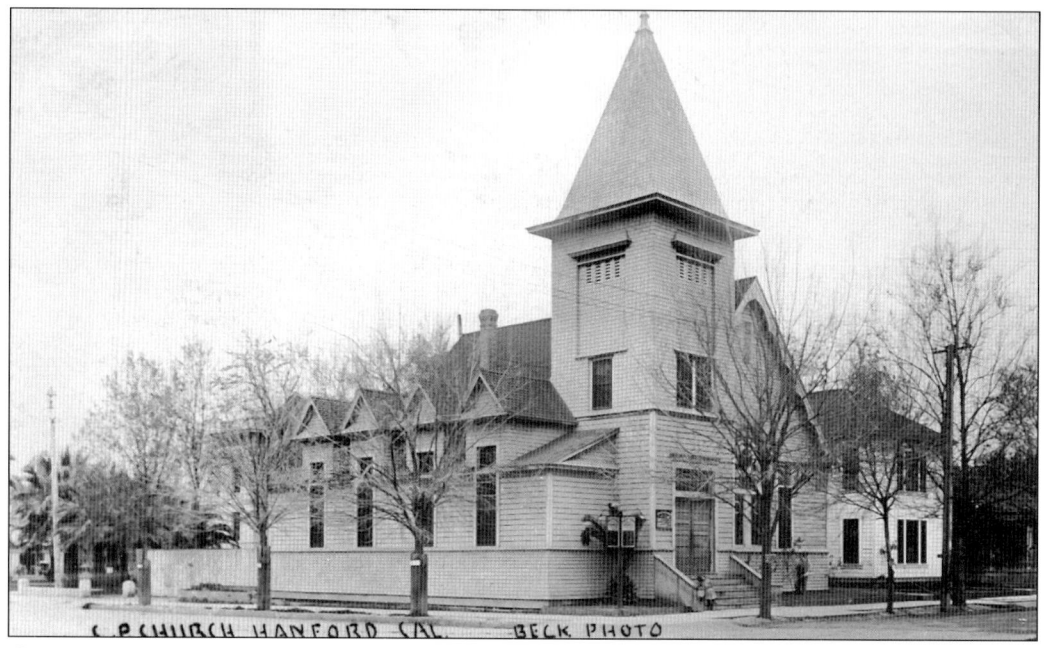

CUMBERLAND PRESBYTERIAN CHURCH. This unused postcard shows the Cumberland Presbyterian Church as it appeared in 1911. The church was founded in 1877 and the building was constructed in 1881. It was located on the northwest corner of Douty and Eight Streets, next to the courthouse.

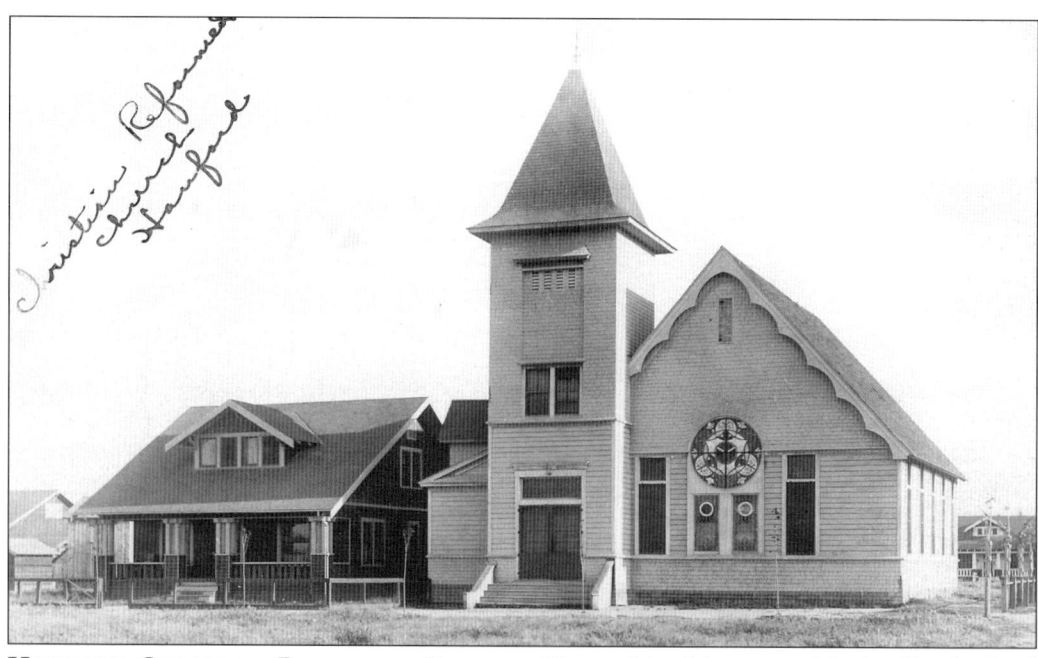

HANFORD CHRISTIAN REFORMED CHURCH. Pictured in this postcard is the Cumberland Presbyterian Church after it was sold to the Christian Reformed Church and moved to the southeast corner of Elm and Park Streets. It is still in use today. (Courtesy Ron Burris.)

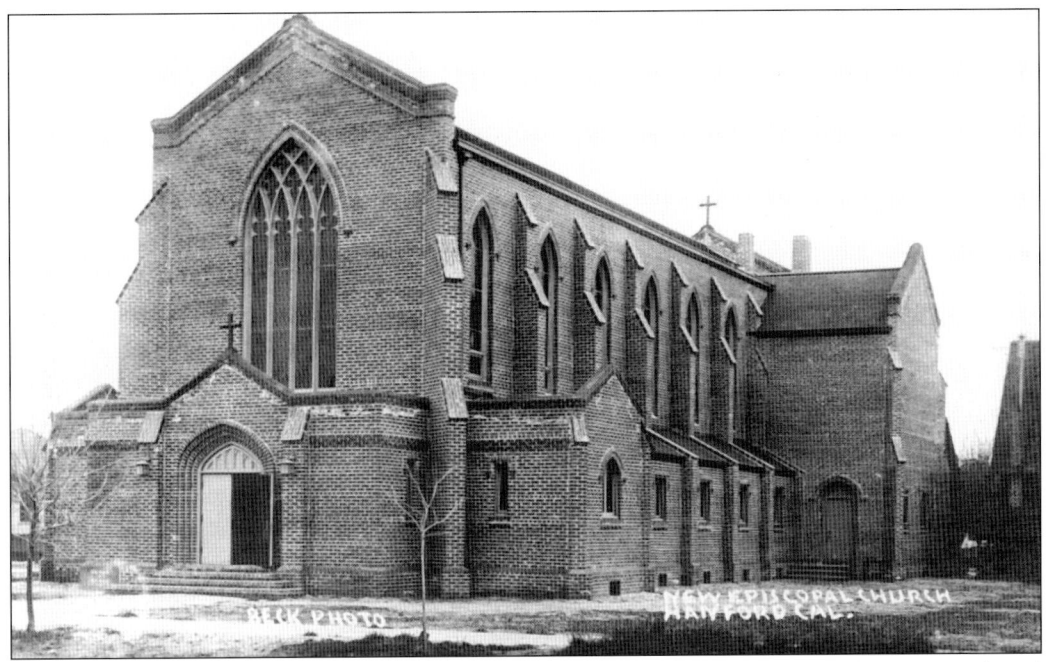

EPISCOPAL CHURCH. The Episcopal Church was founded in 1880 as a mission and developed into a self-supporting parish in 1891. This building, designed by the architectural firm of the McDougal Brothers, was built in 1910. The building is still in use today.

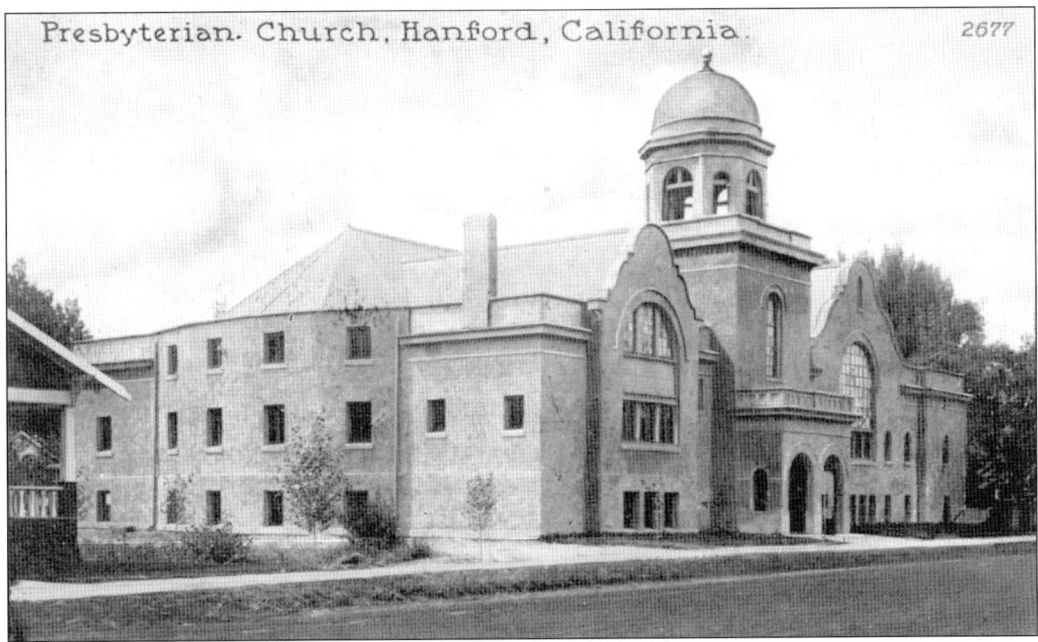

FIRST PRESBYTERIAN CHURCH. Here is First Presbyterian Church as it appeared in 1914. Built in 1913, it was located on the southwest corner of Dewey Irwin Streets. In 1981, the building was demolished.

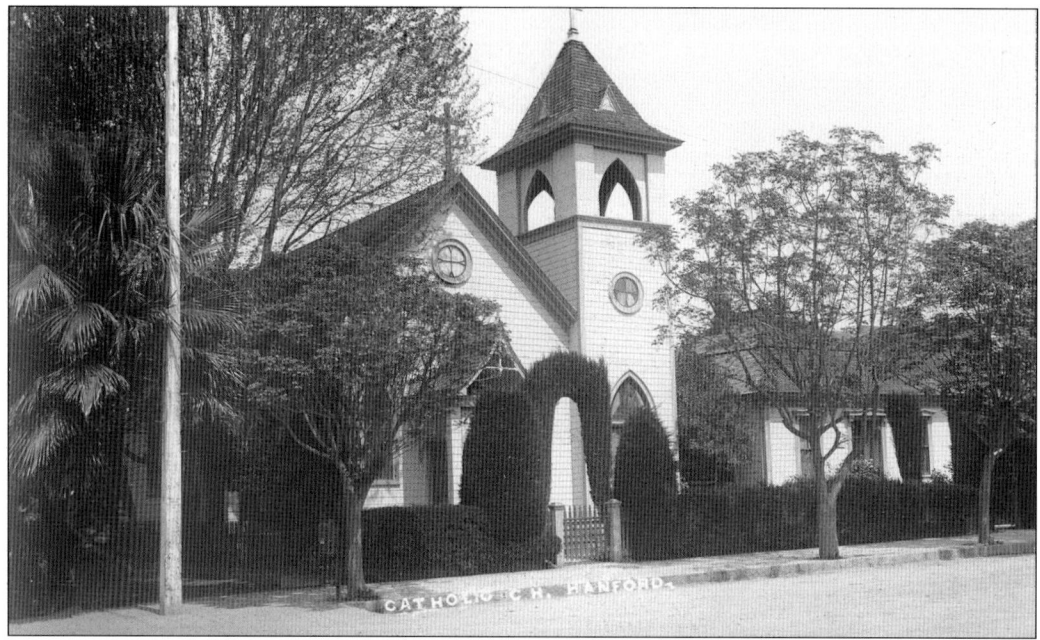

ST. BRIGID'S CHURCH, HANFORD. The original Catholic church in Hanford, this is St. Brigid's Church as it appeared in 1911. Established in 1881, the building was located on the northeast corner of Seventh and Redington Streets. It moved twice—once to the northeast corner of Douty and Florinda Streets and again in 1927, to the corner of Second and Douty Streets. It was renamed Our Lady of Guadalupe.

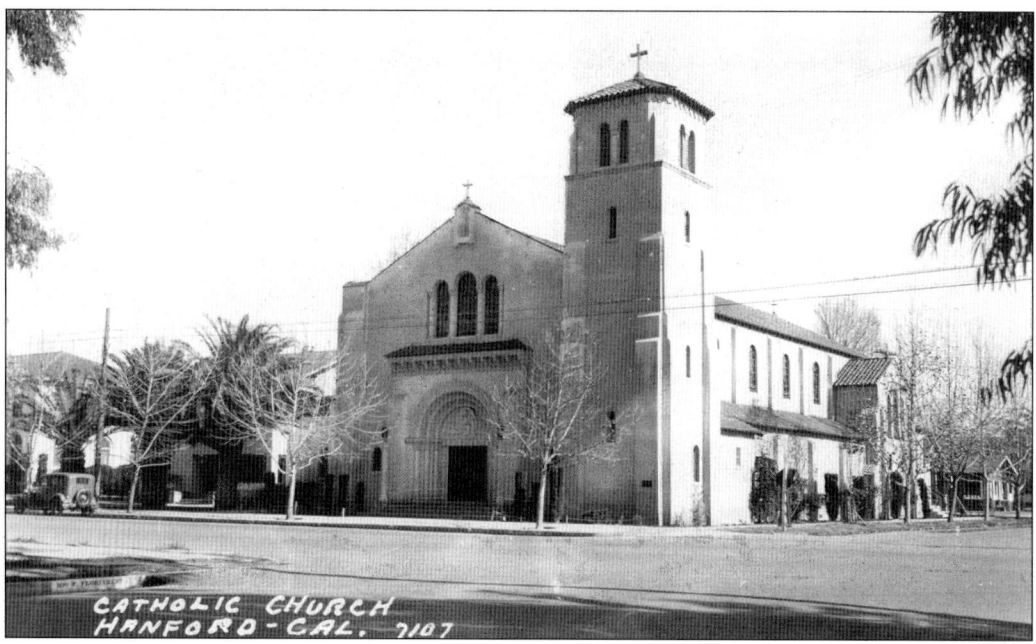

NEW ST. BRIGID'S CHURCH. After the original church was moved off the northeast corner of Douty and Florinda Streets, a new church was built. Designed by Swartz and Ryland of Fresno, it was built at a cost of $65,545 and was dedicated on February 5, 1928. It is still in use today.

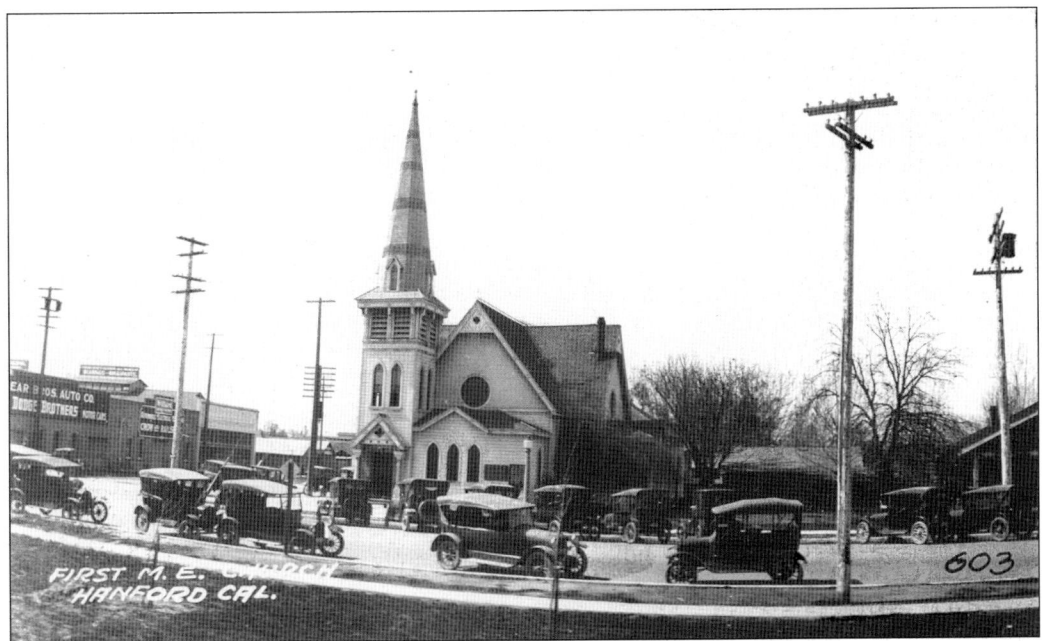

First Methodist Episcopal Church. In 1880, the Methodist Episcopal Church was founded. The building pictured in this 1918 proof postcard was constructed in 1890 at a cost of $8,700. In 1927, the William Fox Company purchased the property and replaced the church with the newly constructed Hanford Fox Theatre, which opened January 1, 1929.

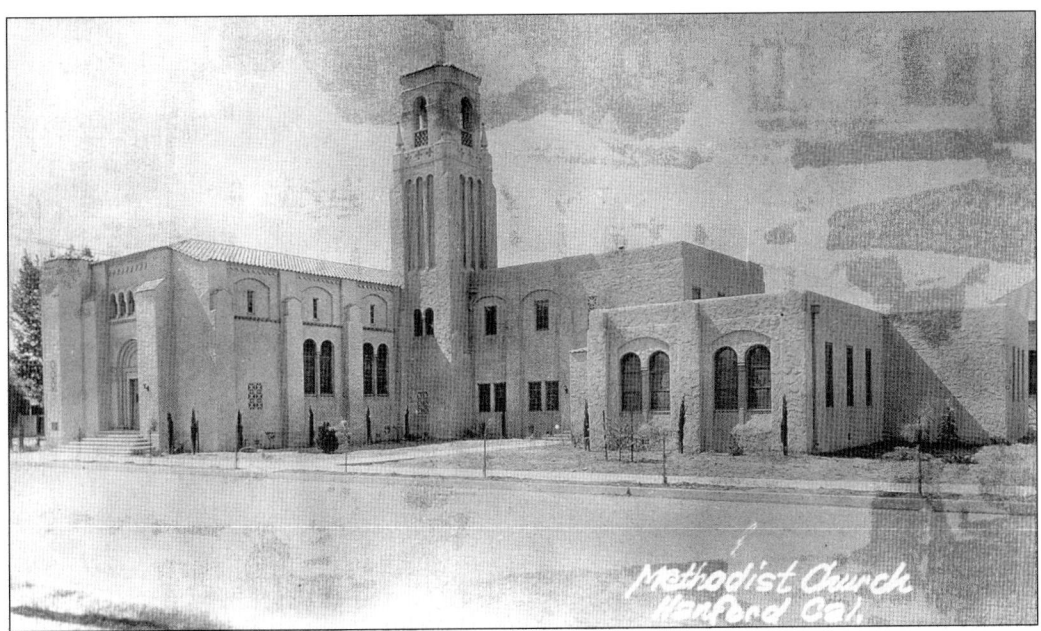

New First Methodist Episcopal. After the Fox Company purchased the original church property, a new church was built on the northeast corner of Center and Redington Streets, where it is still in use today.

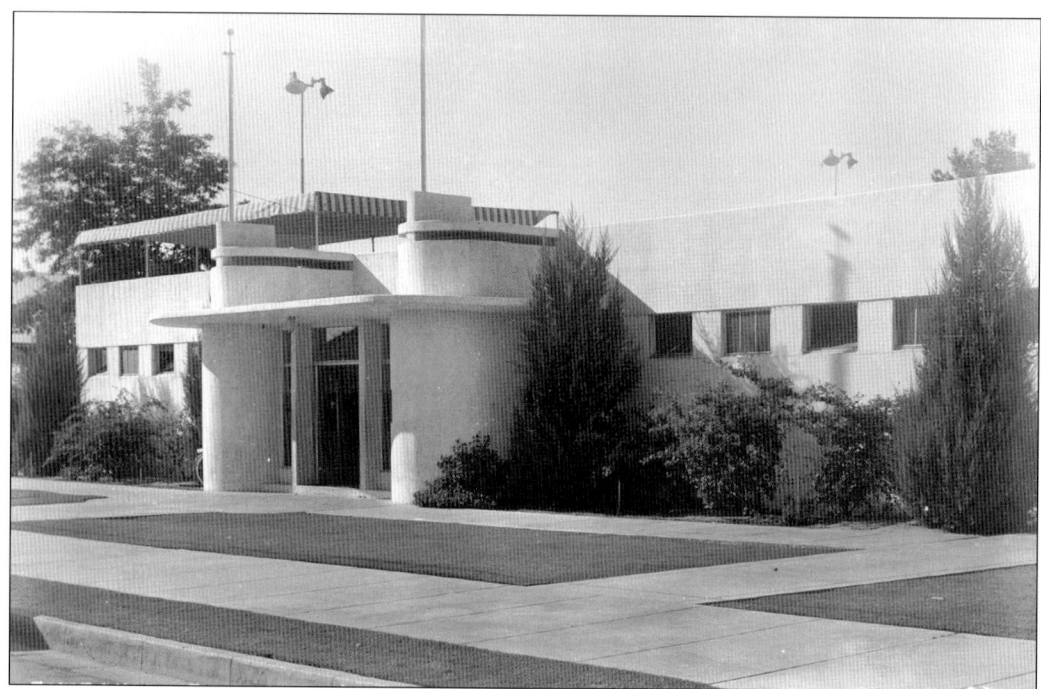

HANFORD POOL. This unused postcard shows the swimming pool building as it appeared in 1942. Built in 1938 by David Horn of Fresno, the structure was a WPA Project and cost $30,000. It was demolished in the late 1980s.

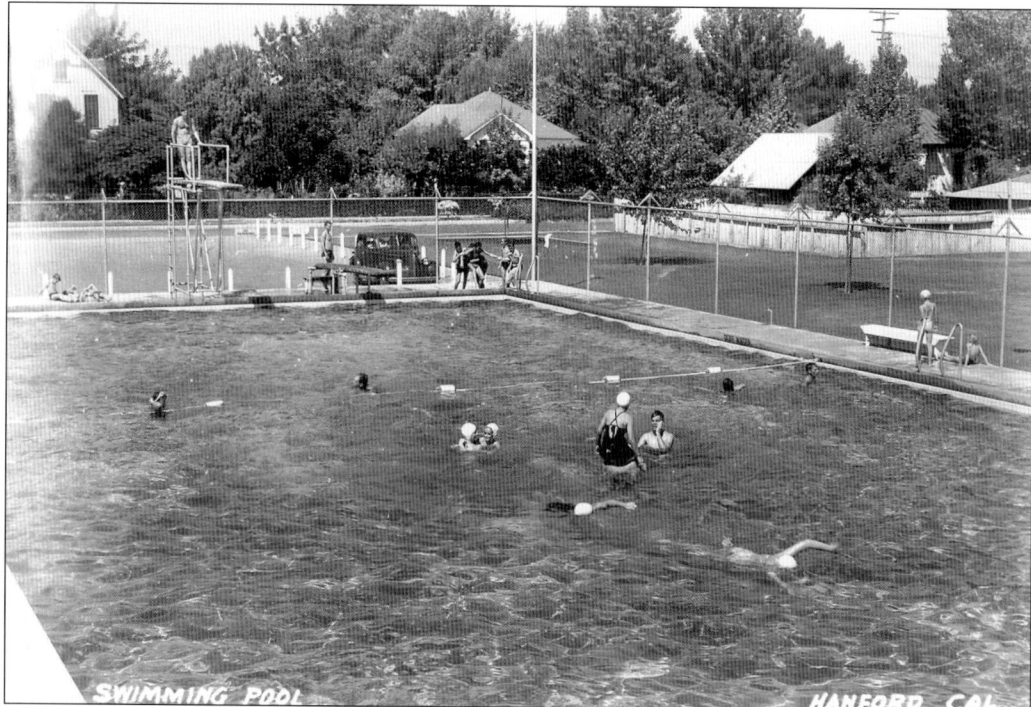

HANFORD PLUNGE. Affectionately known as "The Plunge," the pool was a popular hangout. It was replaced by a more modern pool facility in the 1990s.

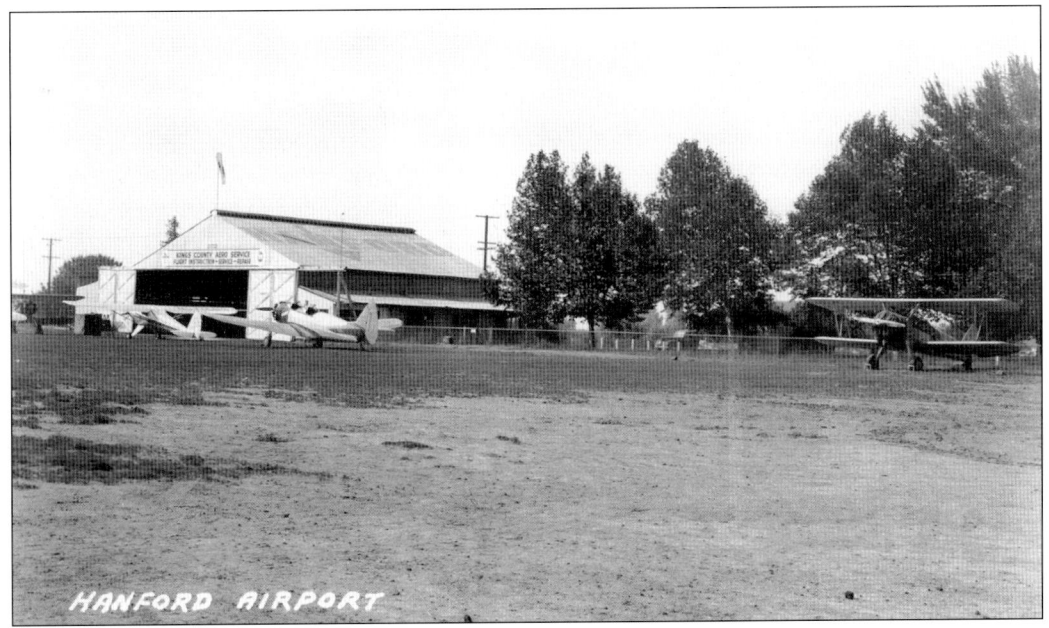

HANFORD AIRPORT. Dedicated in 1930, the airport was considered a major boon to the county. Regular postal air service used the facility along with agricultural spraying companies. A crop dusting flight school was located there for many years.

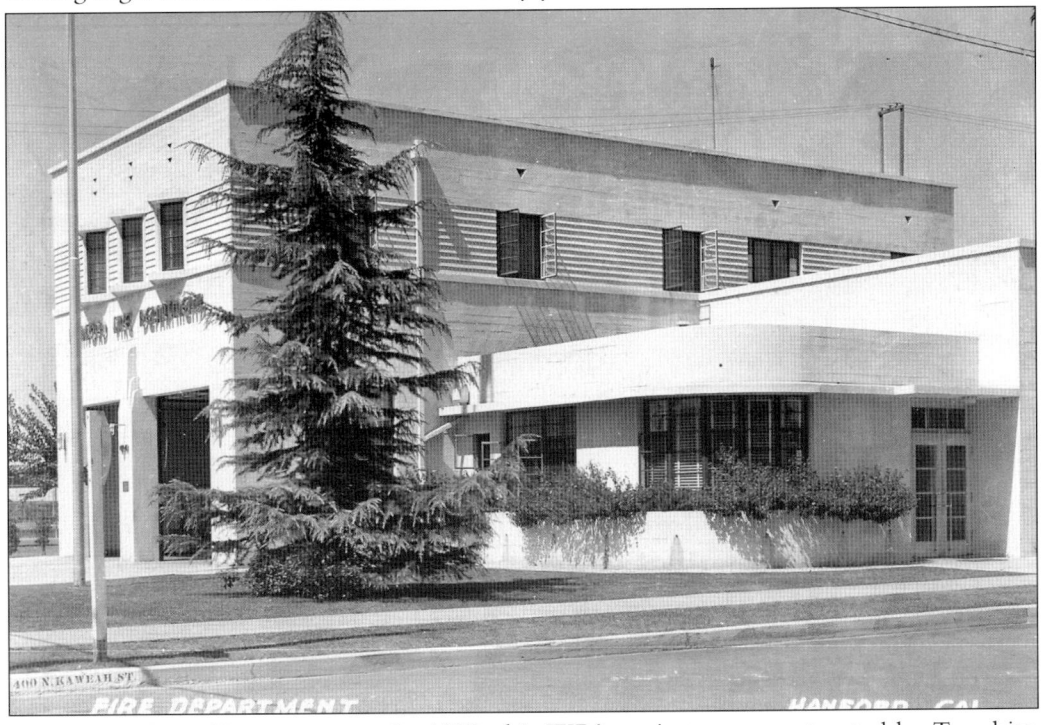

HANFORD FIRE DEPARTMENT. In 1939, this WPA project was constructed by Trewhitt, Shields, and Fisher at a cost of $38,635. The building was the main fire department location until a newer facility was constructed in 1987. Currently the building houses the fire trucks of the Hanford Visitor Agency.

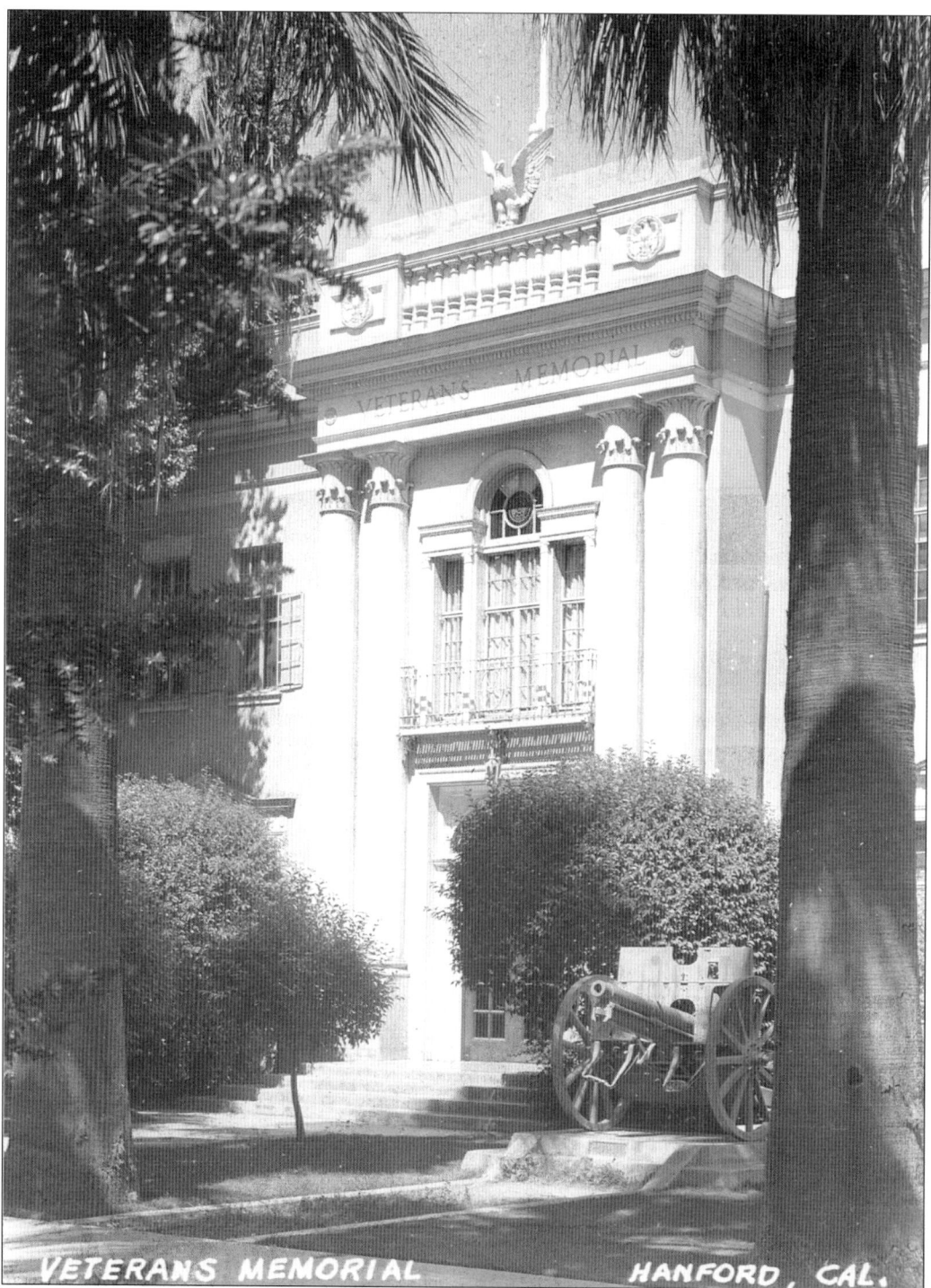

VETERANS' MEMORIAL HALL. The Hanford Veterans' Memorial Hall, seen in this late-1940s postcard, was designed by Swartz and Ryland of Fresno. It was built in 1925 at a cost of $46,000. It is the home of the American Legion, Post No. 3. The cannon in front is a captured German 88 Howizer from World War I. The building is now used as a senior center.

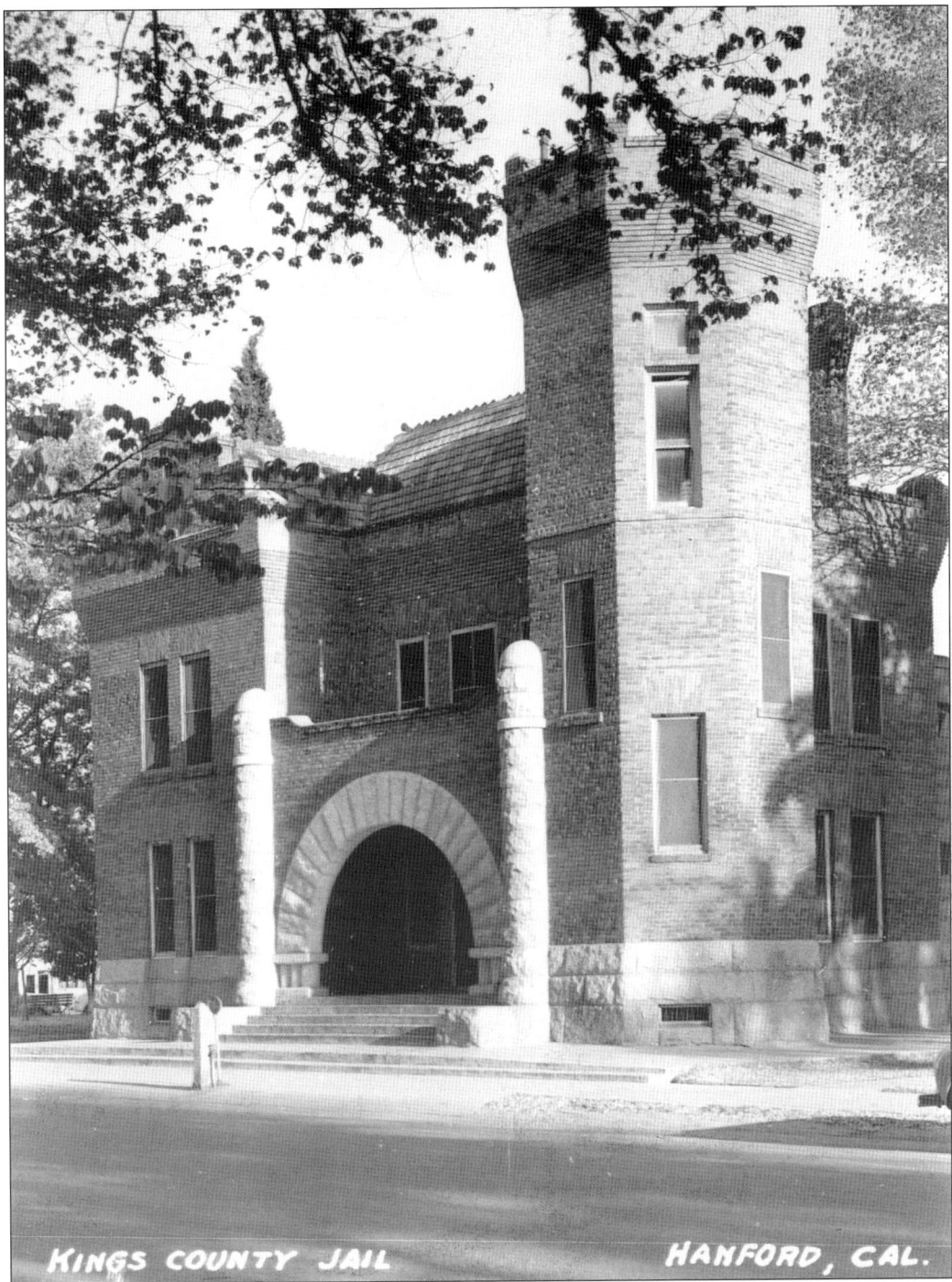

KINGS COUNTY JAIL. One of the more difficult Kings County postcard views to find is that of the jail, designed by McDougal Brothers Architects. It was built by Owens and Griffith of Exeter for $10,663. Construction on the jail began in 1897 and was completed by November 1, 1898. The building served as the county jail until 1964 when a new facility was built. Today the building houses a restaurant and bar. (Courtesy Martha Bentley.)

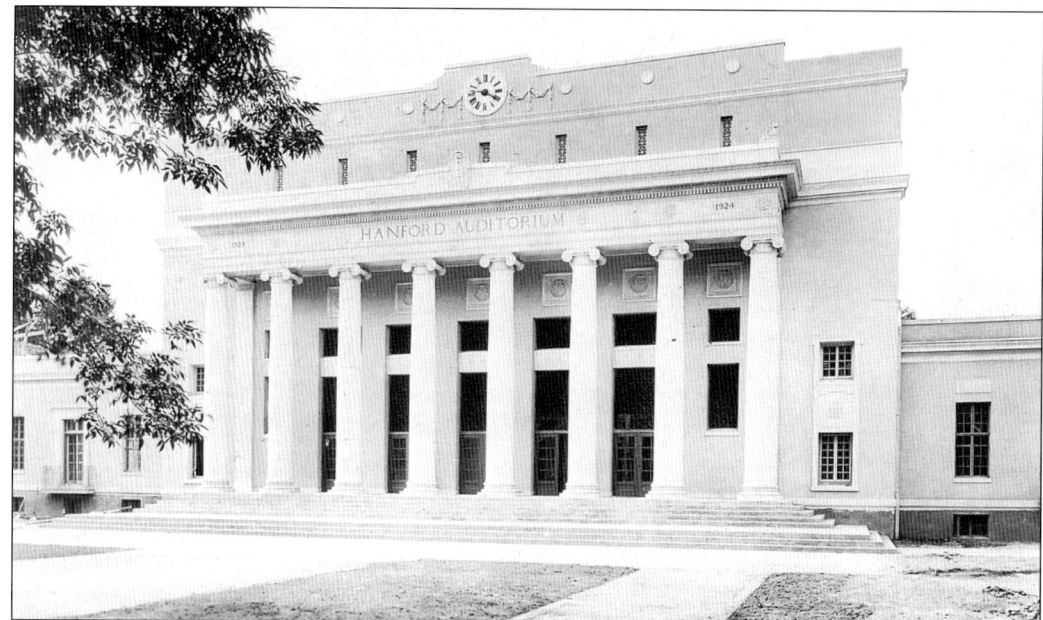

CIVIC AUDITORIUM, HANFORD. In 1923, the citizens of Hanford approved a $195,000 bond to build the Hanford Civic Auditorium. Its purpose was to attract large events to the area. Built at a cost of $217,948.91, the building was designed by Coats and Traver and constructed by Brindle and Bebeau. It was dedicated on May 22, 1925.

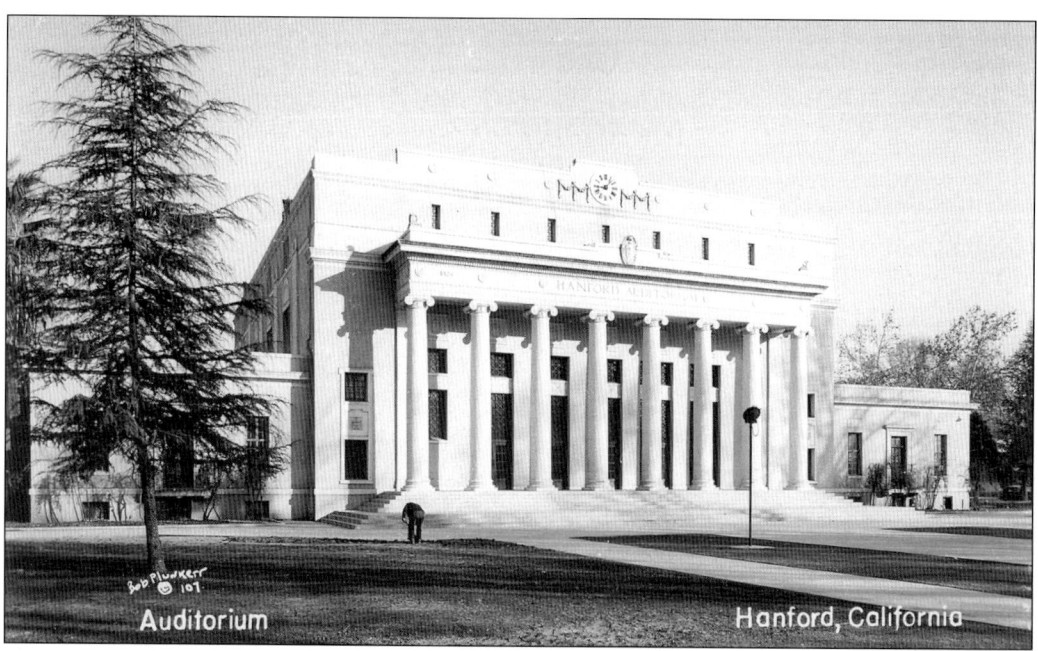

HANFORD CIVIC AUDITORIUM, 1940s. This postcard shows the auditorium in the late 1940s. The clock in the facade came from the Hanford Grammar School, which originally occupied the site.

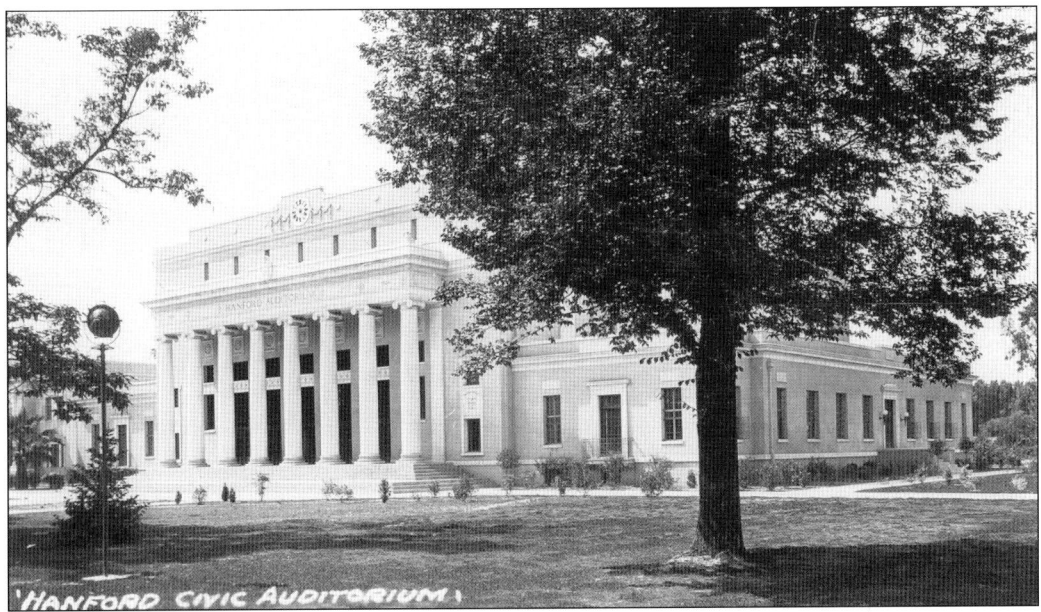

HANFORD CIVIC AUDITORIUM. This postcard view shows the auditorium shortly after its construction. The building was home to the Hanford City offices, the Hanford Police Department, and Company B, 184th Infantry of the California National Guard.

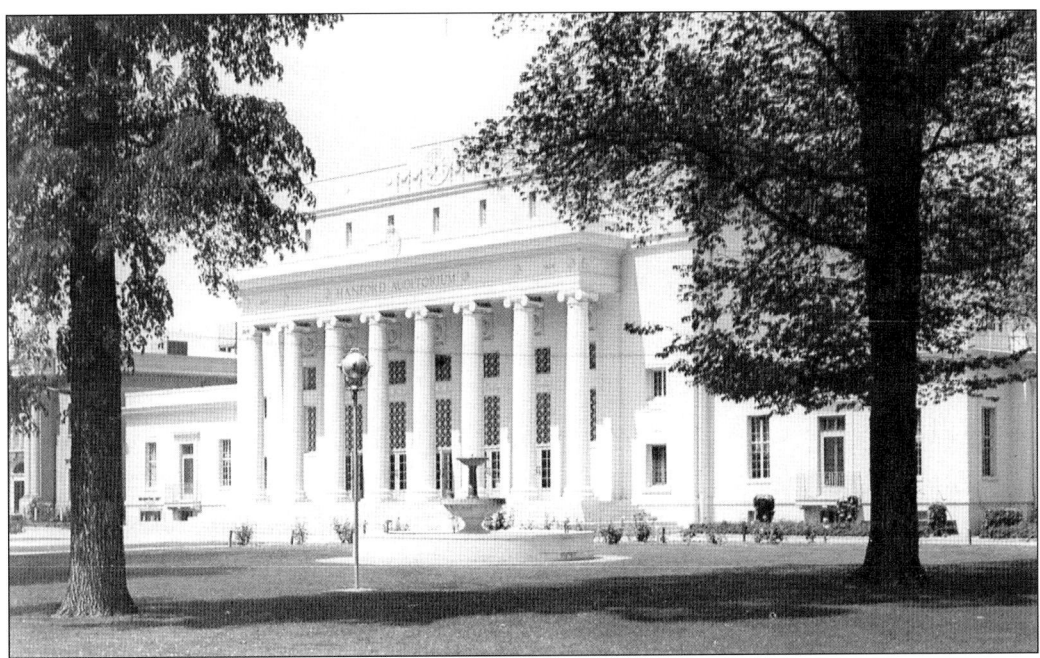

HANFORD CIVIC AUDITORIUM FOUNTAIN. This water fountain was installed in front of auditorium and dedicated to the early pioneers of Kings County. The building is considered to be one of the crowning features of Hanford development. It is still in use today.

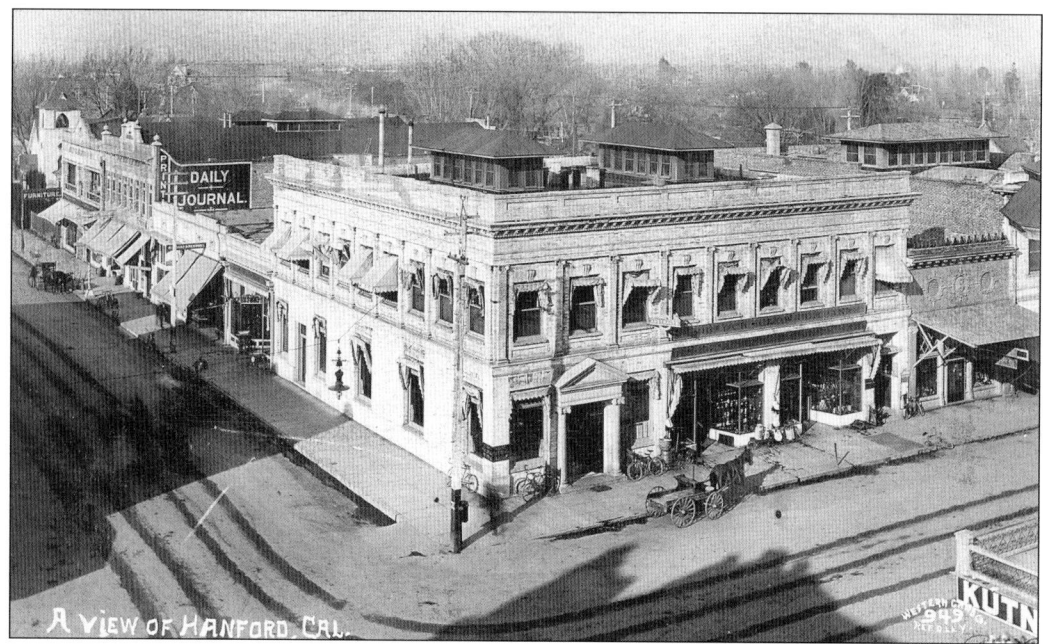

BIRD'S-EYE VIEW, HANFORD. The northwest corner of Seventh and Irwin Streets is seen in this 1911 postcard. To the left is St. Brigid's Church and to its right is the office of the *Hanford Daily Journal*. The building on the corner was the First National Bank of Hanford.

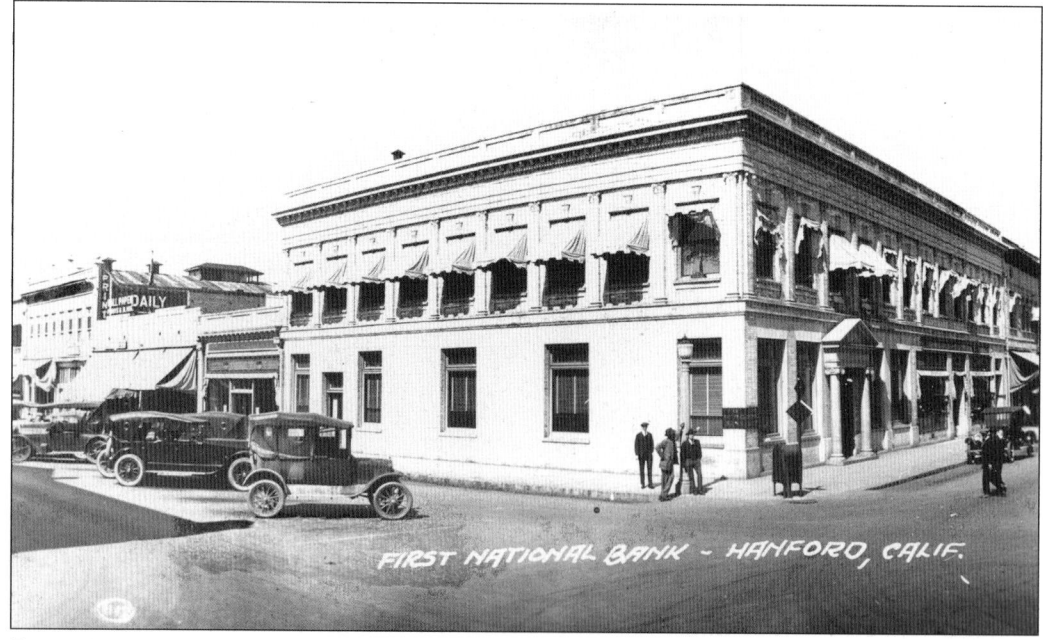

FIRST NATIONAL BANK, HANFORD. This early 1920s postcard shows the First National Bank. During the 1930s, it was known as the Anglo-California National Bank and later the Crocker National Bank. The building was demolished in the late 1950s and replaced with a newer bank building. This site is now occupied by Wells Fargo Bank.

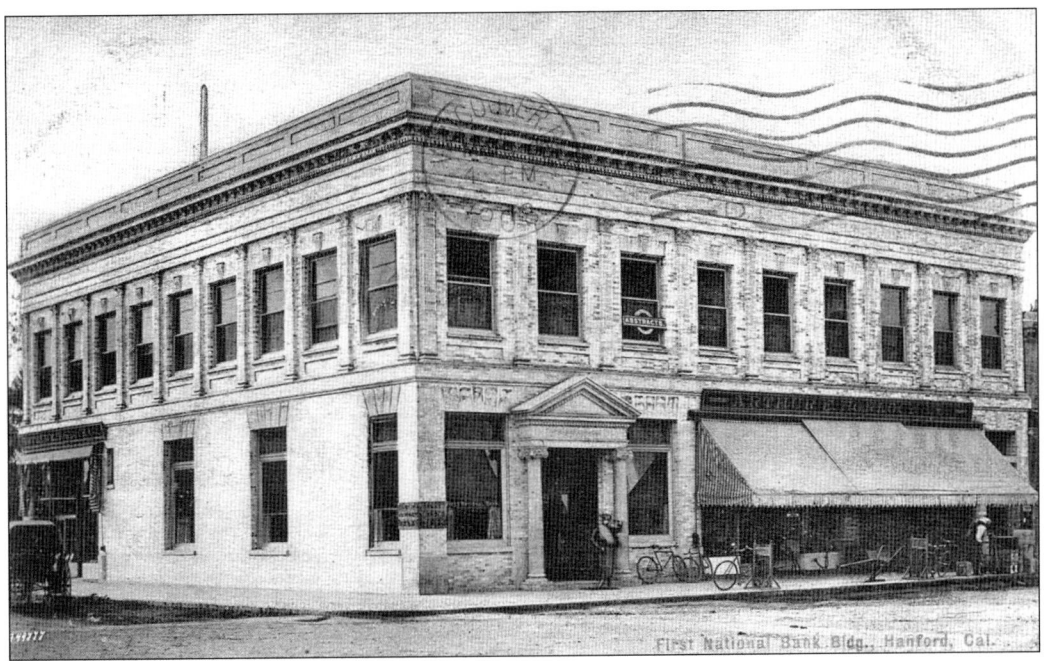

FIRST NATIONAL BANK, 1908. This 1908 postmarked card depicts a close-up view of the First National Bank Building. The intersection of Irwin and Seventh Streets was one of the busiest in the city.

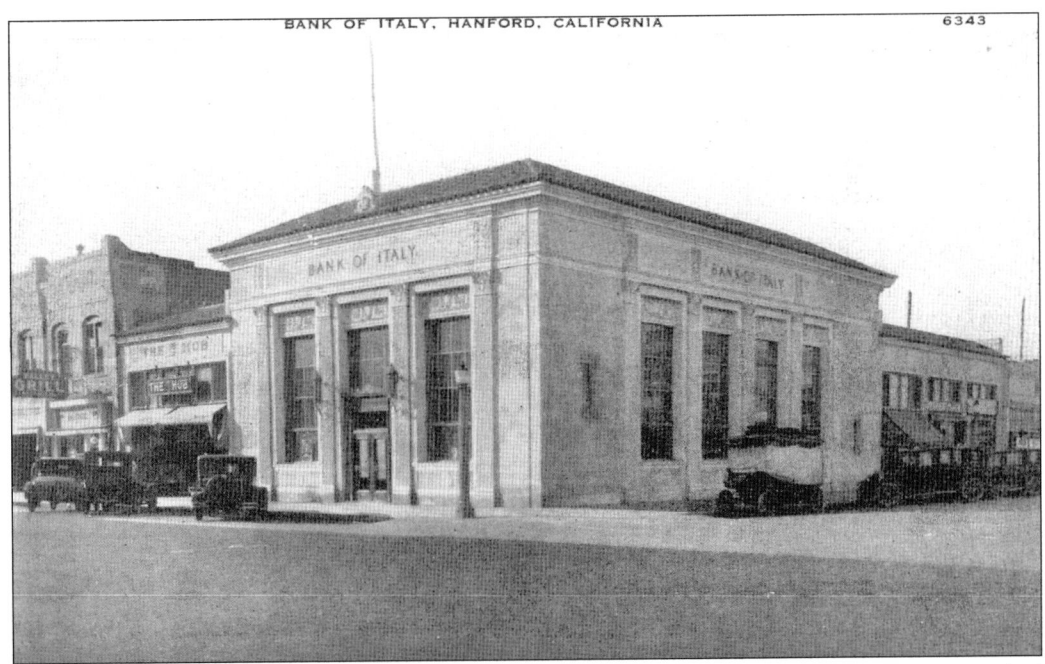

BANK OF ITALY, HANFORD. In the early 1920s, two local banks, The Old Bank and Hanford National Bank, were purchased by the Bank of Italy. This building was built in 1925 at a cost of $175,000 on the old Sharples Building site. By 1930, the bank changed its name to Bank of America.

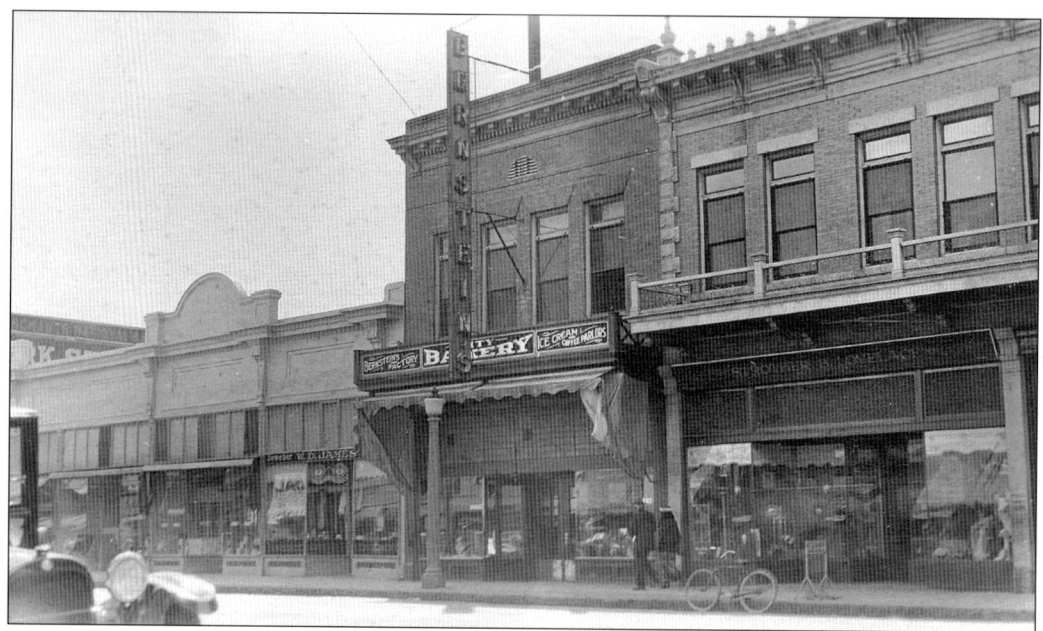

BERNSTEIN'S BAKERY AND CANDY FACTORY. The Bernstein Bakery Building was located at 119 West Seventh Street. The bakery was originally established in 1893 by Fred Bader. In 1903, W. F. Bernstein purchased the business. The business was later purchased by the Peden family, which operated a restaurant and bakery at the same location. It currently houses an antique shop.

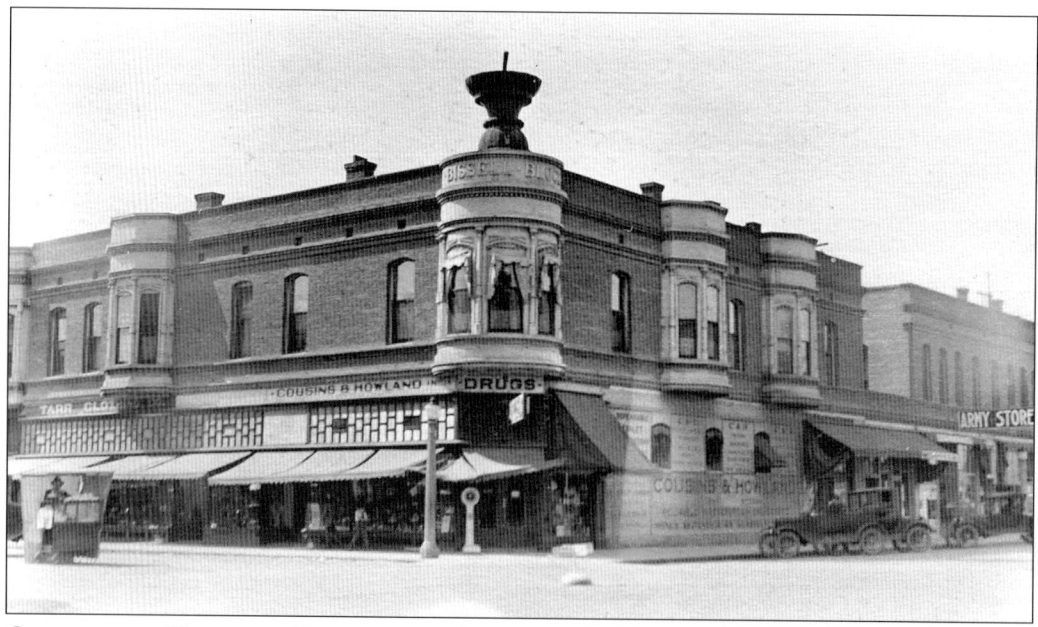

COUSINS AND HOWLAND PHARMACY. This unused postcard depicts the Cousins and Howland Pharmacy that was located on the northwest corner of Douty and Seventh Streets. The building, designed by architect S. E. French, was built in 1899 by San Francisco capitalist F. W. Van Sicklin. Until the early 1990s, a pharmacy occupied this corner. A shoe store occupies the location today.

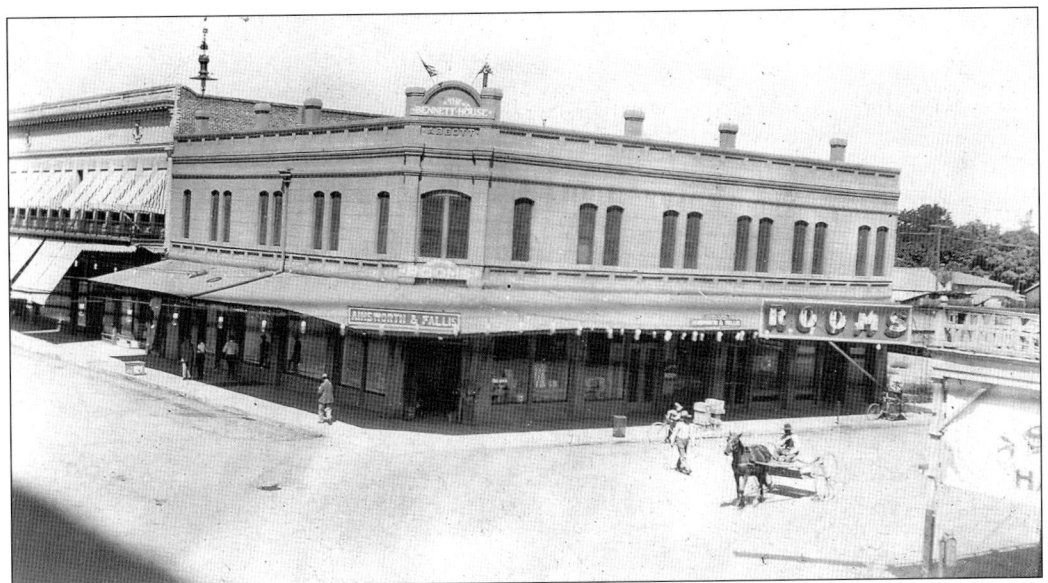

ABBOTT BUILDING. Currently located on the northeast corner of Douty and Seventh Streets, this building was built in 1891 by Kate Jacobs, who operated a hotel at the location until 1899. In 1900, it was renamed the Abbott Building and has had numerous tenants. The building is fully occupied today by numerous local businesses.

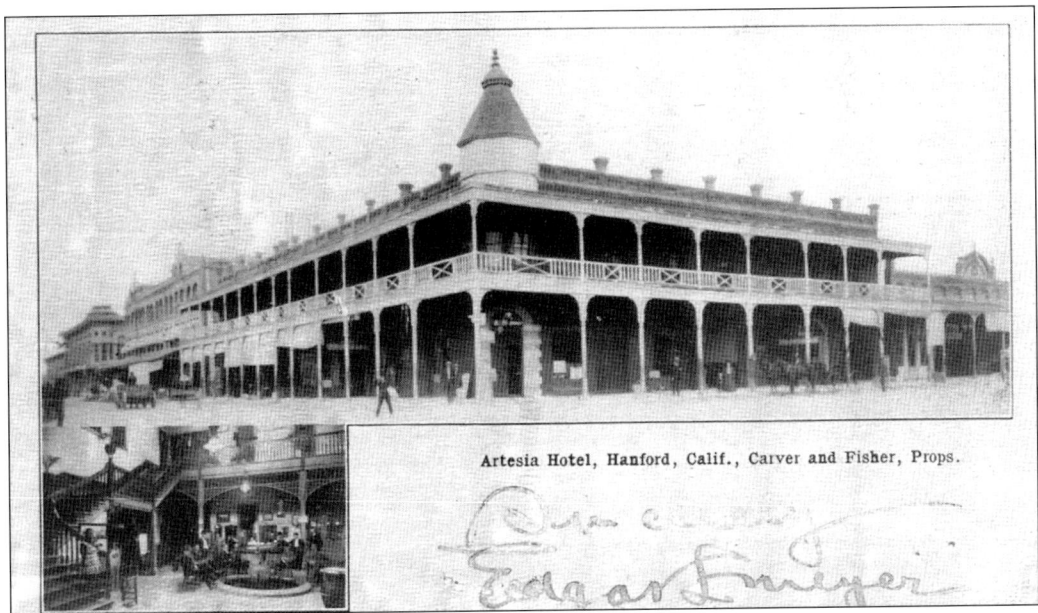

ARTESIA HOTEL. Built in 1891 by the Hanford Development Company, the original hotel burnt in June of that same year and was promptly rebuilt. The building took its name from a natural artesian well that was located in the hotel lobby.

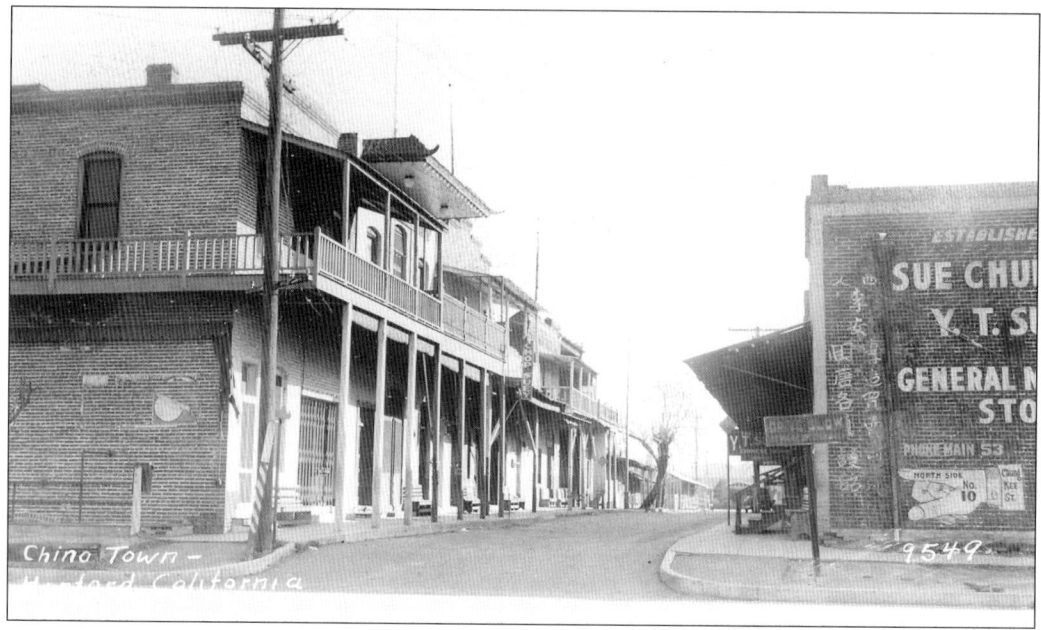

CHINA ALLEY, HANFORD. Kings County was home to the largest Chinese community outside of San Francisco. The center of this community was Chinatown, located in a several block area surrounding Brown Street between Sixth and Ninth Streets in Hanford. Y. T. Sue was a local herbalist who prospered in Hanford. (Courtesy Ron Burris.)

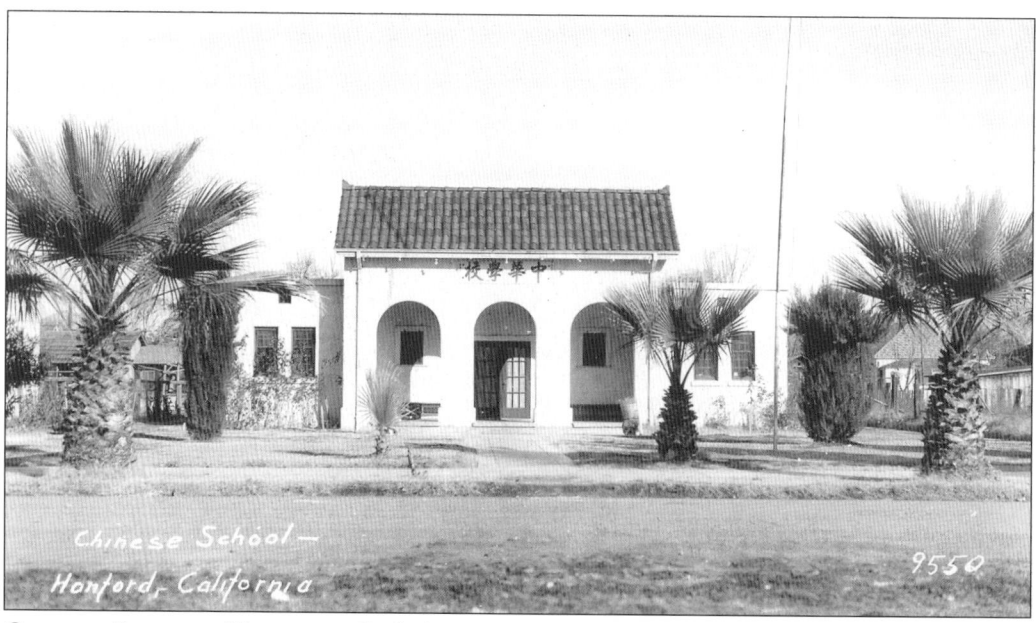

CHINESE SCHOOL, HANFORD. Built in 1922 at a cost of $3,500, Chinese children were sent here to learn the language, history, and culture of their parents. Used continuously until the mid-1950s, it now serves as a community theatre. (Courtesy Ron Burris.)

Two

LEMOORE

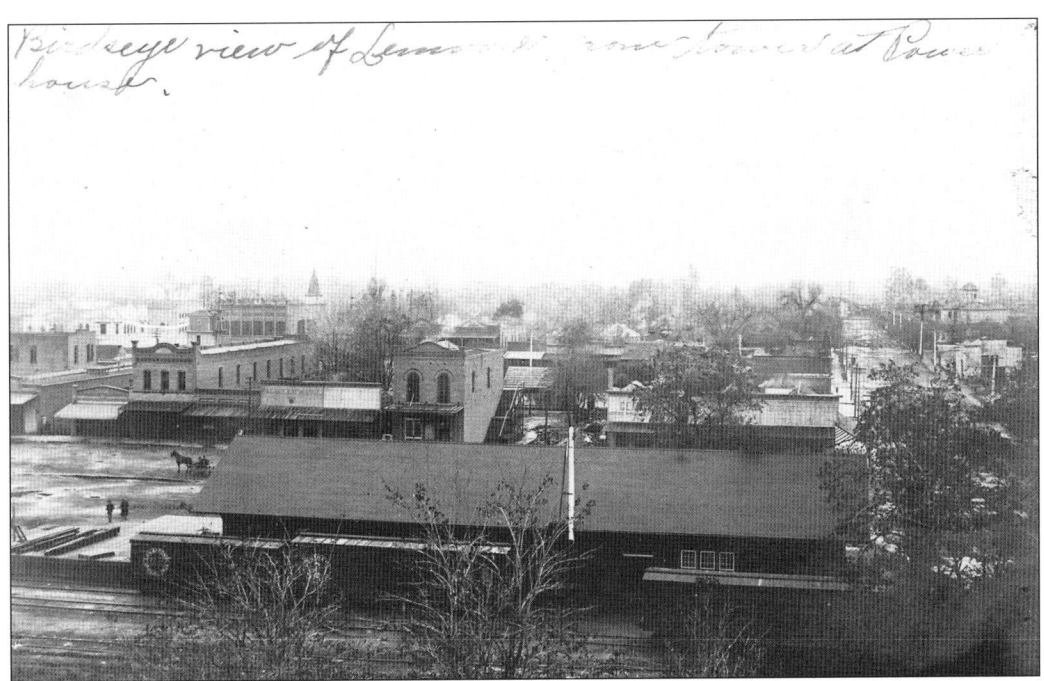

BIRD'S-EYE VIEW OF LEMOORE. This picture, taken on a foggy day, shows Lemoore as it appeared prior to 1912. The building in the foreground is the original Southern Pacific train depot. The street behind it is E Street. The building in the far right is the original Lemoore High School. The buildings shown in the middle are the Lemoore Odd Fellows Building and the Bank of Lemoore. (Courtesy James Hickman.)

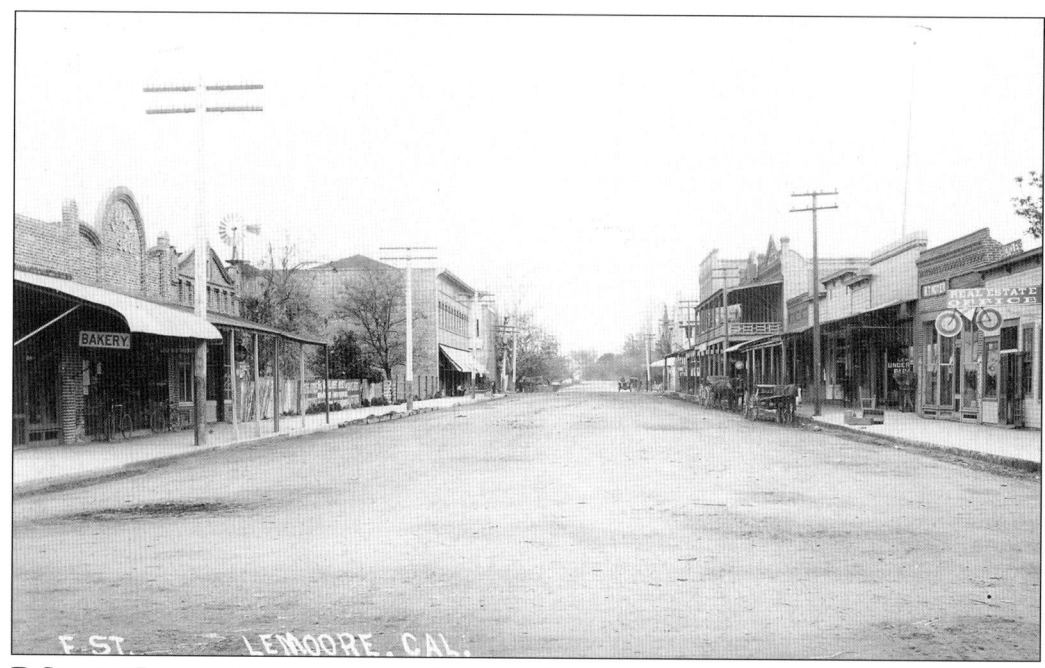

D Street Looking East toward Heinlen Street. This unused postcard shows D Street as it appeared around 1910. The two-story building on the right side with the balcony is the Lucerne Hotel. The card is erroneously identified as F Street.

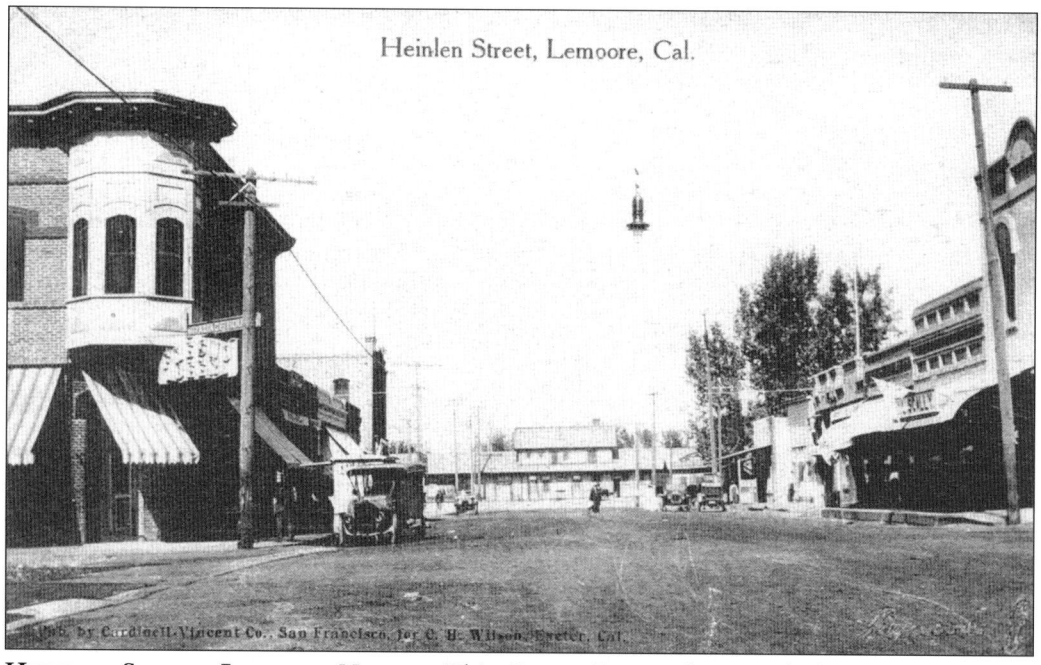

Heinlen Street Looking North. This George Besaw photograph shows Antlers Hotel on the left and the railroad depot in the background. The depot was torn down and recently replaced by another depot brought in from Strathmore, California.

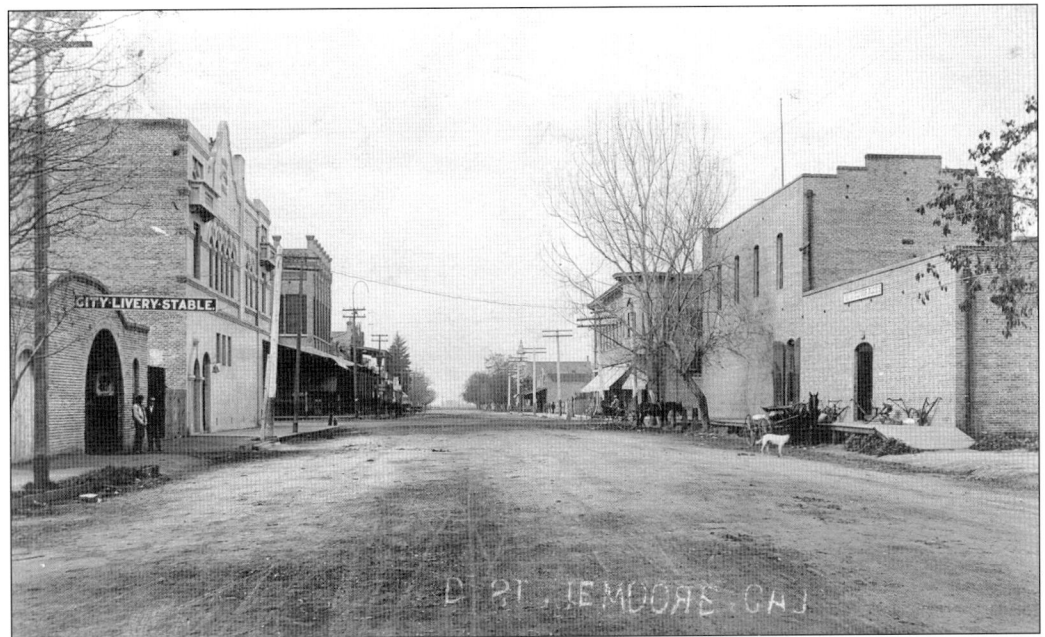

D STREET LOOKING WEST TOWARD HEINLEN STREET. In this 1909 postmarked card, D Street looks west. To the left is the City Livery Stable, built after 1905. Next to it is the Lemoore Odd Fellows Building. Behind the tree on the right side is Antlers Hotel.

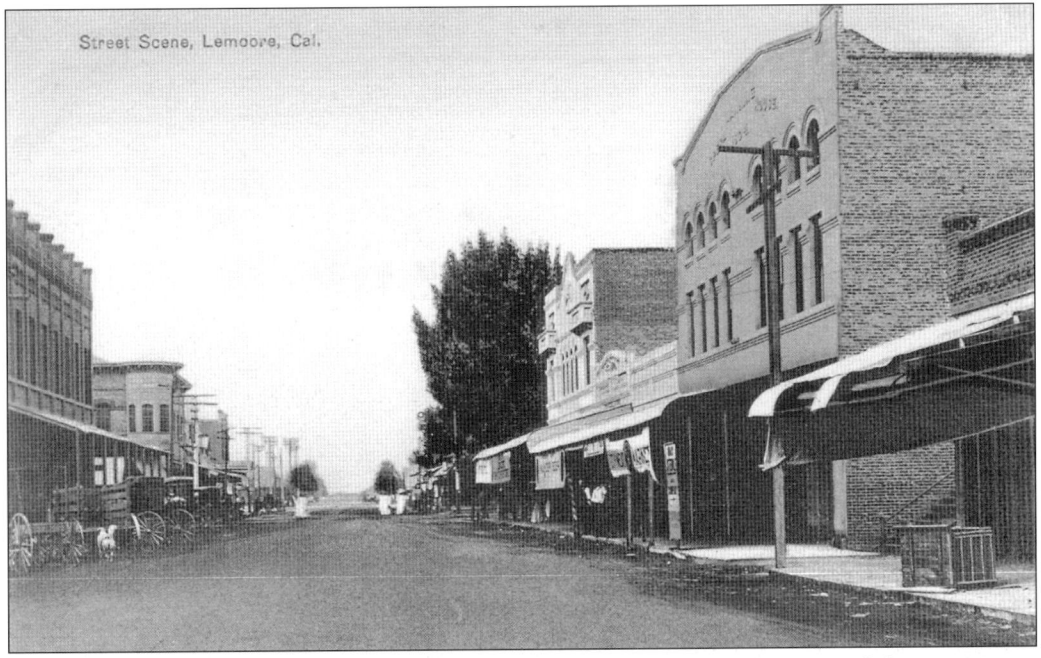

HEINLEN STREET LOOKING NORTH. This postcard view shows many of the prominent buildings of Lemoore as they appeared prior to 1910. To the left is the Bank of Lemoore while the building with the corner turret is the Antlers Hotel. To the right are the Old Fellows Lodge and the Lemoore Opera House.

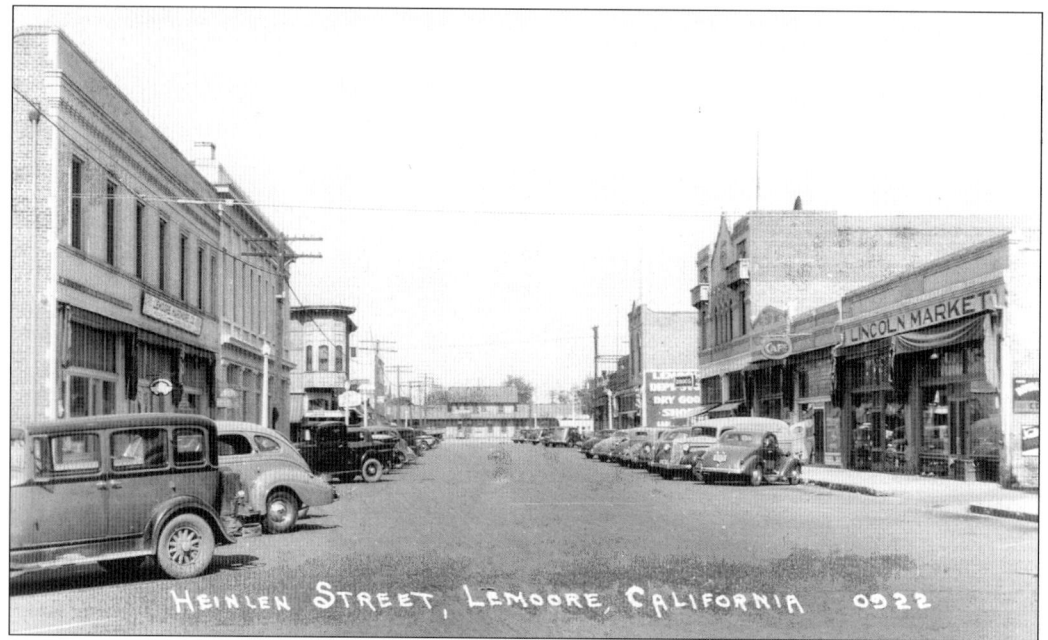

HEINLEN STREET LOOKING NORTH TOWARD D STREET. A busy Heinlen Street scene in the late 1930s shows the Southern Pacific Depot located at the end of the road.

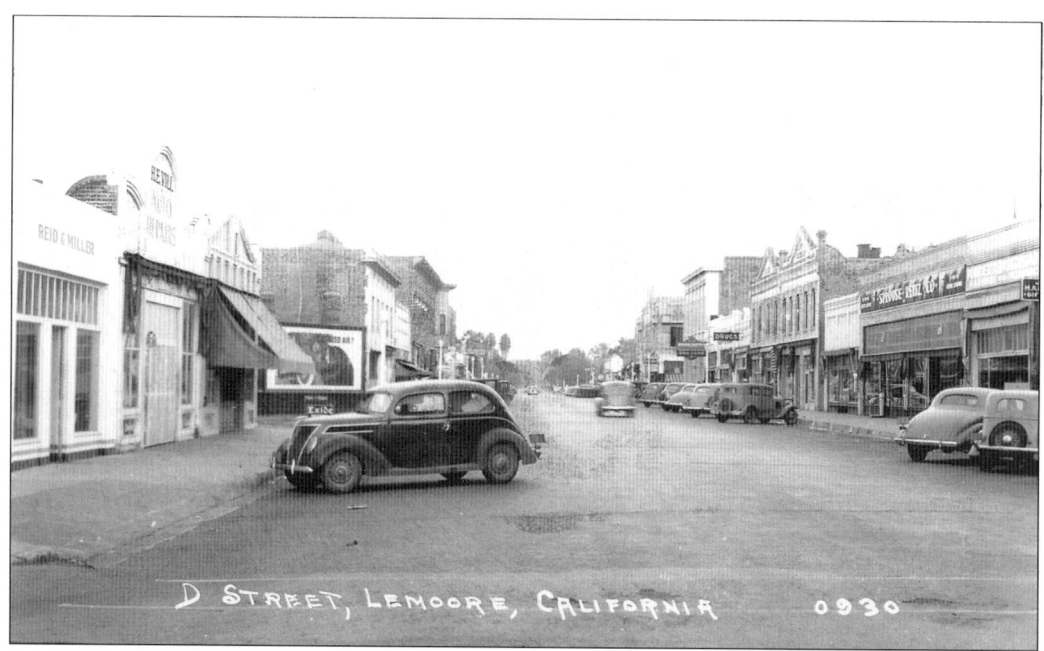

D STREET LOOKING EAST TOWARD HEINLEN STREET. This D Street view shows downtown Lemoore in the late 1930s. Note that the balcony on the Lucerne Hotel has been removed. (Courtesy Ron Lerch.)

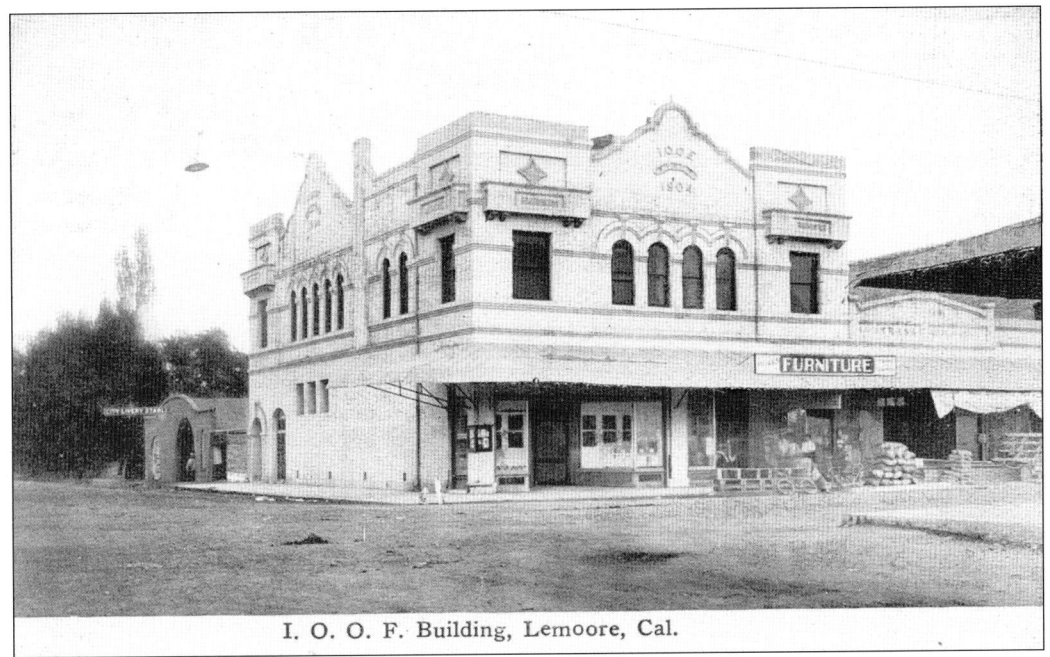

IOOF HALL. Built in 1904, the International Order of Odd Fellows Building was an imposing structure. Located on the southeast corner of D and Heinlen Streets, the building is still home to the Lemoore Odd Fellows Lodge.

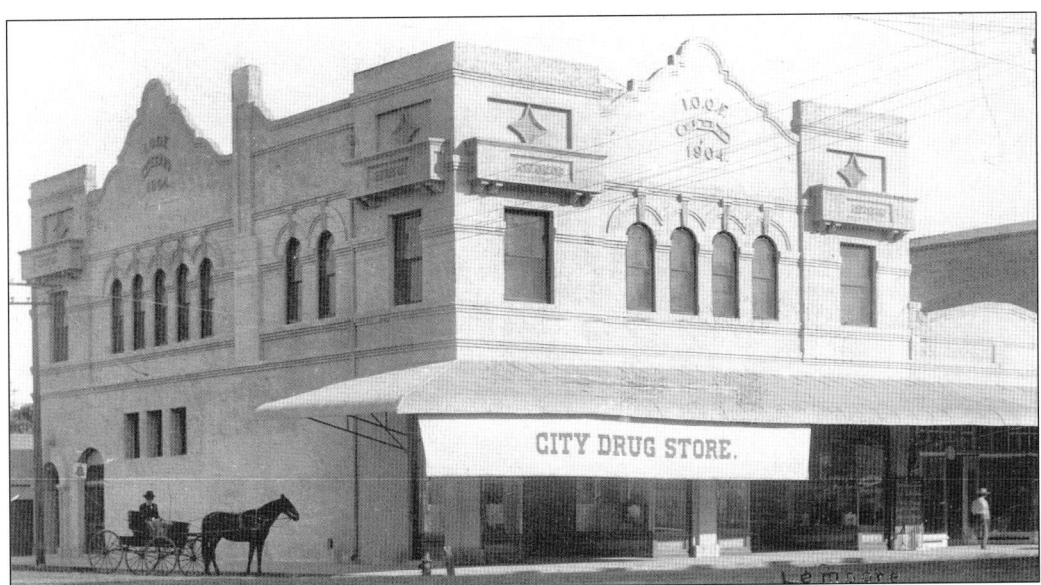

INTERNATIONAL ORDER OF ODD FELLOWS BUILDING, LEMOORE. Pictured in this postcard is the City Drug Store that was located in the ground floor of the building. A drugstore still occupies the same location.

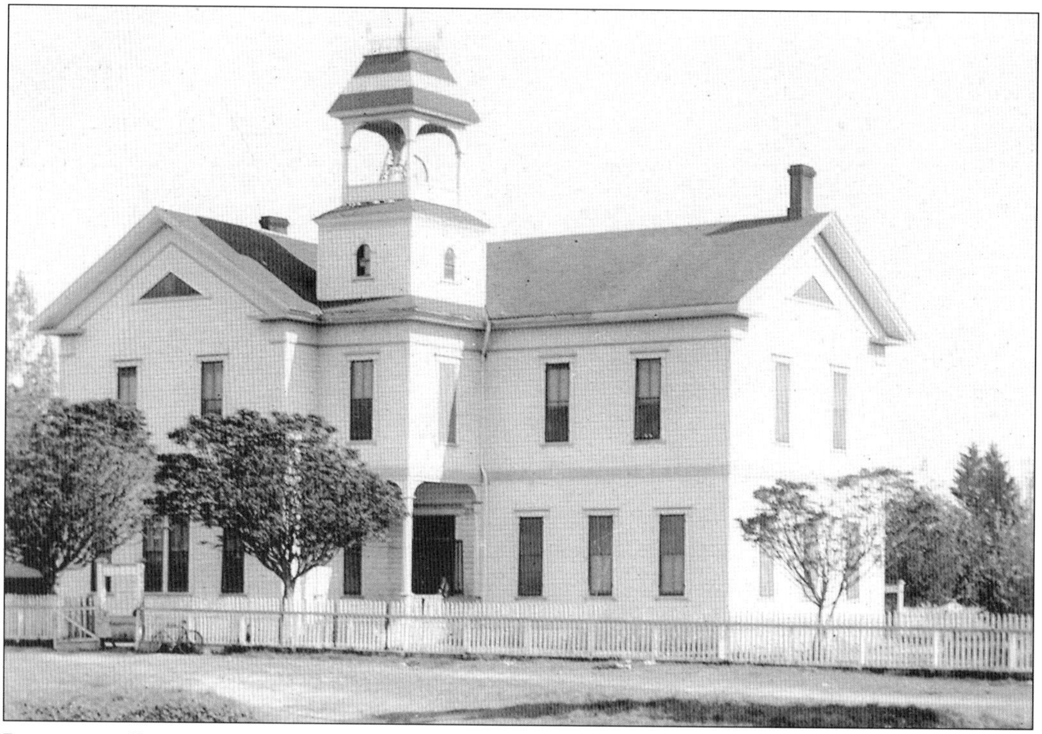

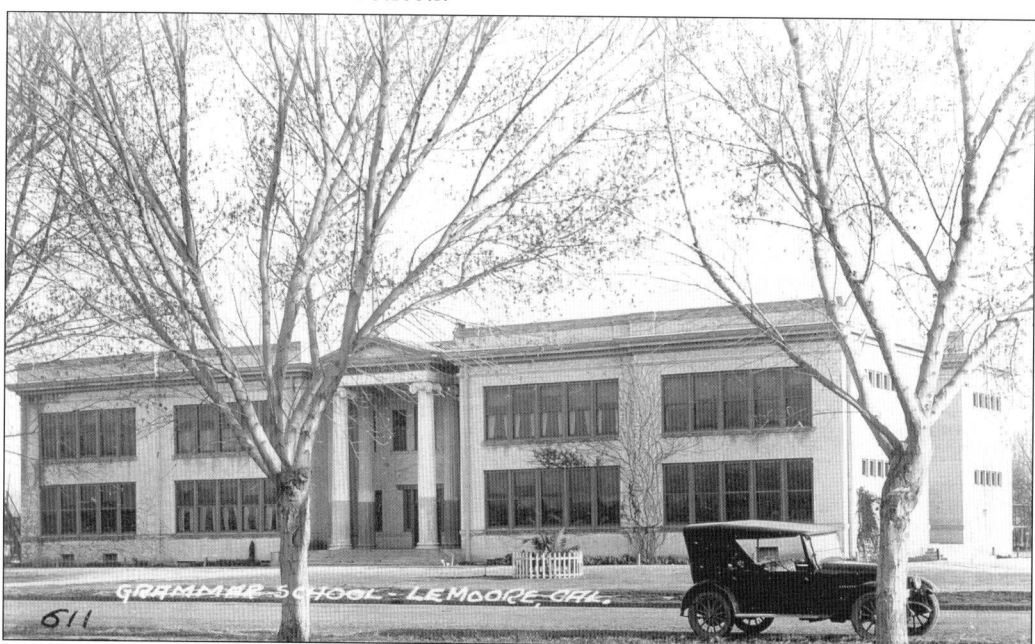

LEMOORE GRAMMAR SCHOOL. Before 1910, this was the original Lemoore Grammar School building. The building shown was built in 1882 at a cost of $10,000 and was located on the northeast corner of Follett and A Streets.

LEMOORE SCHOOL. Pictured in this postcard proof is the replacement Lemoore Grammar School. Built in 1911 at a cost of $40,000, the building was considered one of the best in the state. It occupied the southeast corner of Follett and B Streets.

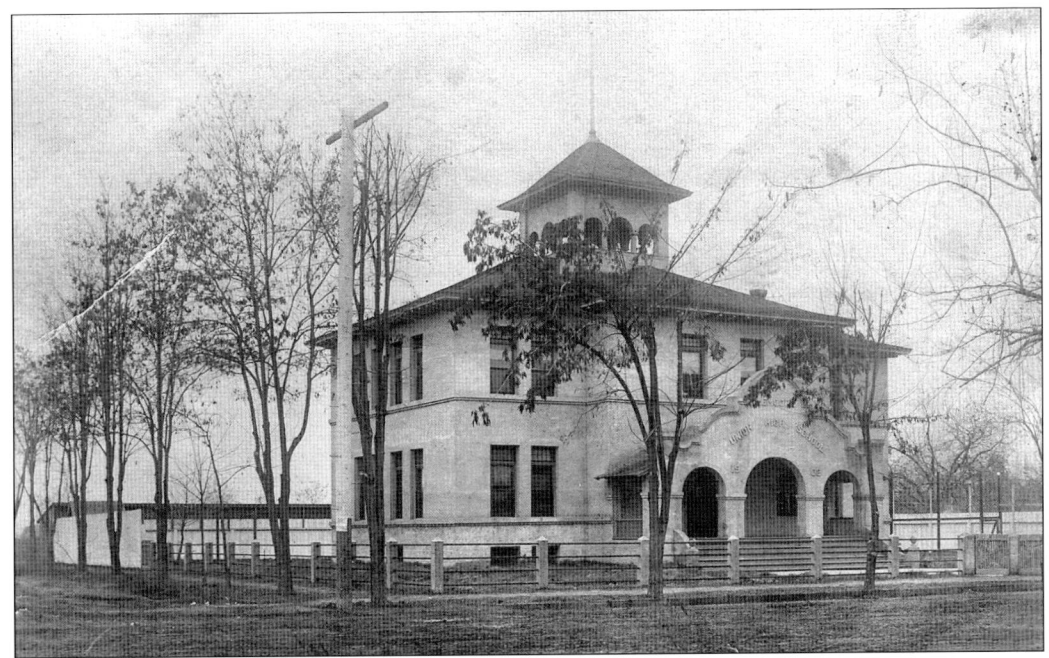

LEMOORE HIGH. This early 1900s postcard depicts the original Lemoore High School Building that occupied the northwest corner of Fox and B Streets. The structure was built in 1902 at a cost of $11,000. (Courtesy Sarah A. Mooney Memorial Museum.)

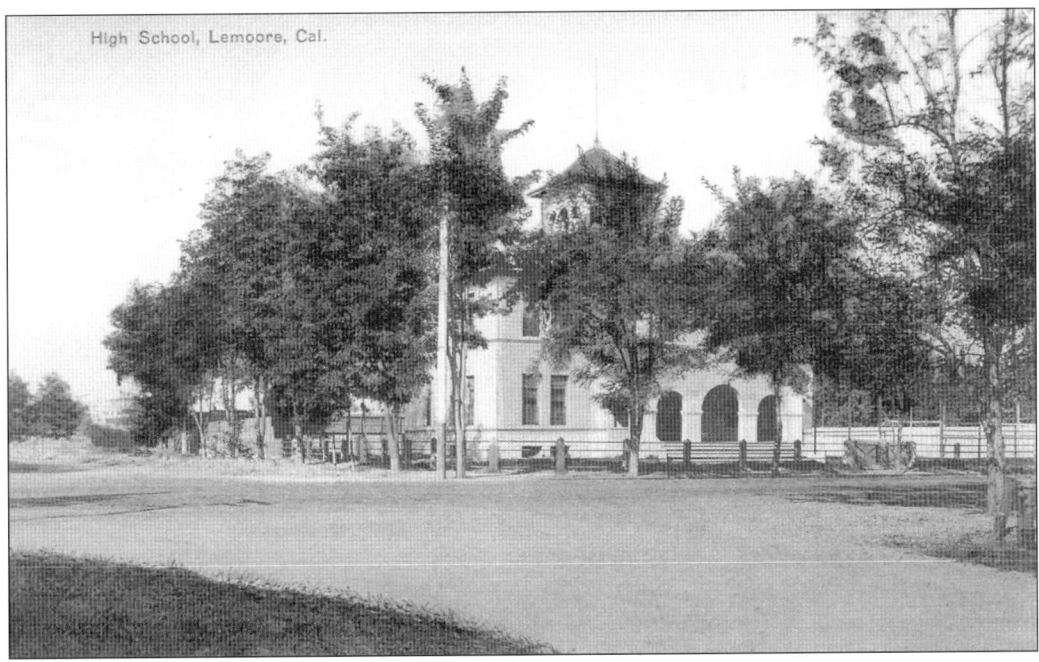

LEMOORE HIGH SCHOOL. The east side of the high school is pictured in this early 1910s postcard. The town's population quickly outgrew the school building and the citizens were faced with moving the school site in 1924.

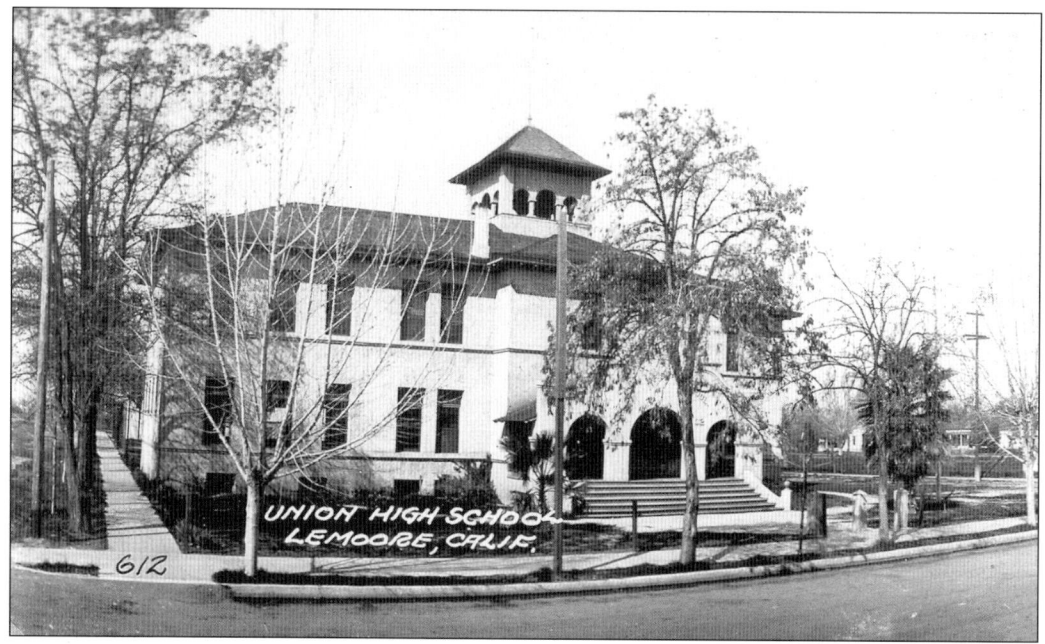

HIGH SCHOOL AFTER EXPANSION. This is the original Lemoore High School building after it underwent an expansion. The school underwent several renovations in its lifetime before being replaced.

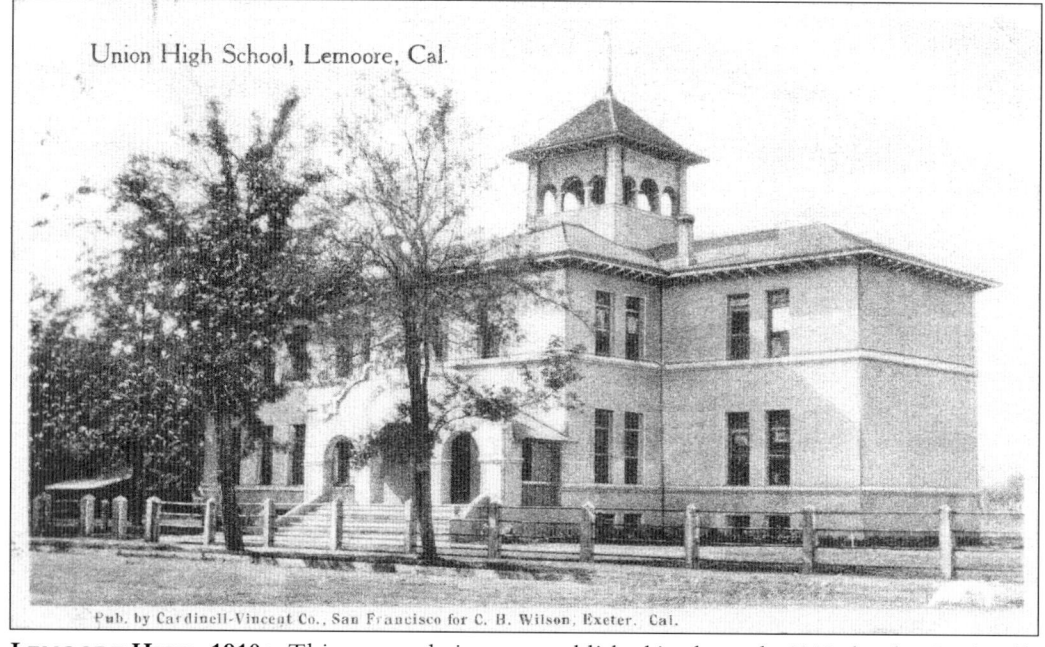

LEMOORE HIGH, 1910s. This postcard view was published in the early 1910s by the Cardinell-Vincent Company of San Francisco. The photograph was taken by George Besaw of Reedley, who later sold his negatives to the San Francisco postcard publisher. It took three bond issue votes, from 1921 to 1924, to get approval for the construction of a new school.

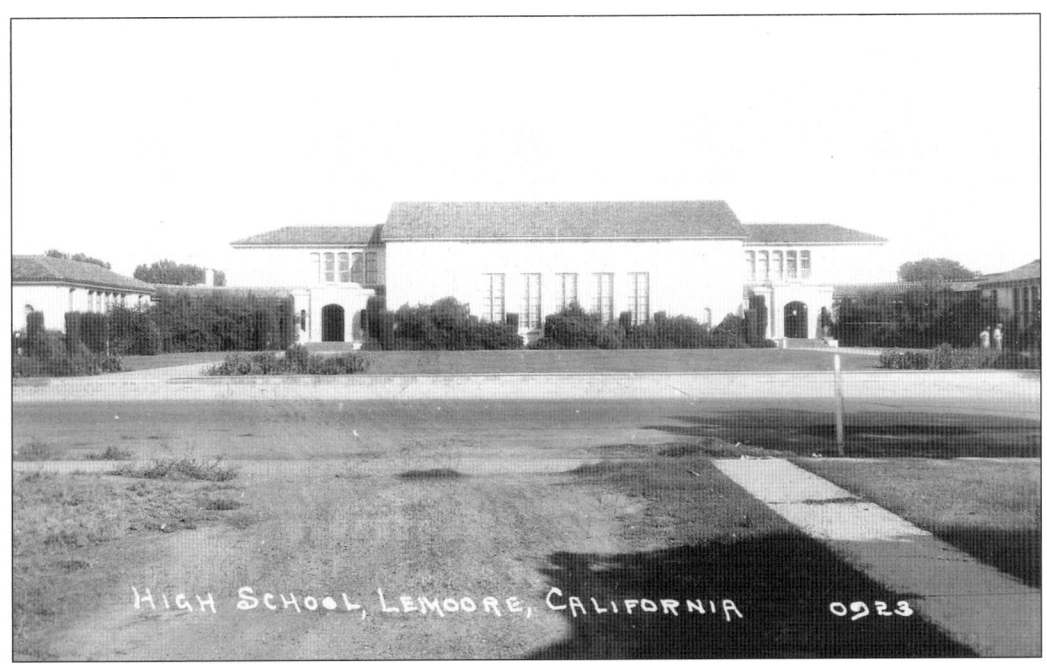

LEMOORE HIGH AUDITORIUM. This view of the auditorium of the Lemoore High School was taken in the mid-1930s. The building was reconstructed in 1975 to meet current earthquake codes and is still in use today.

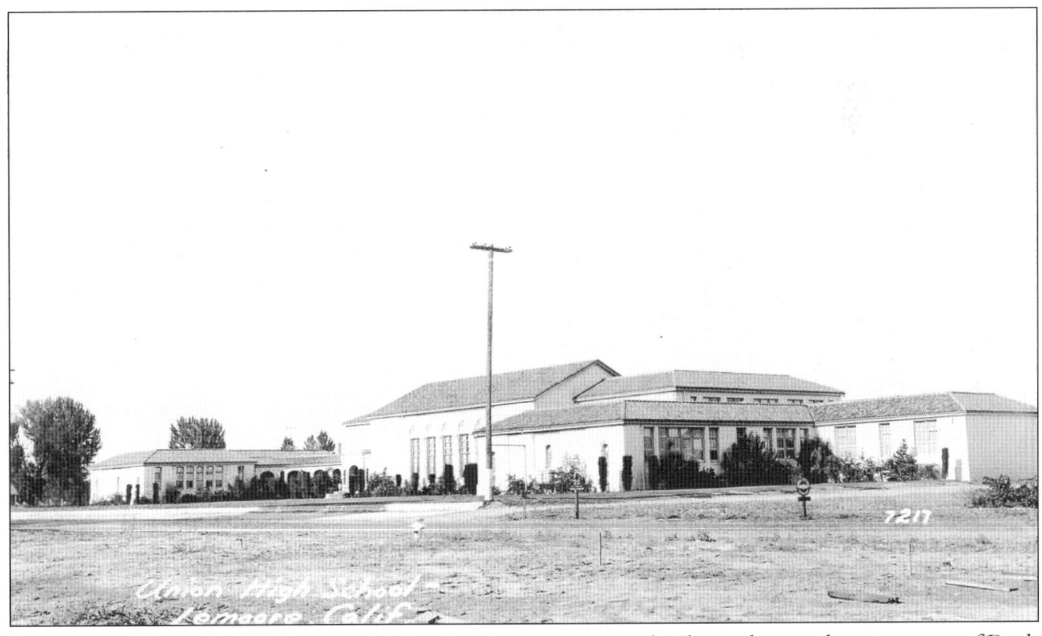

LEMOORE HIGH. In 1925, a new high school structure was built on the southeast corner of Bush Street and Lemoore Avenue. The Mission–style building was designed by William H. Weeks and built by W. J. Ochs for $325,000. It is still in use today.

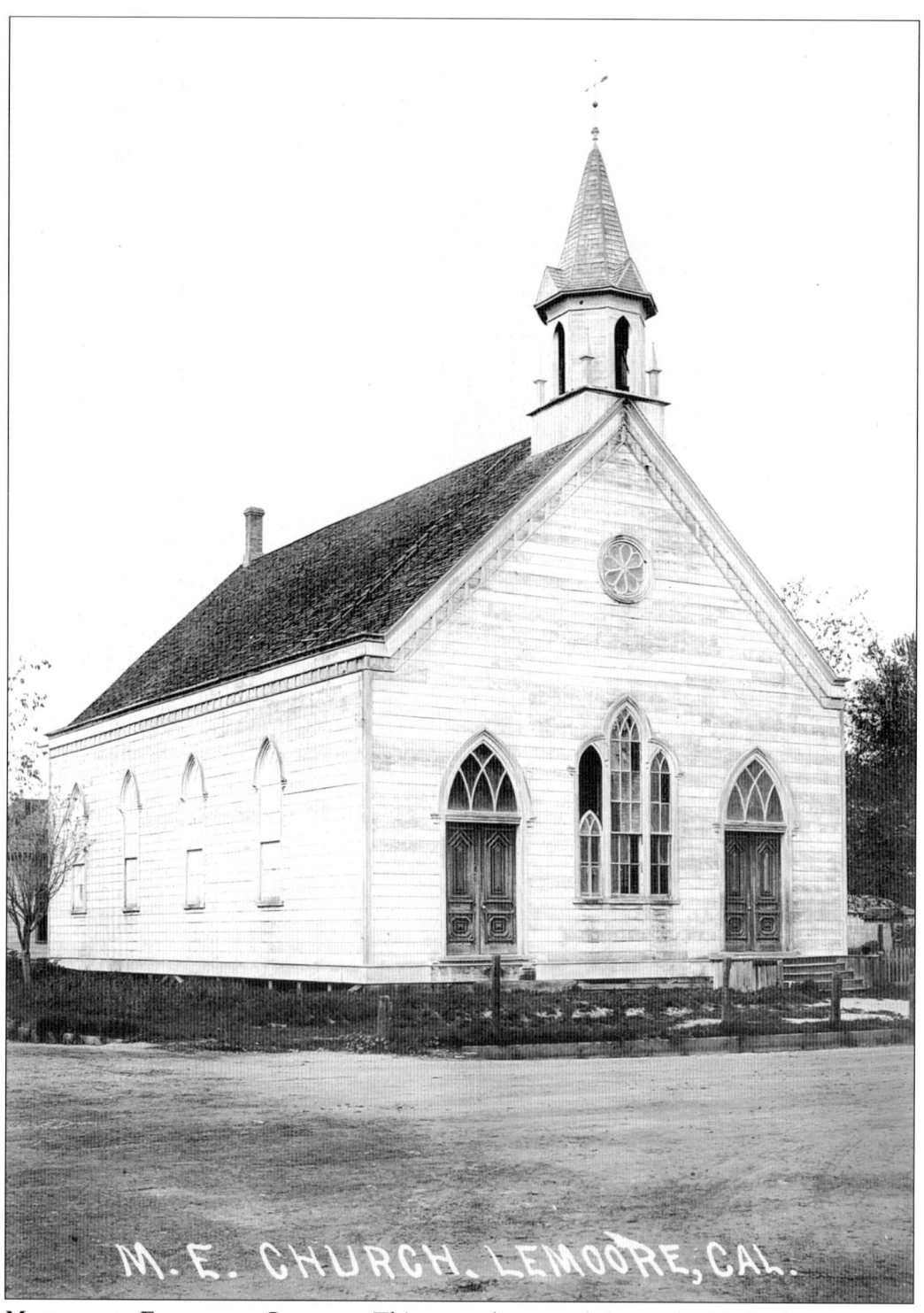

METHODIST EPISCOPAL CHURCH. This unused postcard shows the Methodist Episcopal Church, which was located at Hill and D Streets. Built in 1878, the church was one of the first established in Lemoore.

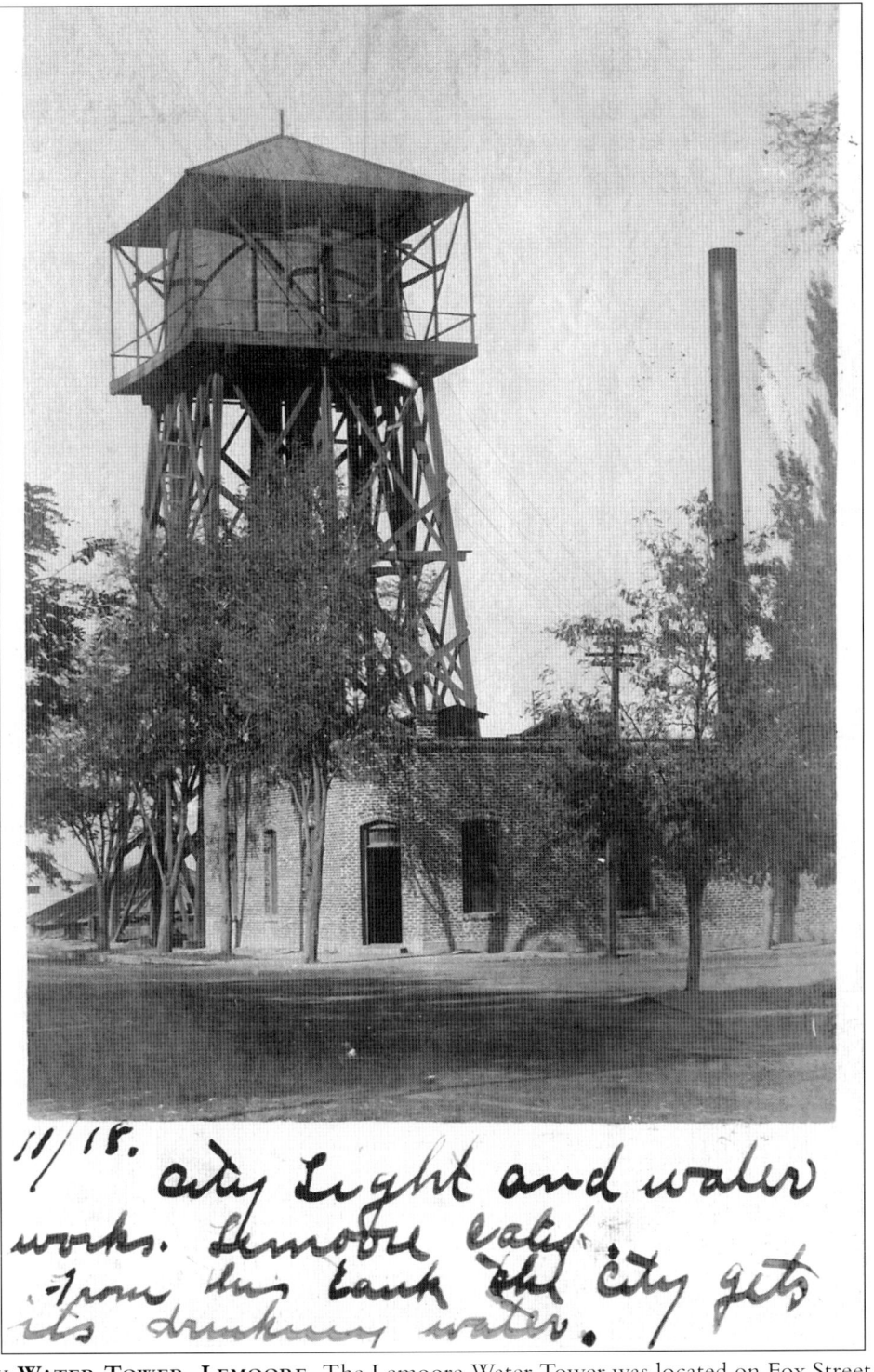

CITY WATER TOWER, LEMOORE. The Lemoore Water Tower was located on Fox Street just north of the Southern Pacific Railroad tracks. The water tower was a prominent landmark of the town for many years. (Courtesy Ron Burris.)

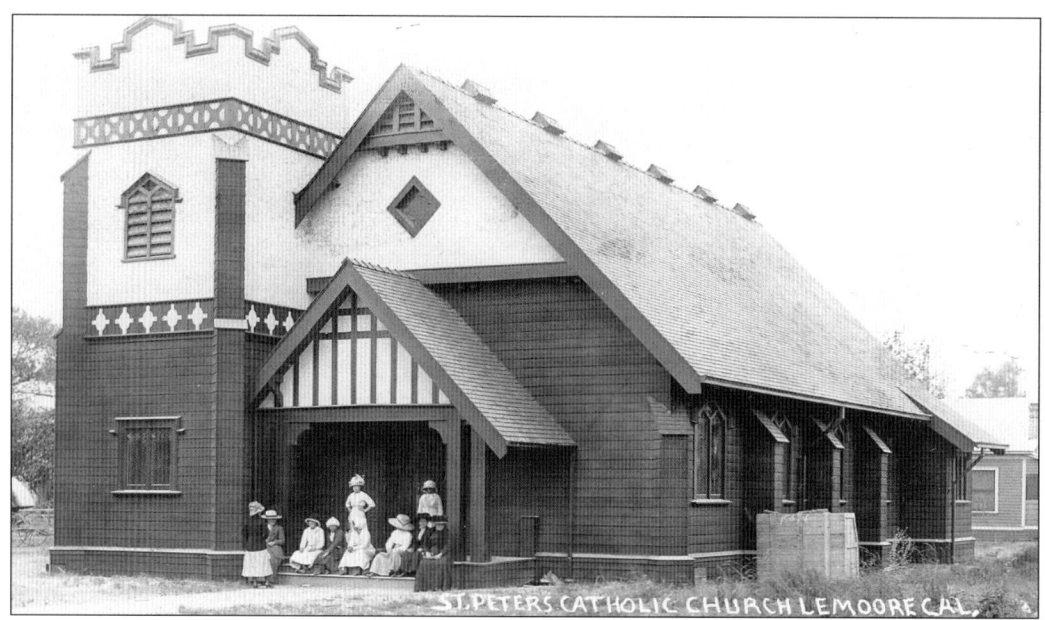

ST. PETER'S CATHOLIC CHURCH. This unused postcard shows St. Peter's Catholic Church immediately after completion in 1912. The box to the right appears to be a crate in which an organ or piano was shipped.

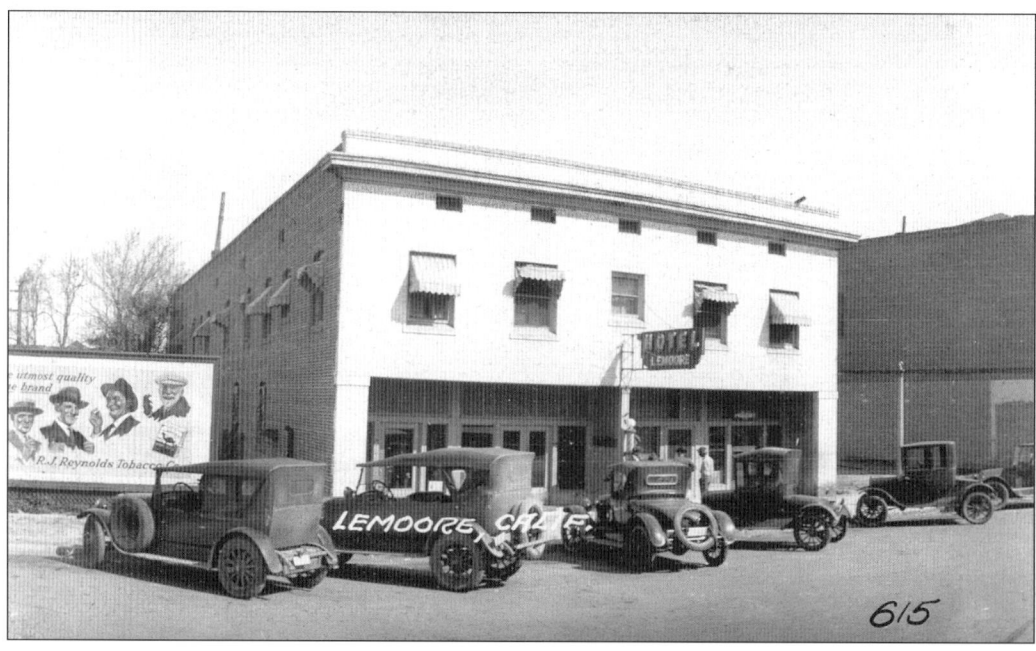

LEMOORE HOTEL. The Lemoore Hotel was located on the north side of D Street between Fox and Heinlen Streets. The billboard on the left advertises R. J. Reynolds Tobacco. A barbershop was located in the first floor of the building.

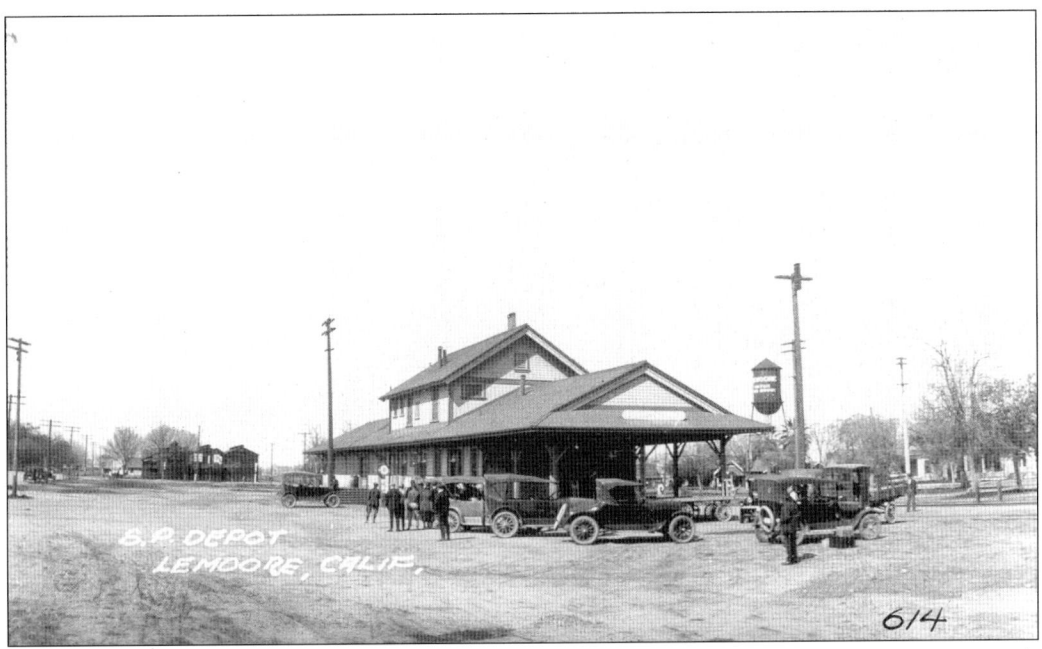

SOUTHERN PACIFIC DEPOT. The Lemoore Water Tower, with the town motto "Lemoore, Watch Us Grow," sat to the right of the Southern Pacific Depot, pictured here in the early 1920s.

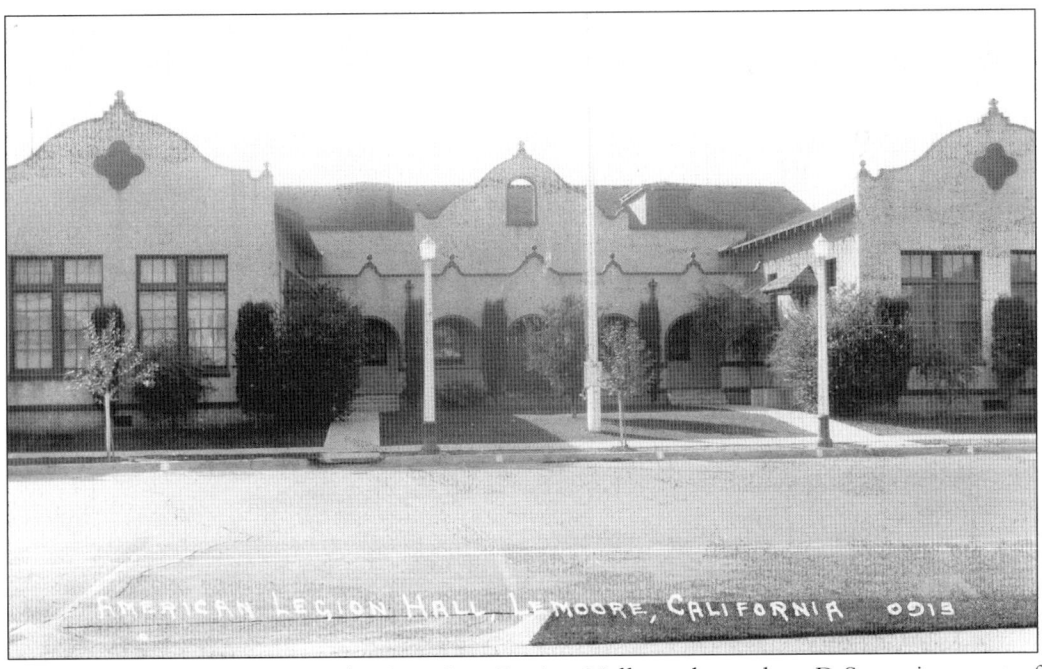

AMERICAN LEGION HALL. The American Legion Hall was located on D Street just west of Fox Street. It was built in 1922 at a cost of $10,000 and housed the American Legion Post No. 100. Lemoore veterans made the bricks used to erect the building.

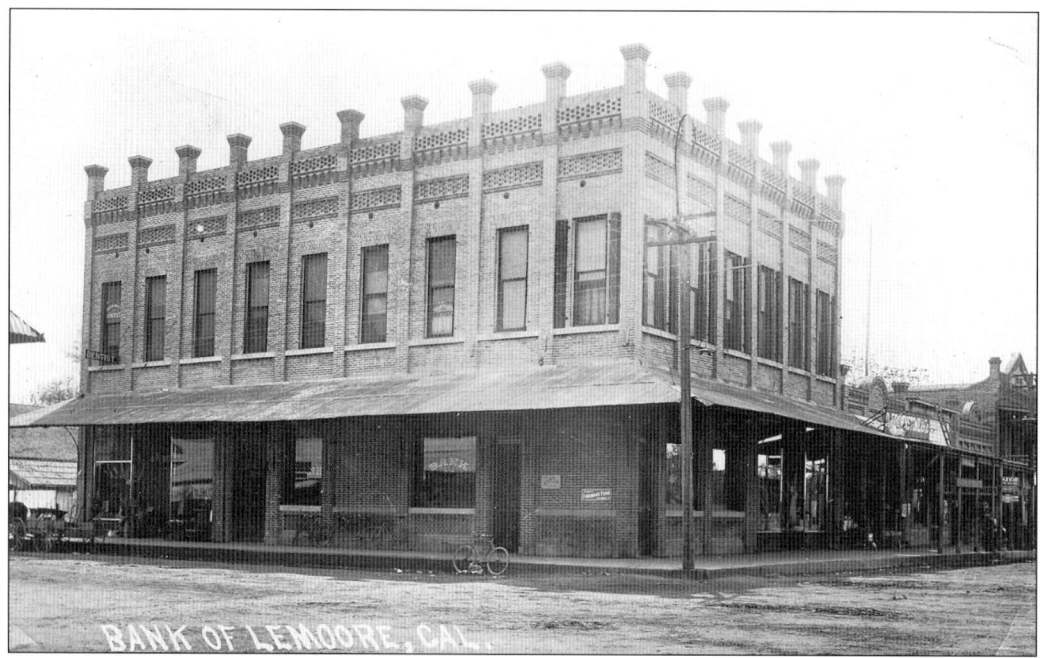

BANK OF LEMOORE. Pictured in this postcard is the Bank of Lemoore, located on the southwest corner of Heinlen and D Streets. The bank, incorporated on December 28, 1891, was Lemoore's only bank until 1905. (Courtesy James Hickman.)

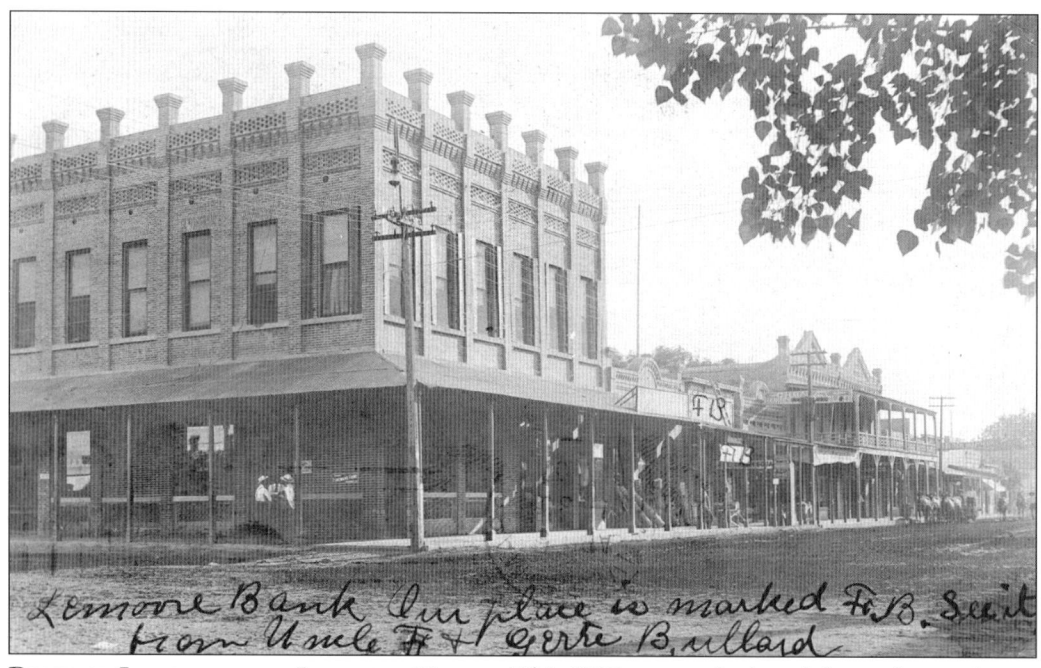

BANK OF LEMOORE AND LUCERNE HOTEL. This 1907 postmarked card shows the southwest corner of Heinlen and D Streets. On the corner is the Bank of Lemoore. The two-story structure with the balcony is the Lucerne Hotel.

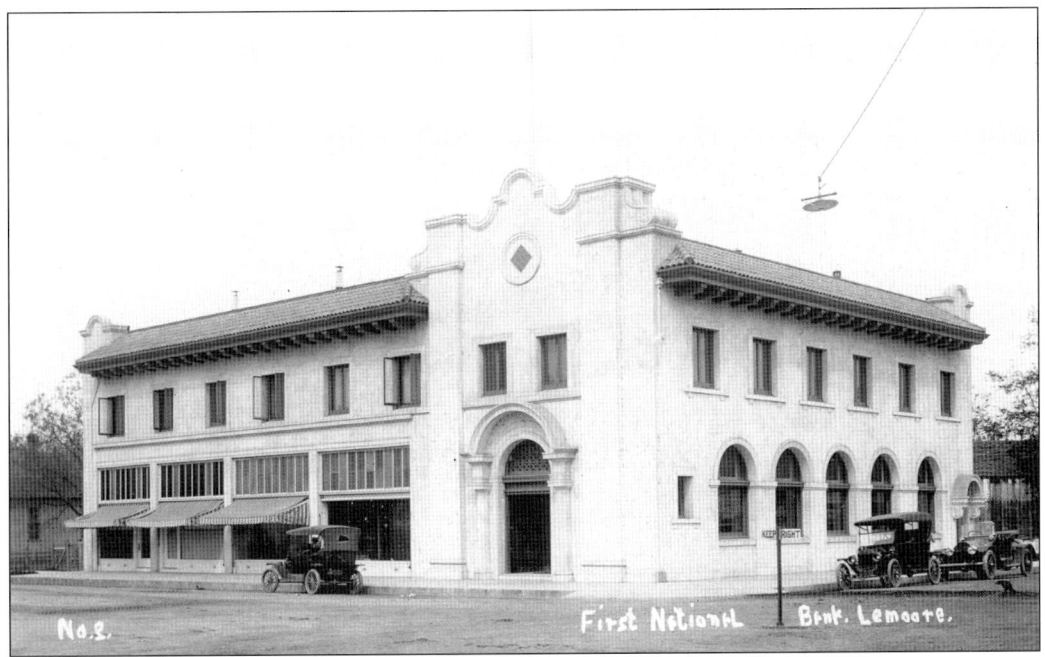

FIRST NATIONAL BANK OF LEMOORE, EARLY 1920S. The First National Bank's advertisements of the time boasted of its security systems, stating that "the building is modern in every way, having modern double lock safe deposit boxes and the American Bank Protection Burglar Alarm System for the double protection to their vault and safe." (Courtesy Ron Lerch.)

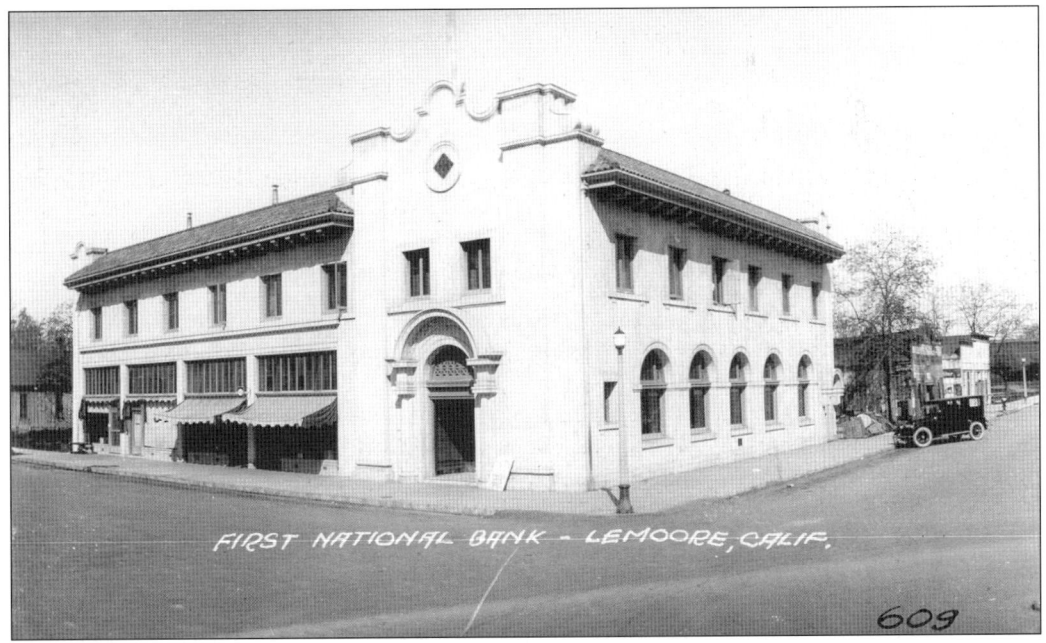

FIRST NATIONAL BANK OF LEMOORE. Pictured in this unused postcard is the First National Bank of Lemoore. The bank was chartered in June 1905 and was originally located on Heinlen Street. In January 1913, the bank moved to this location.

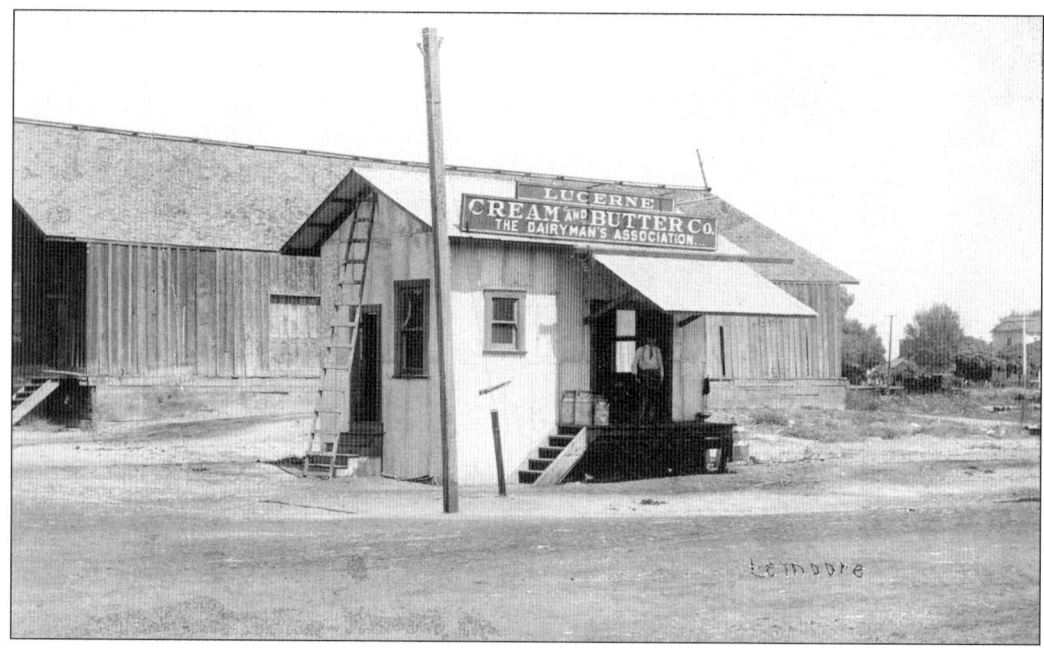

LUCERNE CREAM AND BUTTER COMPANY RECEIVING STATION. The Lucerne Creamery was located in Hanford and had a Lemoore receiving station located on the northeast corner of Heinlen and E Streets. The building behind it is the J. R. Heinlen Grain Warehouse.

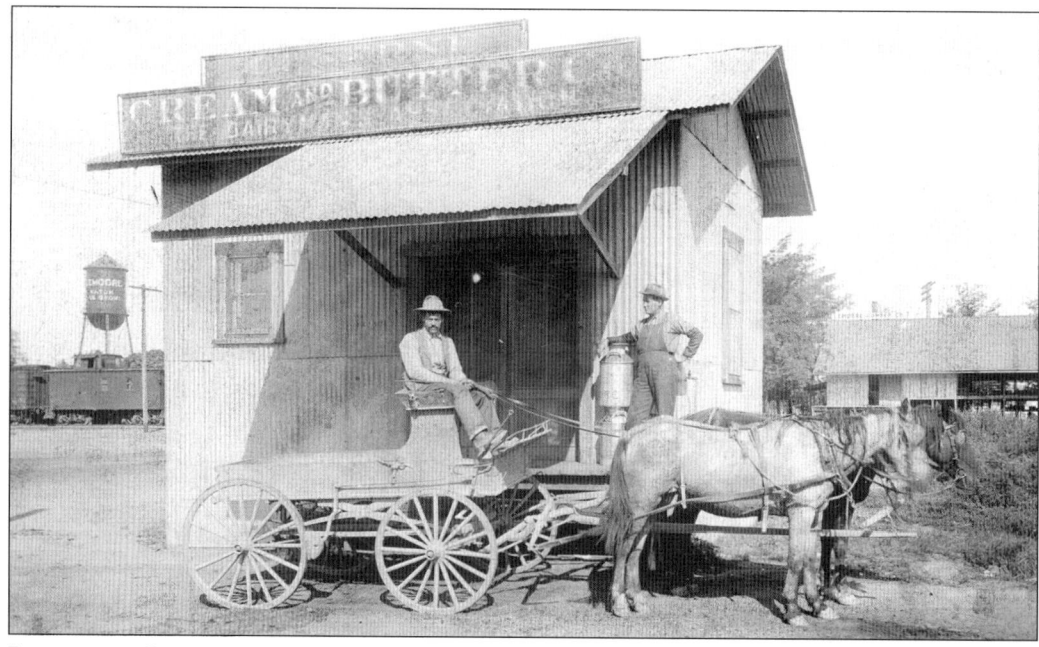

LUCERNE CREAM AND BUTTER. This later view of the receiving station shows a customer delivering his milk to the station manager. Note the advertisement on the water tower. To the right is the Lemoore Lumber Company, which was located across the tracks. (Courtesy Louie Silva.)

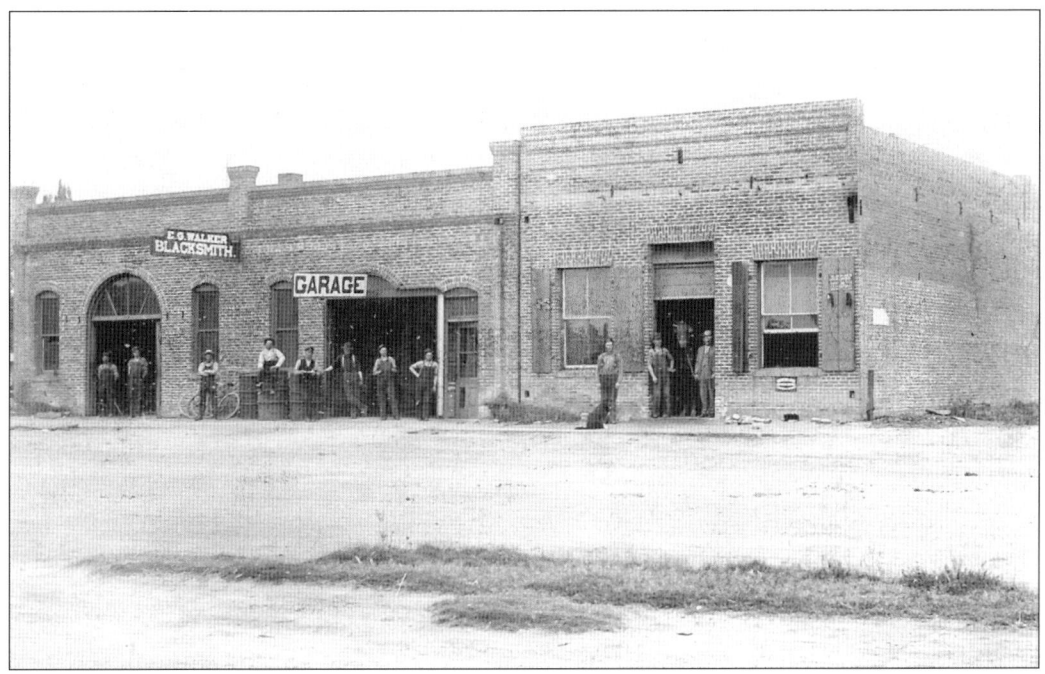

E. G. Walker Blacksmith and Garage. This 1910 postmarked card shows the Walker Blacksmith shop.

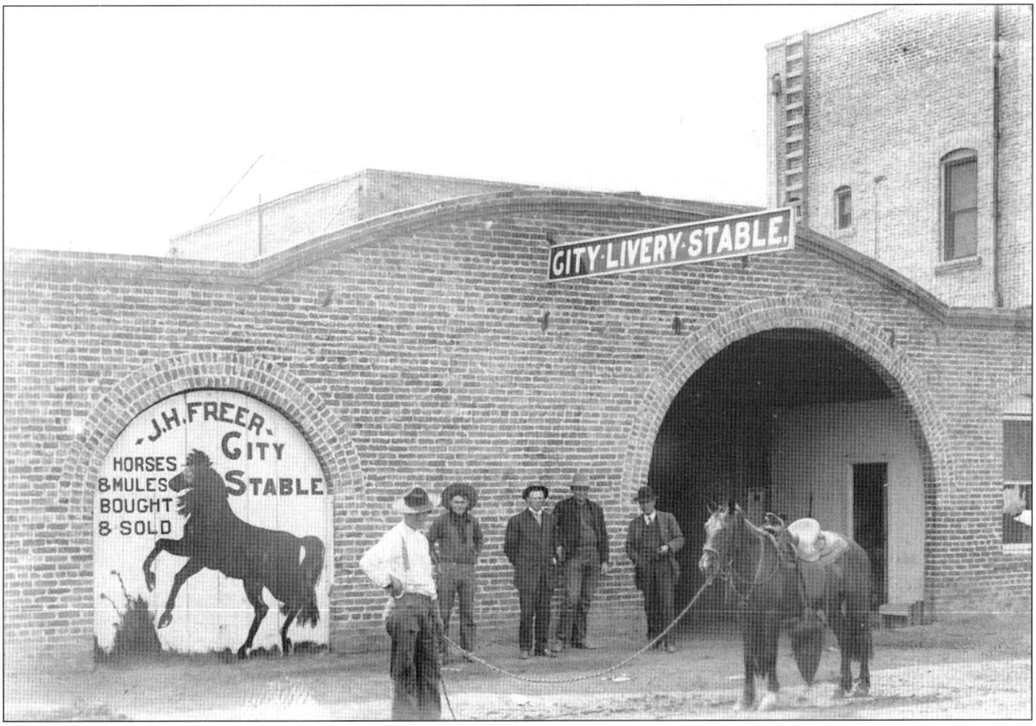

J. H. Freer Stables. Pictured in this unused postcard is the stable building that sat just east of the Old Fellows Building on D Street, also known as the City Livery Stable. Stables were a common site in early Kings County. (Courtesy Sarah A. Mooney Memorial Museum.)

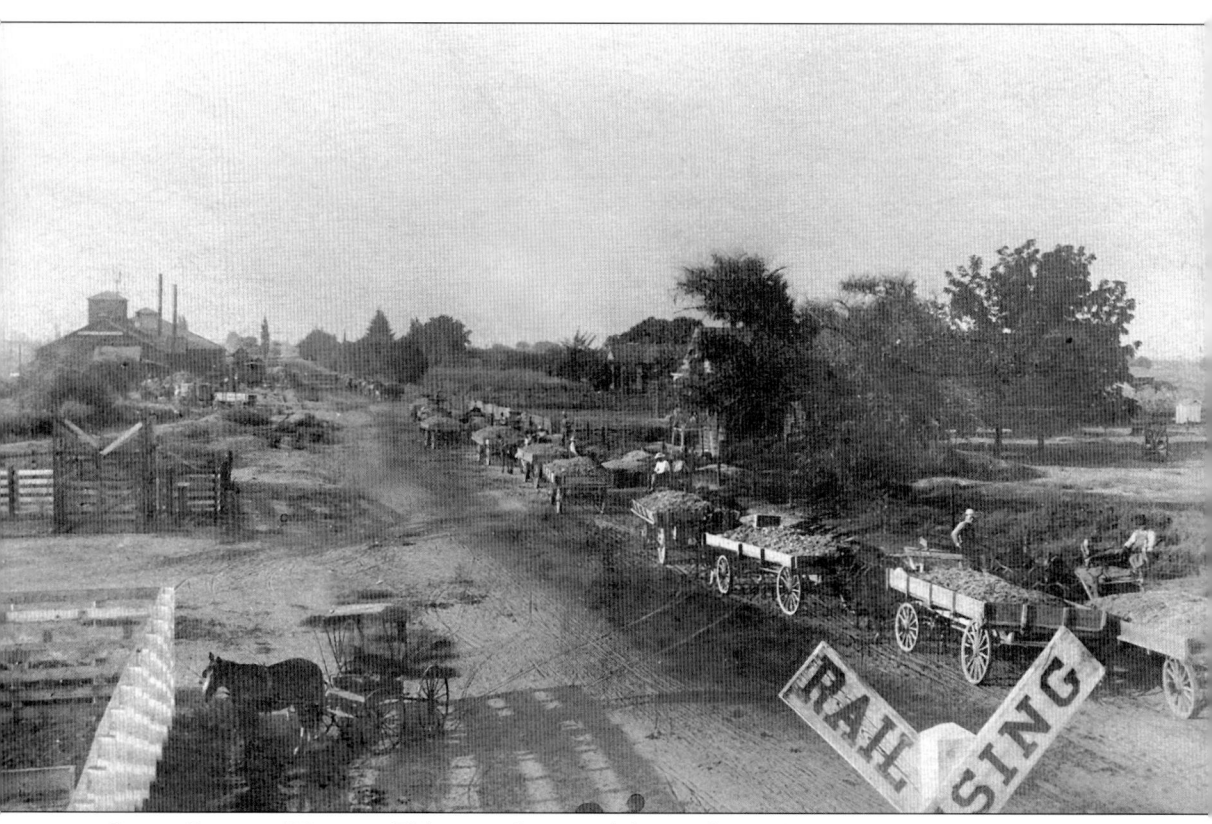

SWISS COLONY WINERY. This unused postcard shows a busy winery scene in Lemoore. Wagons of grapes were brought to the winery for processing. The building was located on the west side of Lemoore Avenue north of the Southern Pacific Railroad tracks.

Three

CORCORAN

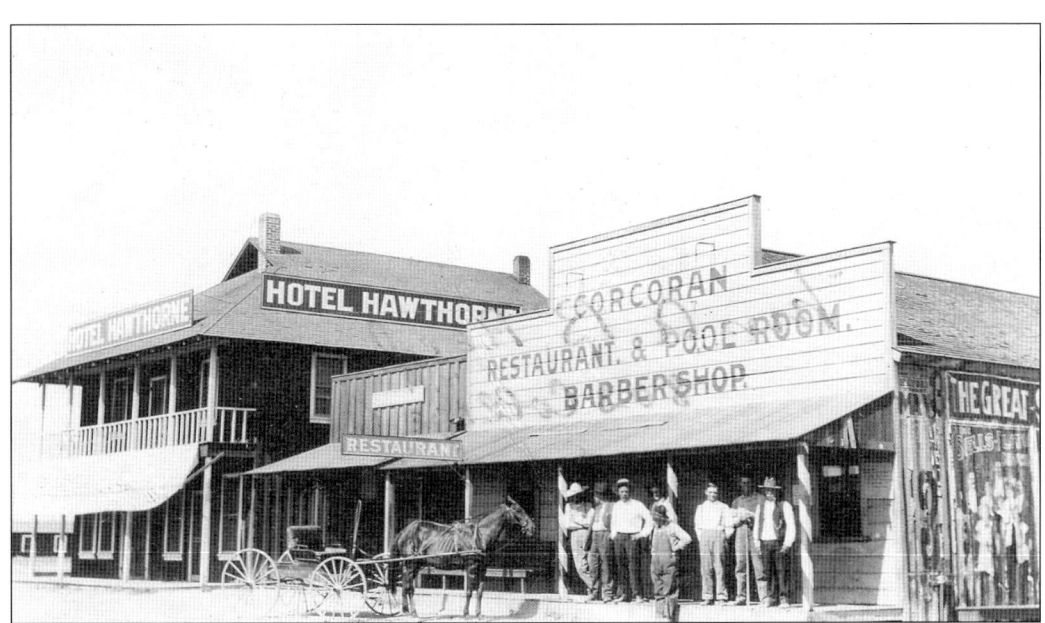

HOTEL HAWTHORNE AND CORCORAN RESTAURANT. Two of the earliest businesses that operated in Corcoran—the Hotel Hawthorne and the Corcoran Restaurant—were located across the street from the Corcoran Creamery. The banner to the right advertises a circus coming to Hanford on Tuesday, May 3, 1910.

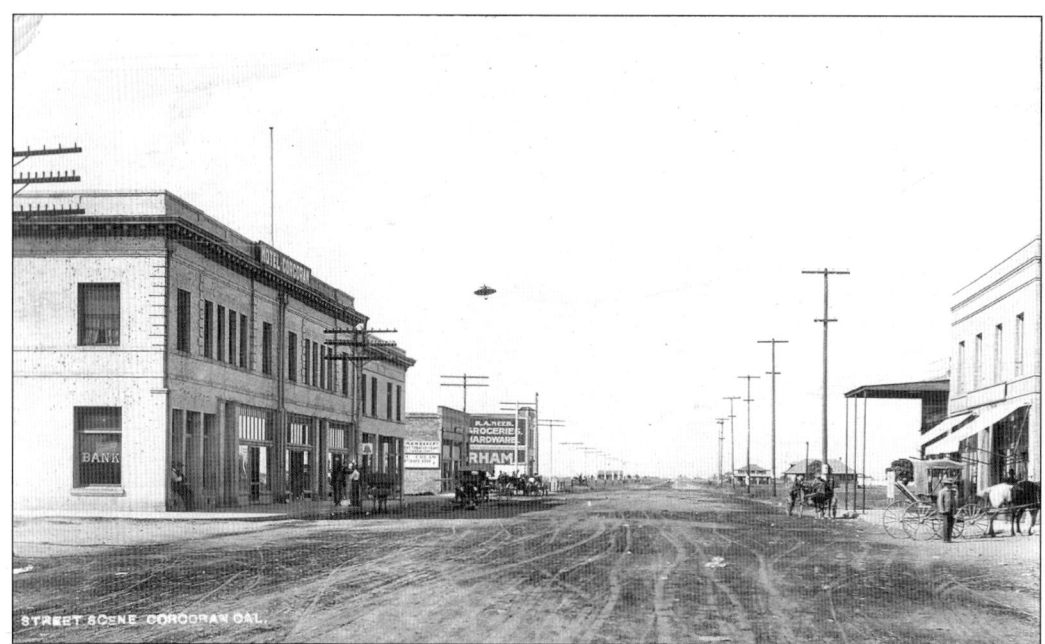

WHITLEY AVENUE LOOKING WEST, CORCORAN. This early 1910s view shows Corcoran's main street. Whitley Avenue was named for H. J. Whitley, a Los Angeles real estate speculator who purchased the town site in 1905.

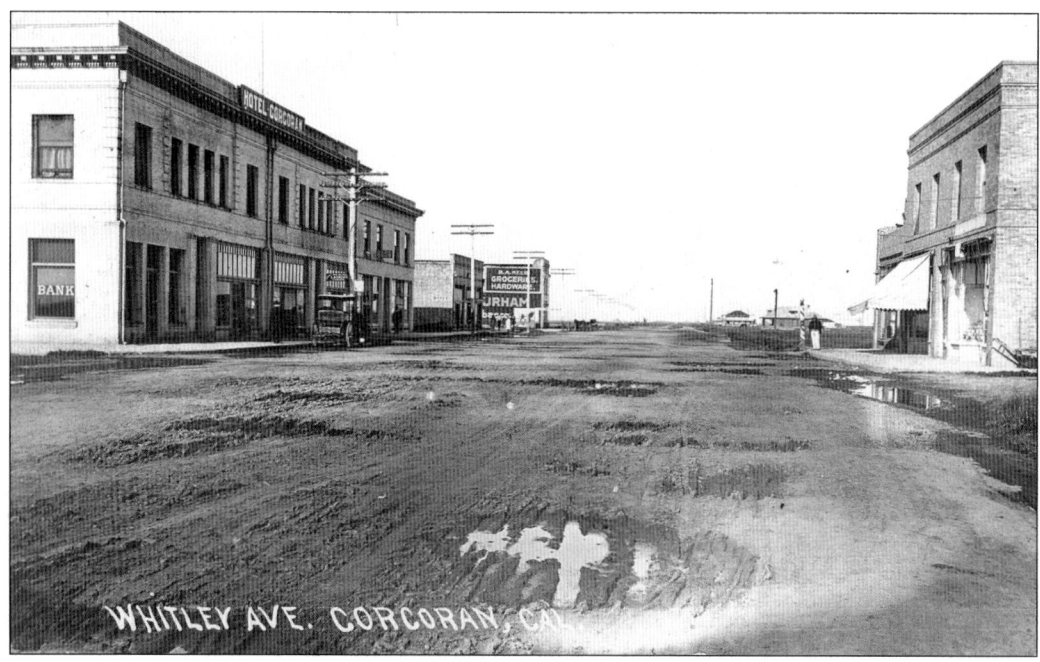

WHITLEY AVENUE LOOKING WEST, CORCORAN. This view is almost identical to the previous one—except for the muddy streets. Corcoran is situated on the shores of Tulare Lake, a body of water that has since been reclaimed as farmland. The fertility of the land is unmatched in California.

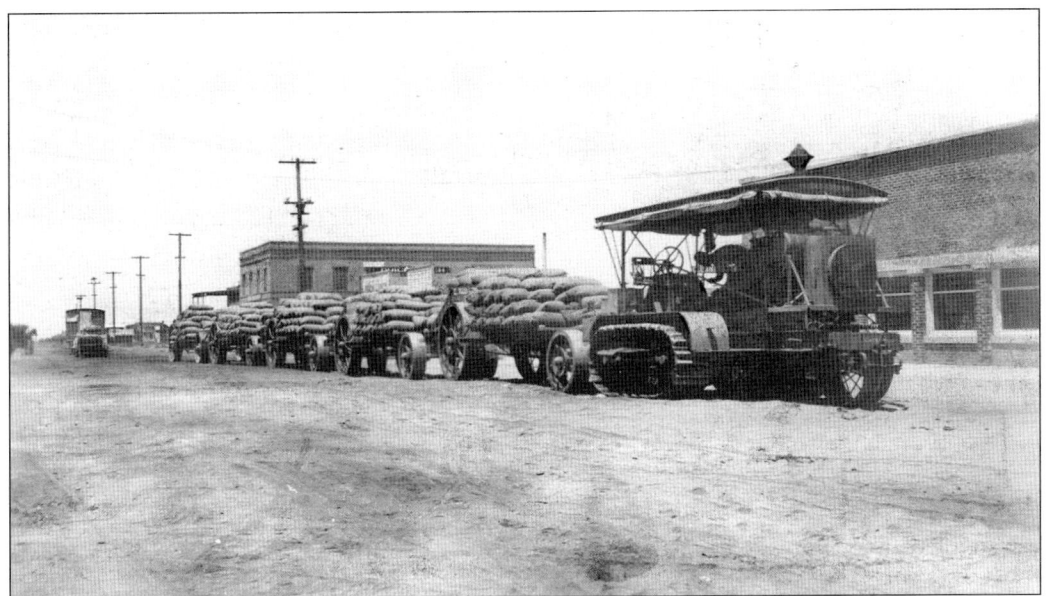

HAULING WHEAT IN CORCORAN. The printed message on the back of this card states, "This is the way that wheat and barley is hauled to market in Corcoran, Kings County, California (48 tons each trip)."

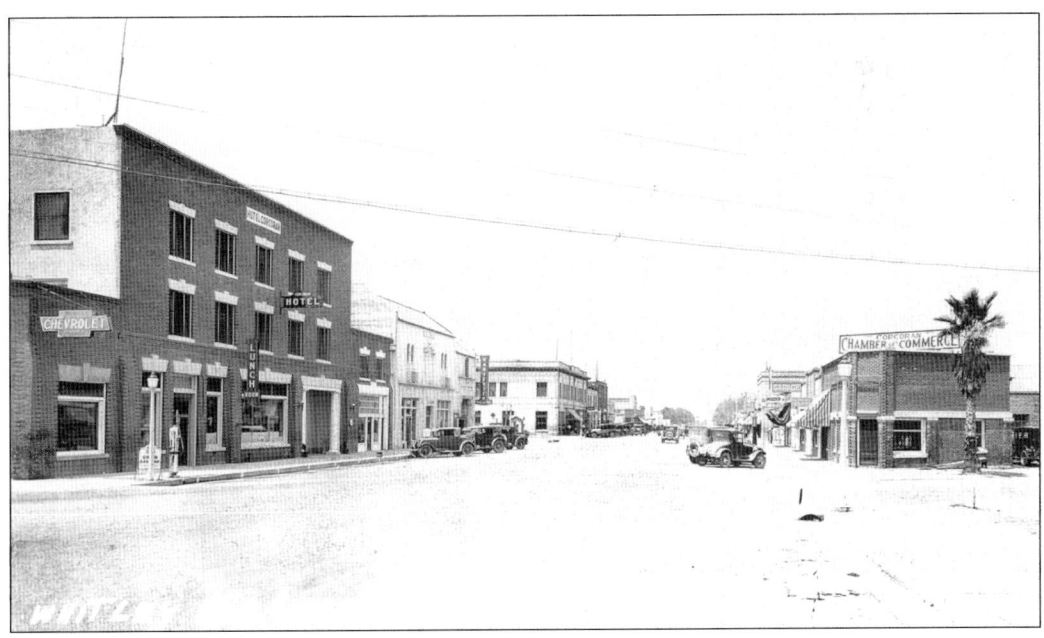

WHITLEY AVENUE LOOKING WEST, CORCORAN. In the mid-1920s, this is the town of Corcoran as it appeared from the train depot. (Courtesy James Hickman.)

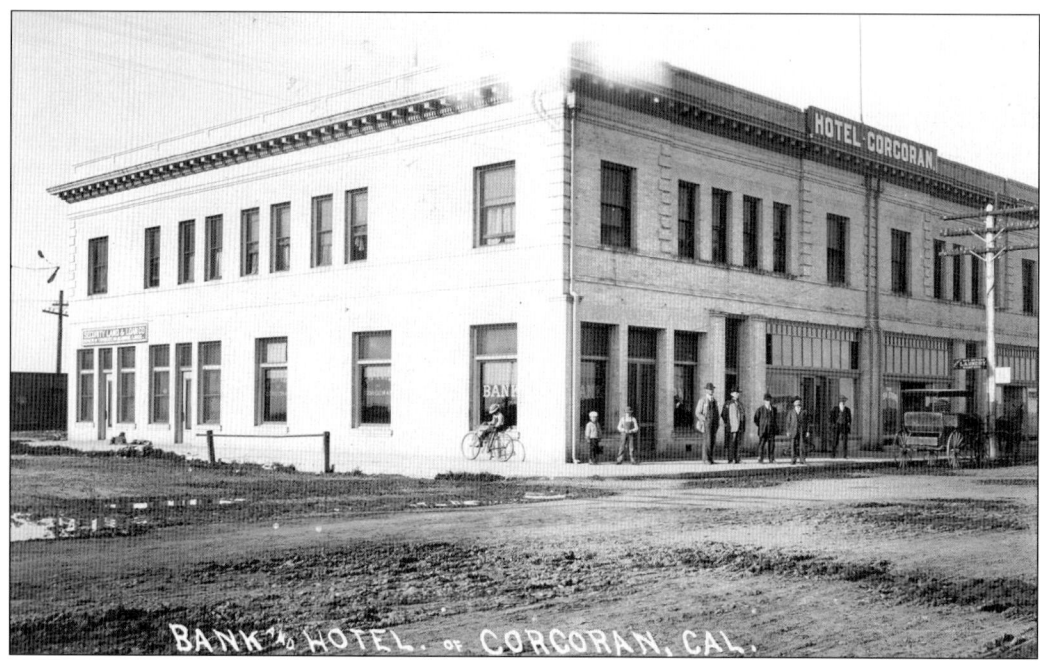

BANK AND HOTEL, CORCORAN, 1910. The first major building constructed in Corcoran housed the Land Office on the left and the Bank of Corcoran in the corner.

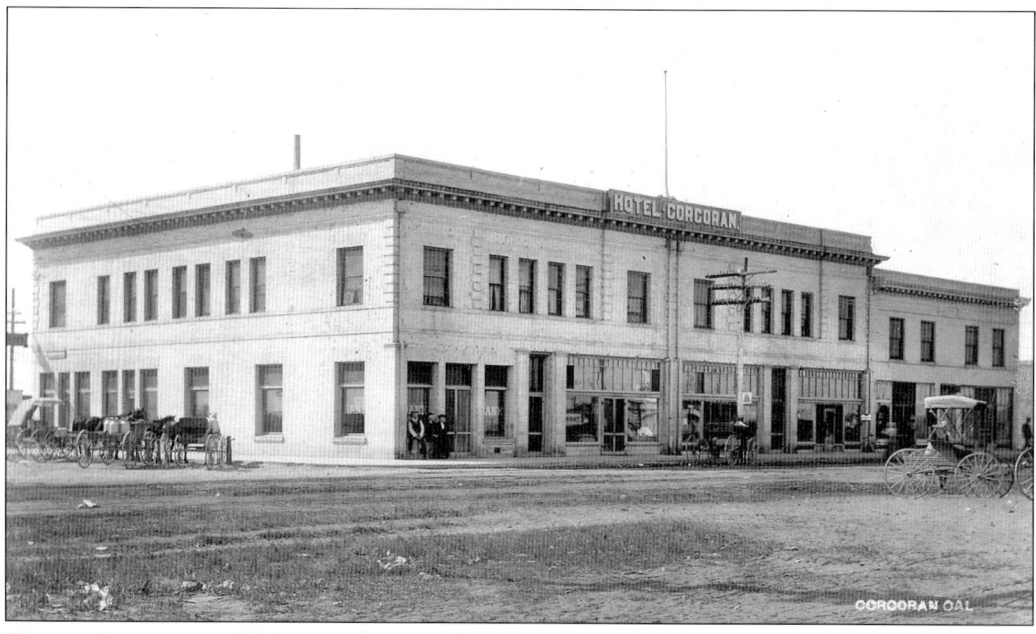

HOTEL CORCORAN. This unused postcard shows the Hotel Corcoran soon after its construction in 1910. Located on the southwest corner of King and Whitley, the building's first floor housed the local bank, a grocery store, and pool hall. (Courtesy Ron Burris.)

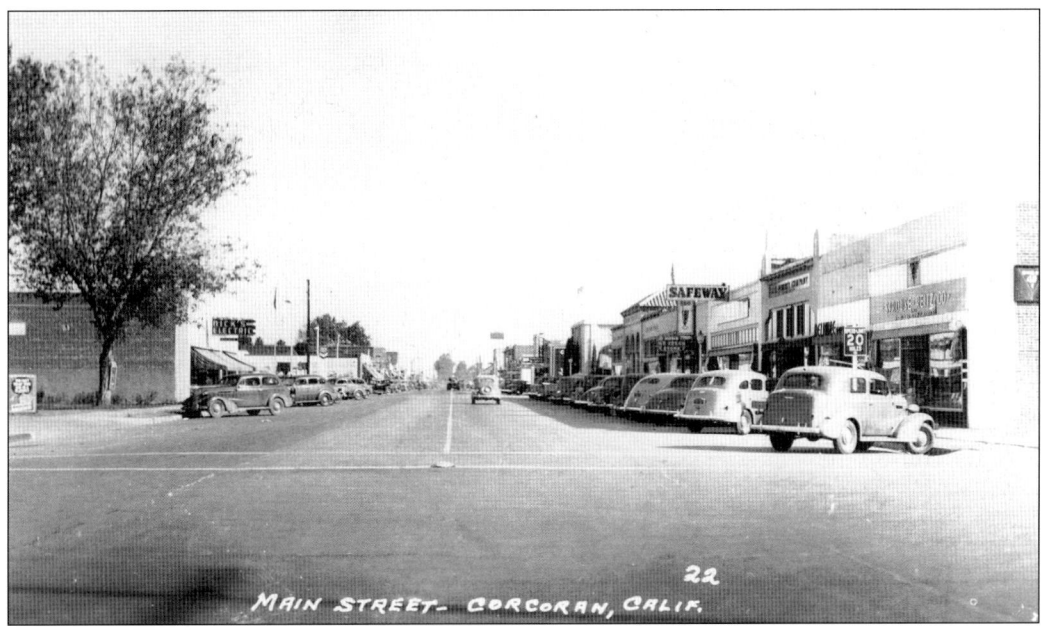

WHITLEY AVENUE LOOKING EAST, CORCORAN. This 1930s postcard shows the main street of Corcoran on a busy day. (Courtesy James Hickman.)

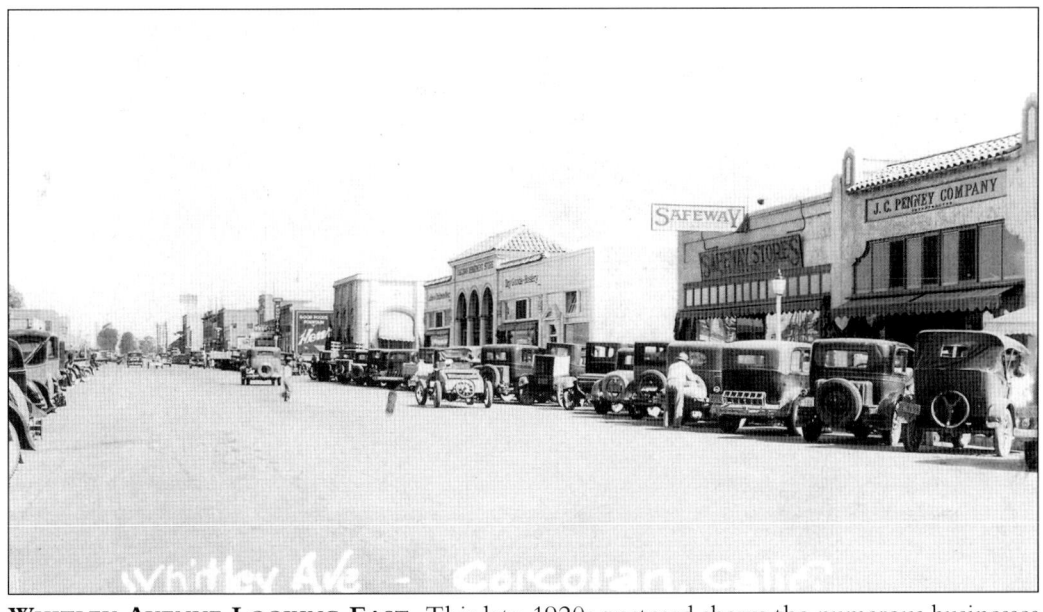

WHITLEY AVENUE LOOKING EAST. This late-1920s postcard shows the numerous businesses that occupied the town during the time. Corcoran was the nearest town to the farm labor camps and provided all sorts of goods and services to migrant farmers. Pictured in this view are the Bank of America, Safeway Stores, and the J. C. Penney Company.

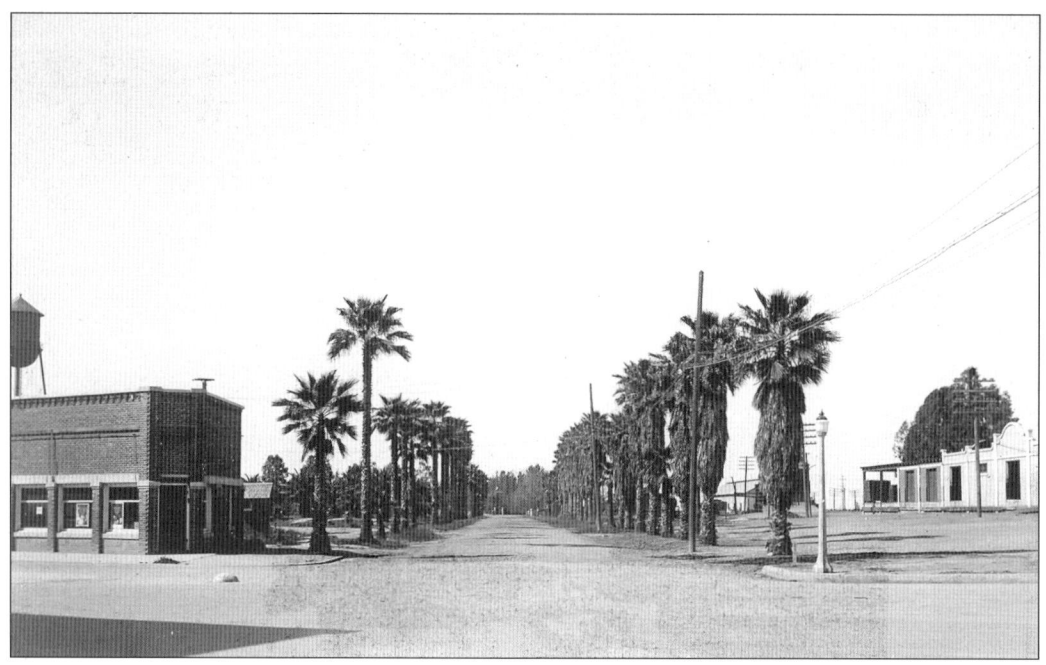

OTIS AVENUE LOOKING NORTH, CORCORAN. Corcoran's original name was supposed to be Otis, who was a friend of H. J. Whitley. However, the name never took. The source of the name of Corcoran is in dispute. Two competing stories have it named after a military officer or a local railroad official. (Courtesy Ron Burris.)

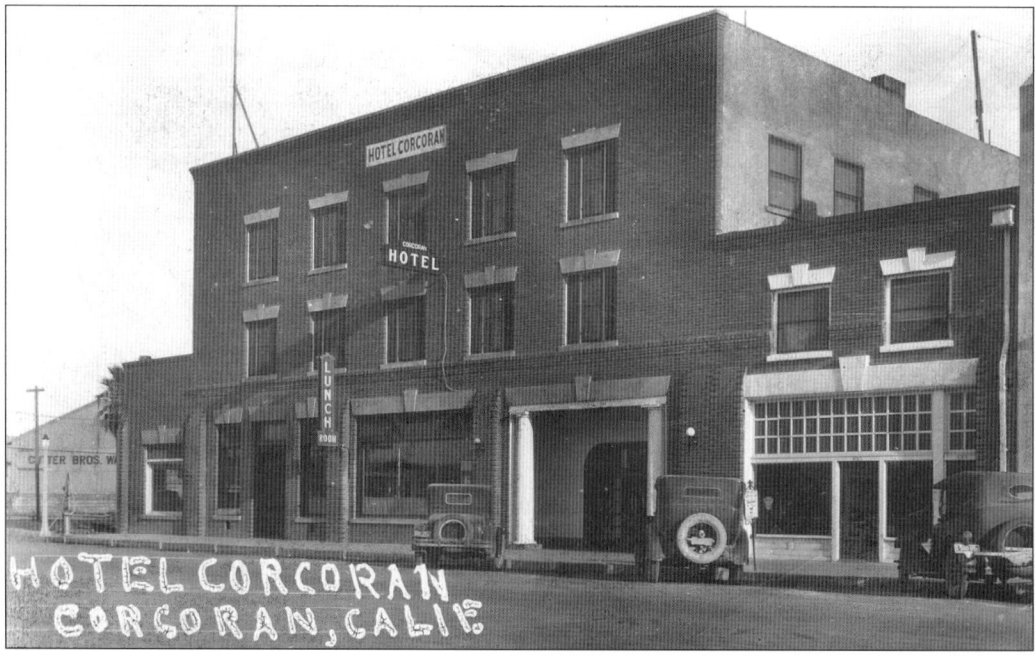

HOTEL CORCORAN. In 1914, a second hotel Corcoran was built on the southeast corner of Otis and Whitley Avenues. It was touted as "one of the best hotels in the valley," according to a March 1914 *Corcoran Journal*. Double rooms went for $2 a night, while a single room cost $1.50. It was the only hotel in town that offered a private bath.

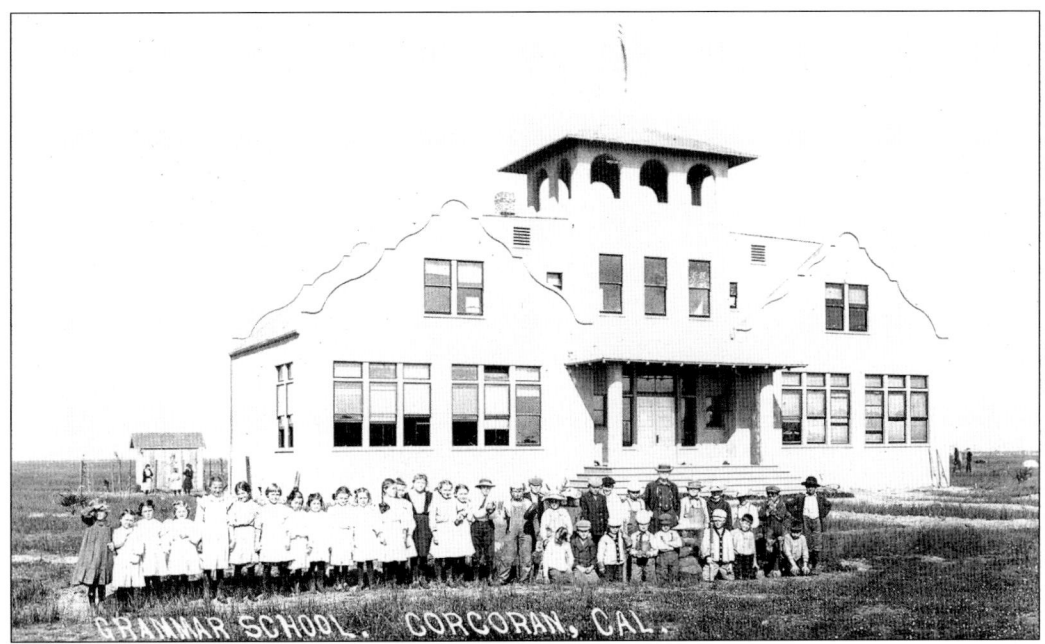

CORCORAN GRAMMAR SCHOOL. Pictured in this 1909 postcard is the Corcoran Grammar School. Completed in 1906 by contractor C. D. Walker, the school was located on Van Dorsten Avenue, just north of Whitley. In 1921, it was converted to house the Corcoran City Hall. It was torn down as a WPA project in the early 1930s.

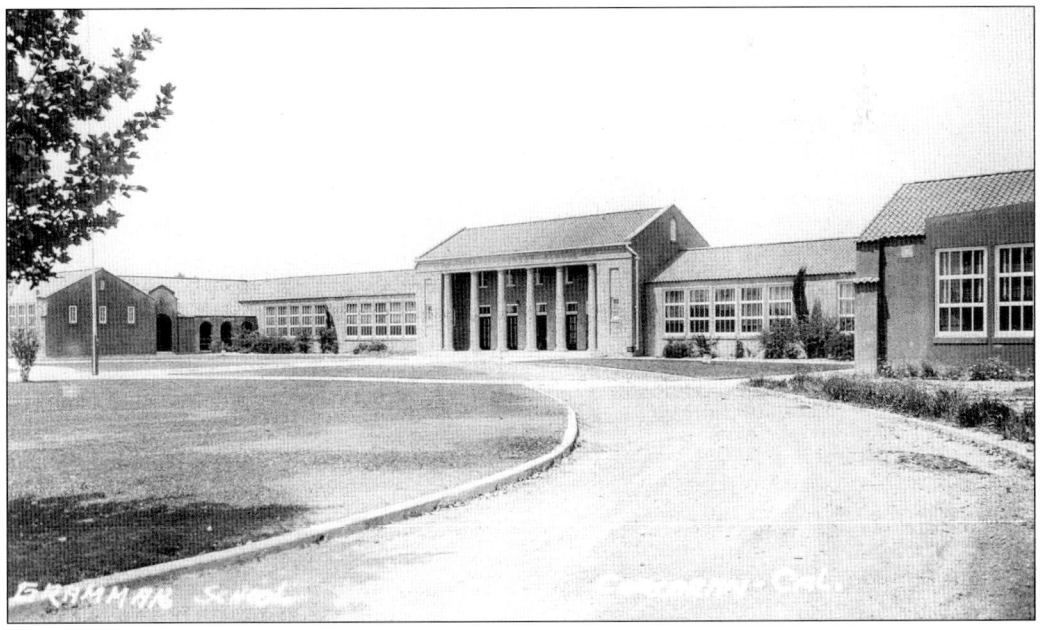

GRAMMAR SCHOOL, CORCORAN, 1930s. Built in 1921 by M. P. Renfro of Porterville, the Central Grammar School cost $60,000. It was located on Letts Avenue, south of Corcoran High School.

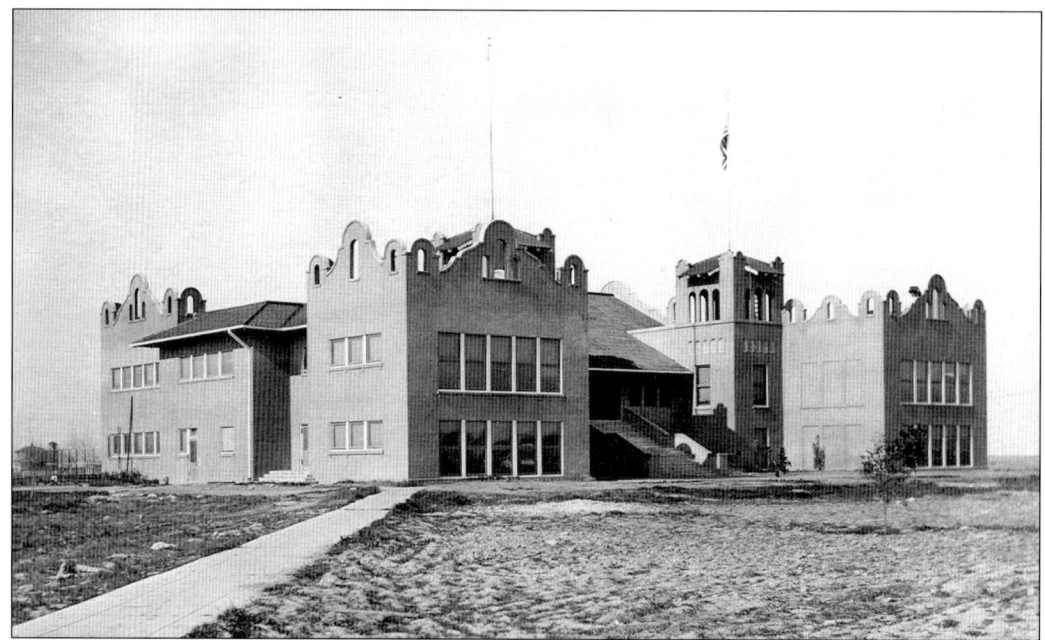

Corcoran High. The building pictured was completed in late 1914 at a cost of $39,984. Located on the southwest corner of Whitley and Letts Avenue, it was used as the local high school until 1939 when it was torn down. (Courtesy Hanford Carnegie Museum.)

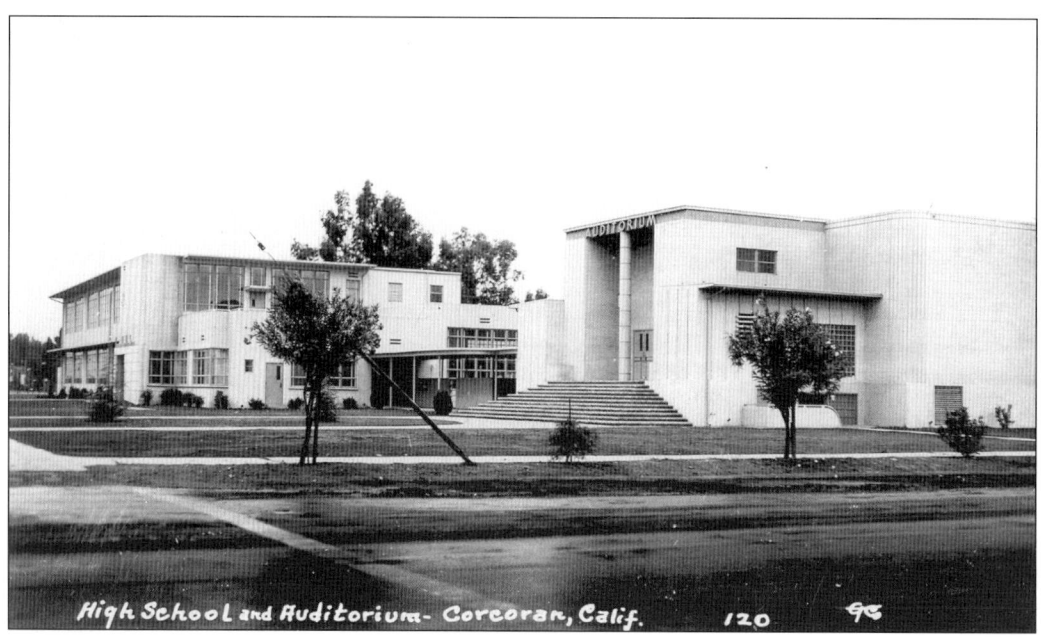

Corcoran High School, Corcoran. This unused postcard shows the new high school shortly after it was built in 1939 for $287,000. The contractor was W. W. Petley of Los Angeles. The new building was constructed around the outside of the original school. It is still in use today.

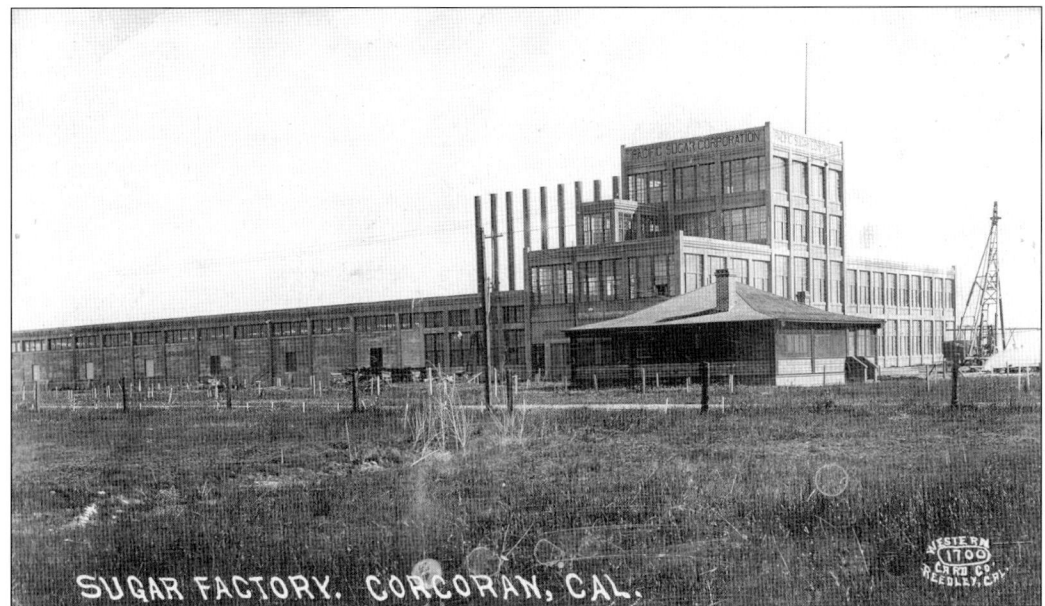

PACIFIC SUGAR COMPANY FACTORY, CORCORAN. Sugar beets were an early crop in the Corcoran area. In order to process the beets, a factory was built in 1908 at a cost of $1 million. During World War II, the building was used as a German prisoner of war camp. The building was razed in the late 1980s. (Courtesy James Hickman.)

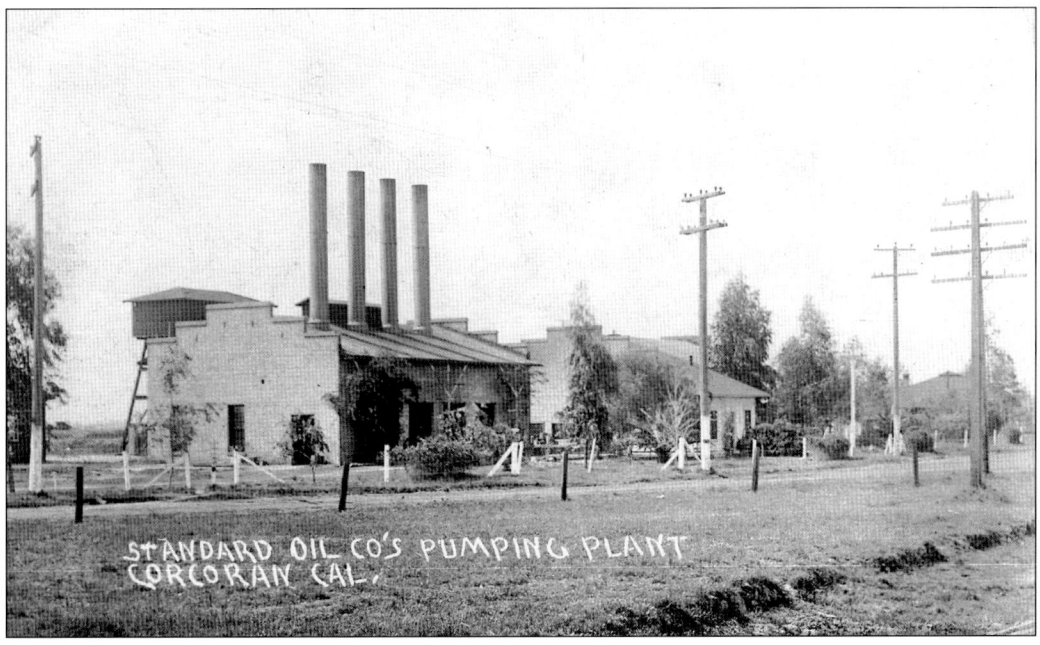

STANDARD OIL PUMPING STATION, CORCORAN. The pumping station, built in 1905, was located on Otis Avenue north of the Corcoran Railroad Depot. Standard Oil operated a series of pumping stations that moved oil along the Southern Pacific railroad right-of-way from Kern County north to the San Joaquin Delta.

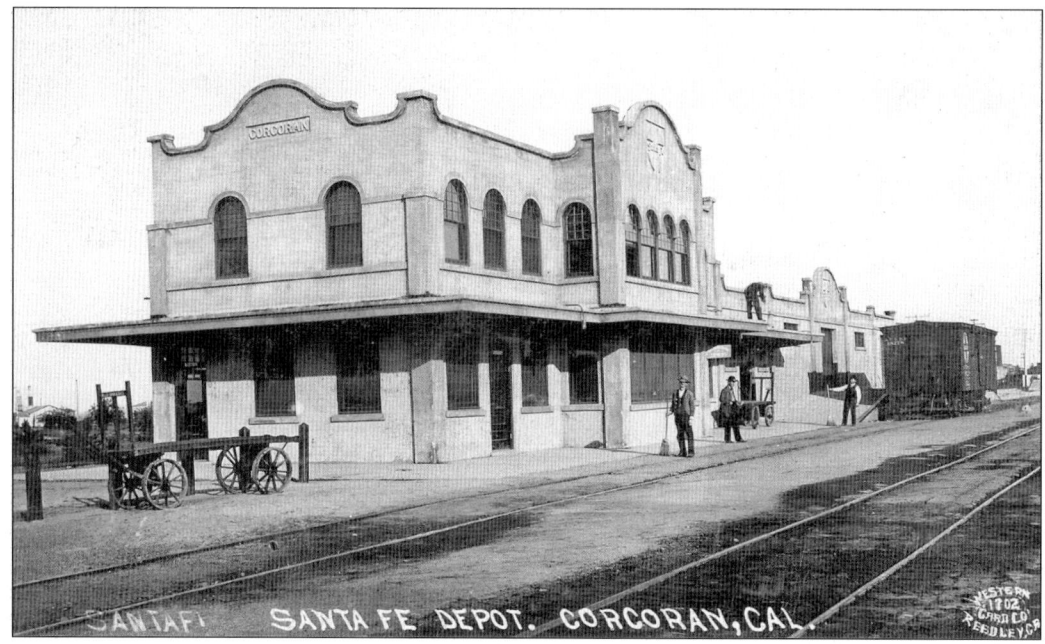

SANTA FE DEPOT AND CORCORAN EMPLOYEES. Published by George Besaw of the Western Card Company of Reedley, California, this card pictures railroad employees performing a clean-up of the depot and the surrounding grounds.

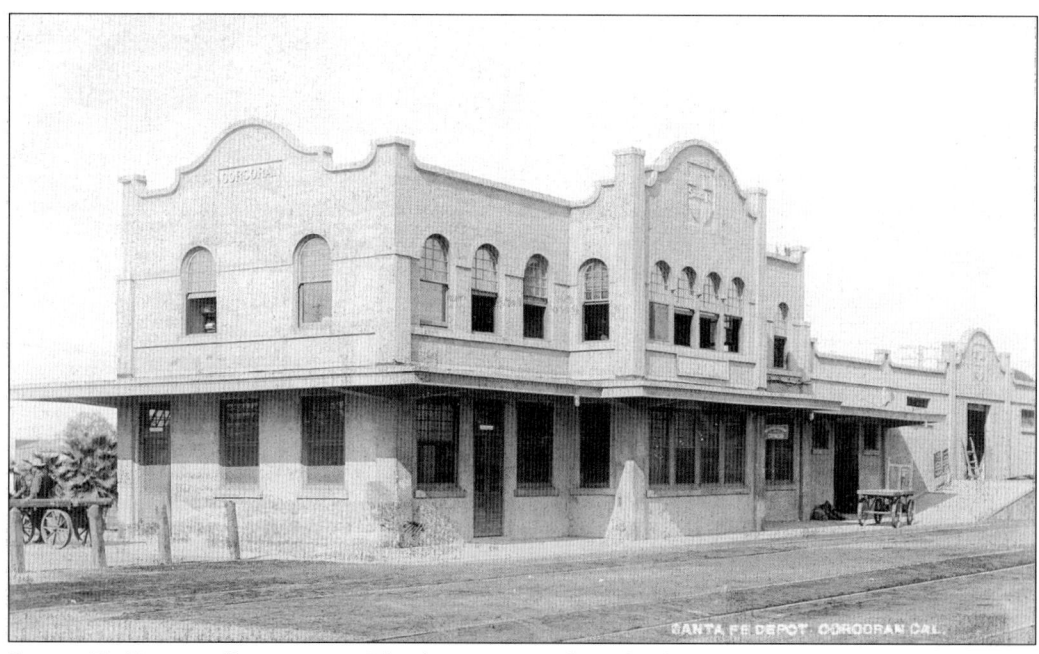

SANTA FE DEPOT, CORCORAN. The depot pictured was built in 1907 by the Atchison, Topeka, & Santa Fe Railroad at a cost of $20,000. The building was made from reinforced concrete and was considered to be one of the finest along the route.

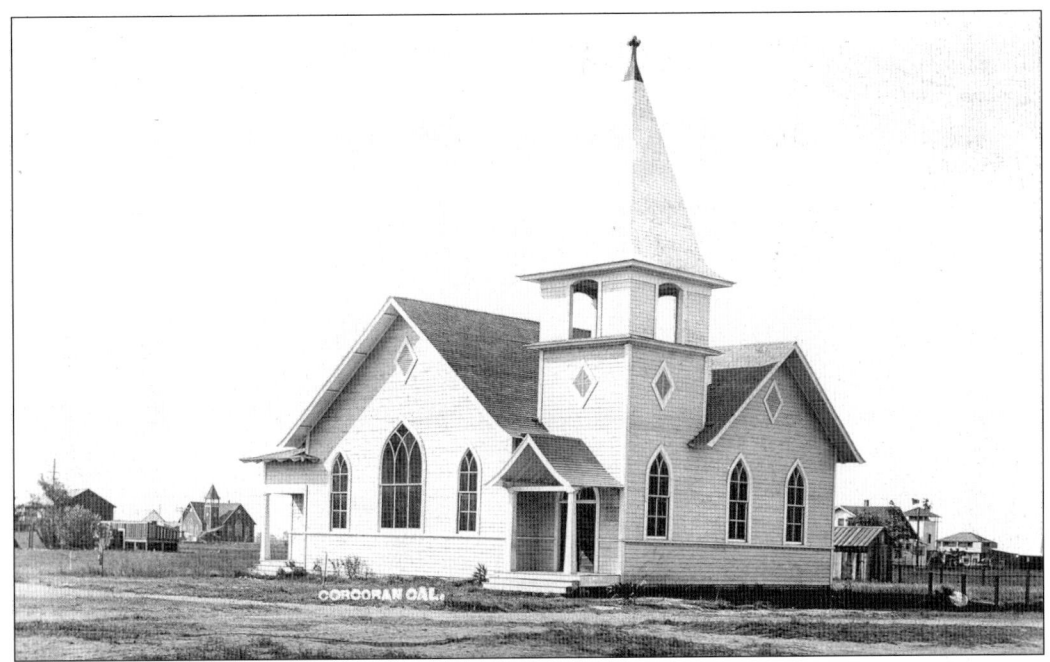

First Presbyterian Church. This 1910 postmarked card shows the First Presbyterian Church that was located on the southwest corner of Hanna and Chase Avenues. The church community was organized on February 4, 1906, and the building was dedicated on January 10, 1910. It cost $4,000 to build.

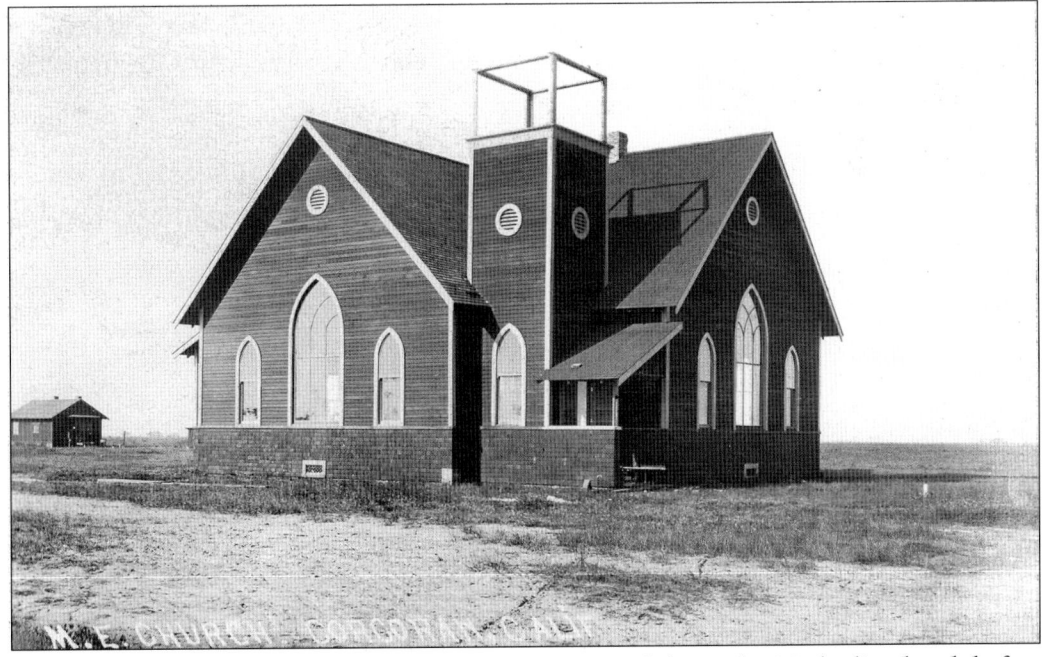

First Methodist Church. This 1910 postmarked card shows the Methodist church before the bell tower was completed. This building occupied the southwest corner of Jepson and Van Dorsten Avenues. In 1907, the church community was organized in Corcoran. The building pictured was dedicated on September 5, 1909, and cost $2,500 to build.

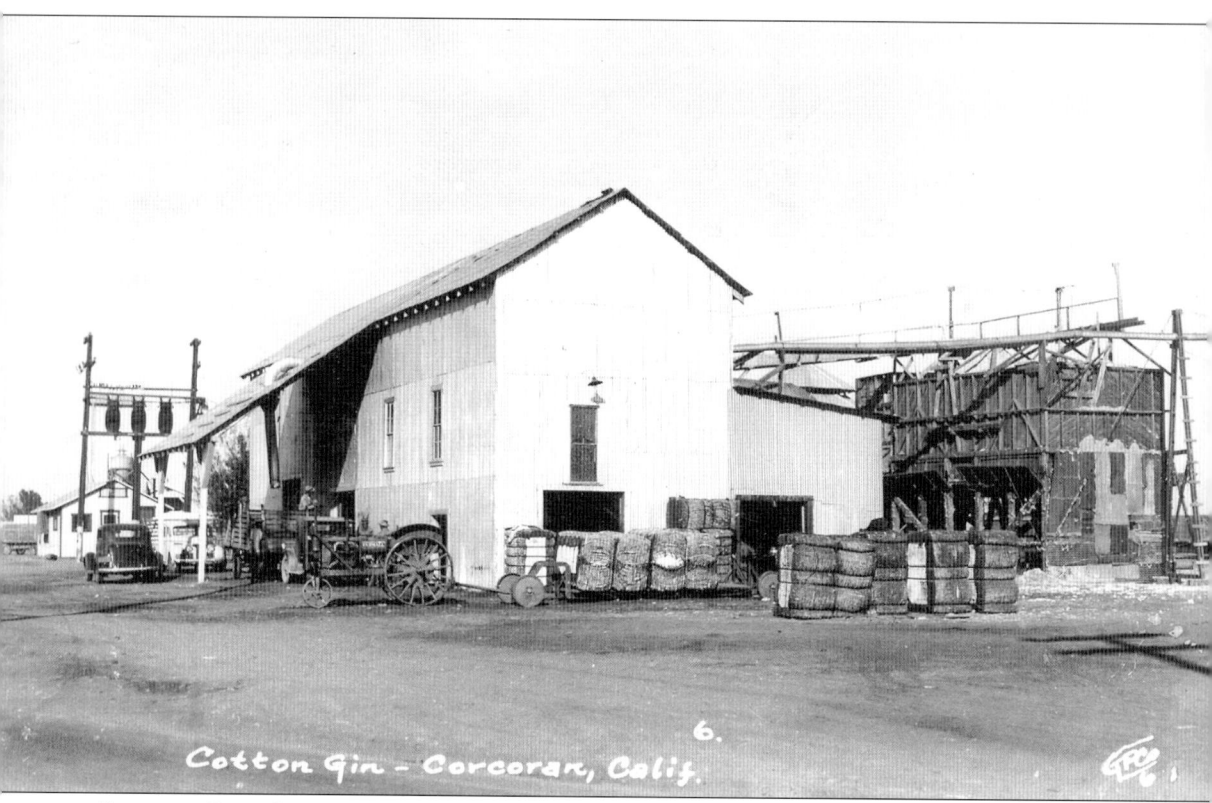

Cotton Gin, Corcoran. The term "Cotton is King" is no better suited than when applied to the Corcoran farming area. Cotton was introduced to the area in 1920 by the J. W. Guiberson Company and flourished. Vast fortunes were created from growing the crop since the climate and soils were ideal. Corcoran is currently home to some of the largest cotton farming operations in the United States. (Courtesy Ron Burris.)

Four

AVENAL

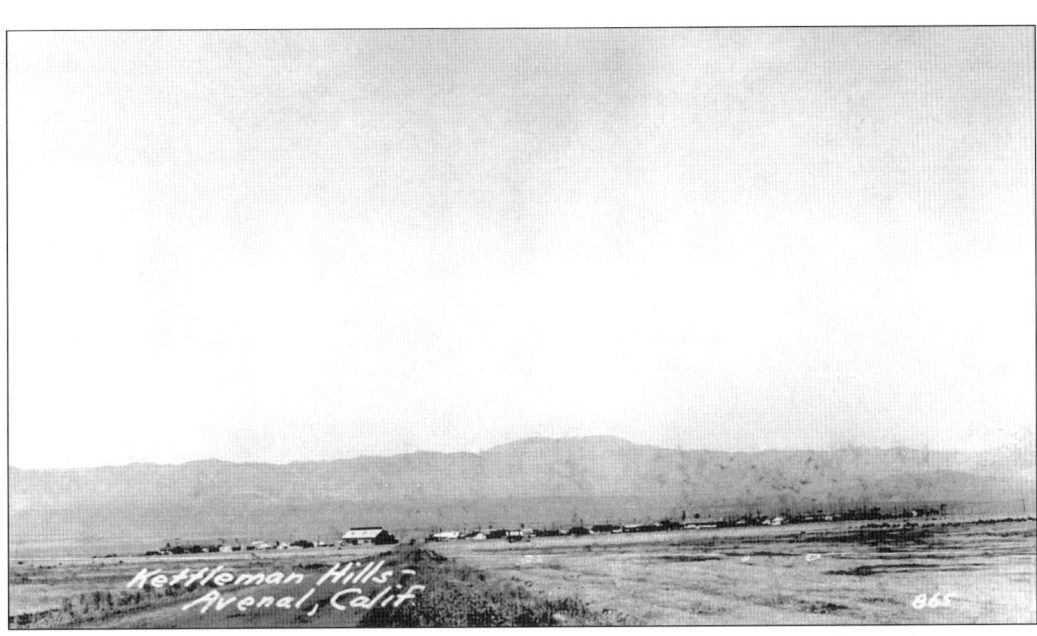

AVENAL TOWN VIEW. Avenal was established in 1928 on the west side of Kings County. In 1929, oil was discovered in the local hills and the town became a major center of oil production in California. This postcard is looking west toward the town. The tall, flat hill in the background is named "The Black Hole" and was used by rustlers to hide stolen cattle.

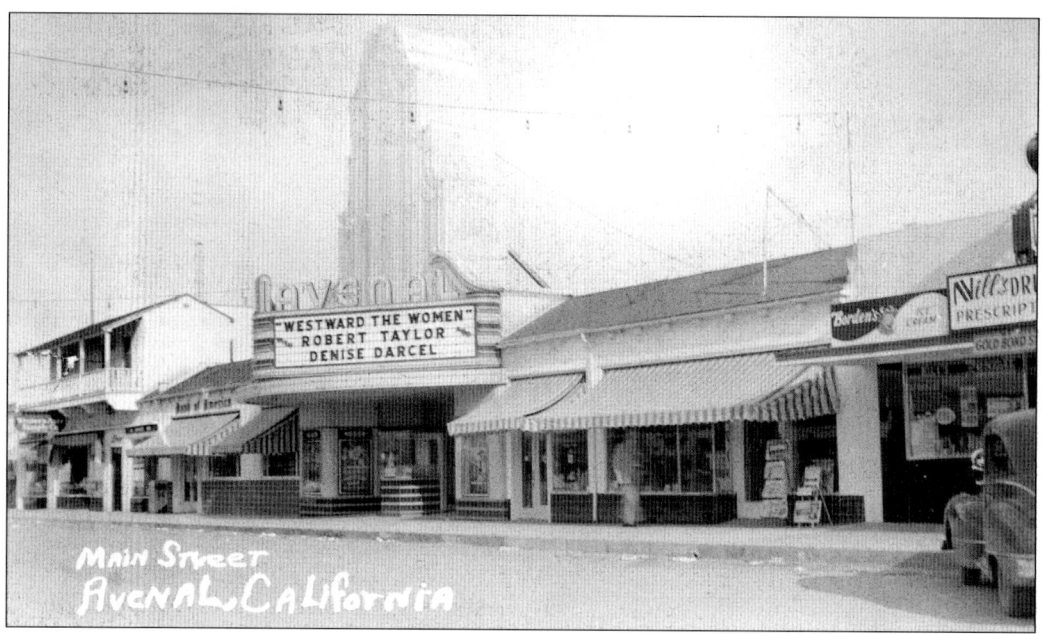

AVENAL THEATRE. The centerpiece of Avenal was the Avenal Theatre, designed by architect W. D. Coats and built in 1935 by R. D. Moore Construction. In 1998, the City of Avenal partnered with private investors to restore the building. Unfortunately, it burned down in 2003. *Westward the Women* debuted in 1951. (Courtesy Ron Burris.)

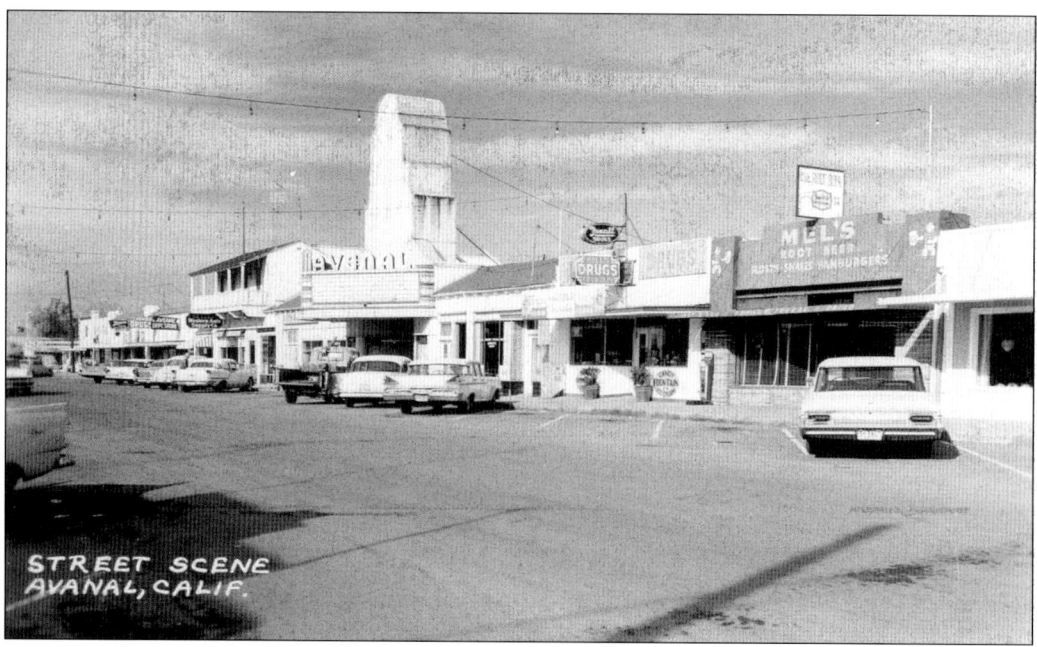

KING STREET, LOOKING WEST. A busy downtown scene in the early 1960s clearly shows two drugstores, a hardware store, the theatre, and a soda shop.

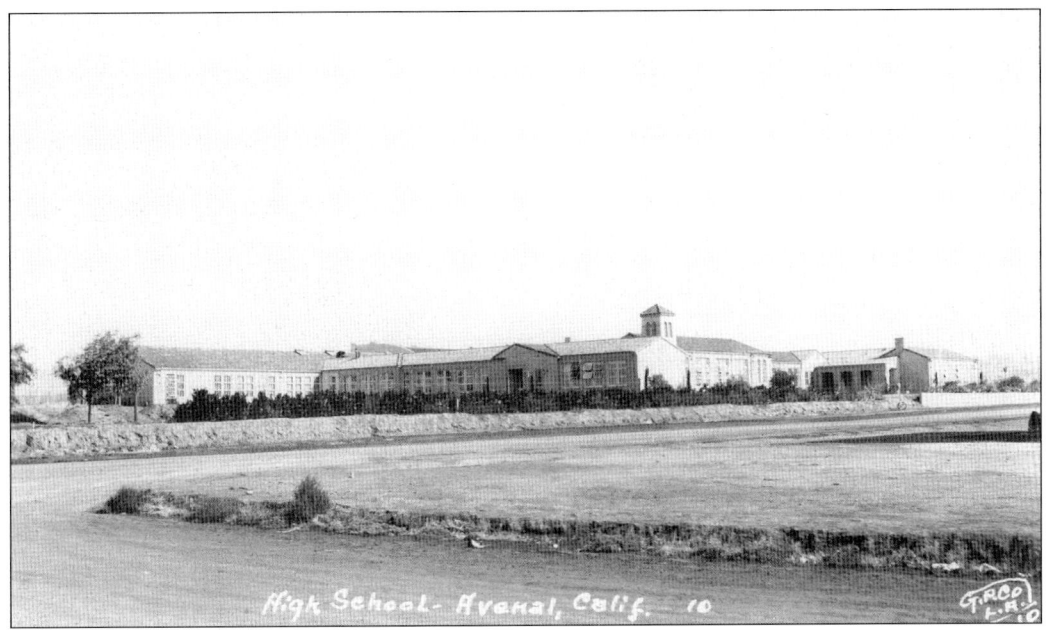

AVENAL HIGH SCHOOL. Here is Avenal High School in 1937 shortly after it was built. The building was designed by William H. Weeks, who planned it to match the architecture of Lemoore Union High School. The district enjoyed a large tax base due to the discovery of oil within its boundary.

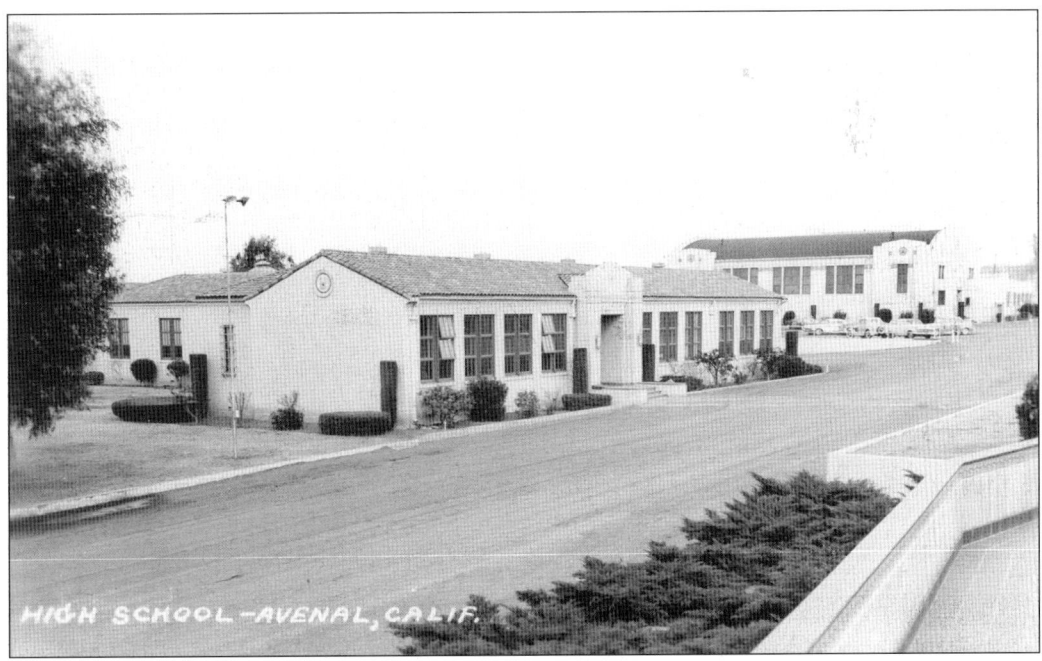

AVENAL HIGH WITH GYM. This postcard shows the administration building in the foreground and the gymnasium in the background. Avenal High School was unified with the local elementary school in 1979 and the district is now called the Reef-Sunset Unified District.

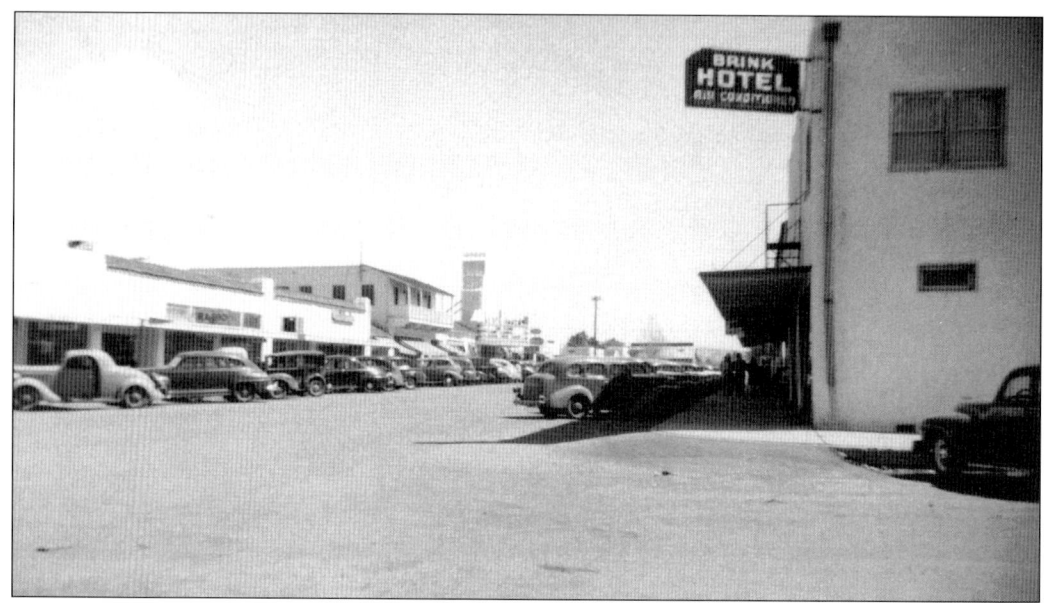

KING STREET, AVENAL. This easterly view of King Street shows the Avenal Theatre in the background and the Brink Hotel. (Courtesy Ron Burris.)

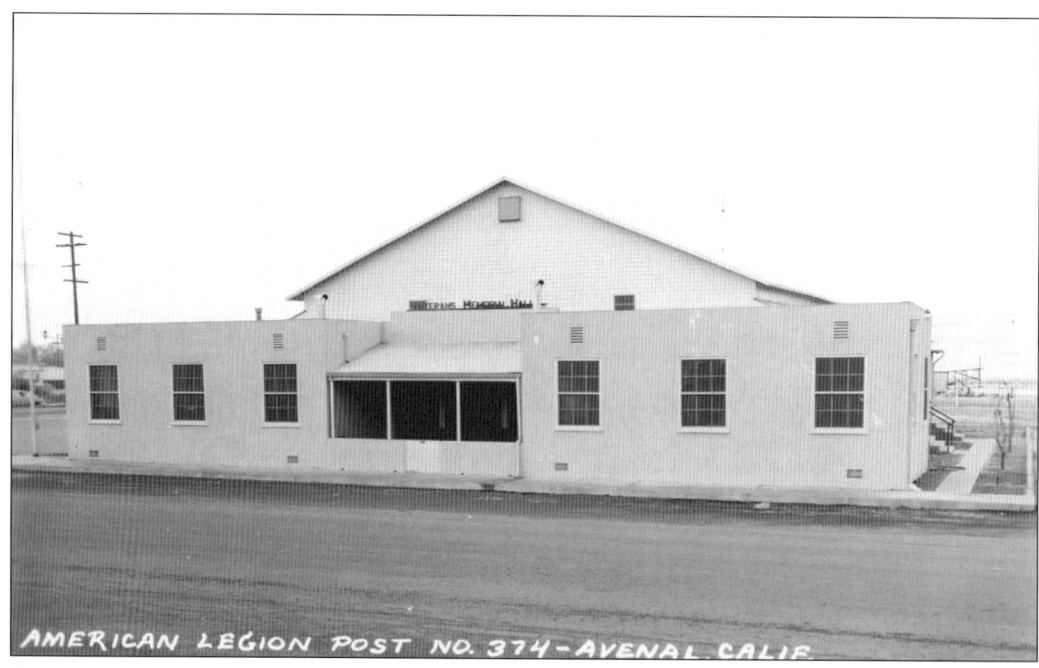

AMERICAN LEGION POST NO. 374. The building depicted on this card was originally located on Tulane Street, south of the downtown area. It was destroyed by fire in the early 1970s. (Courtesy Ron Burris.)

Five

Armona and Hardwick

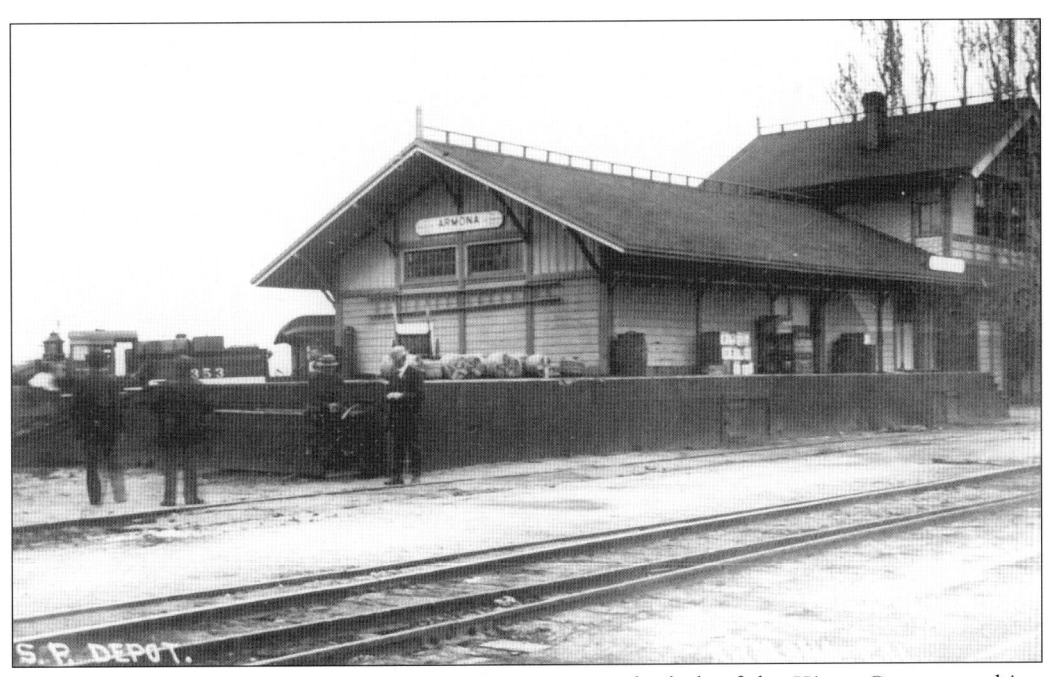

Southern Pacific Depot, Armona. Armona was the hub of the Kings County packing industry. The railroad provided the transportation necessary to delivery the packed agricultural products to market. On the left side of this image is a train parked on the Hardwick spur line.

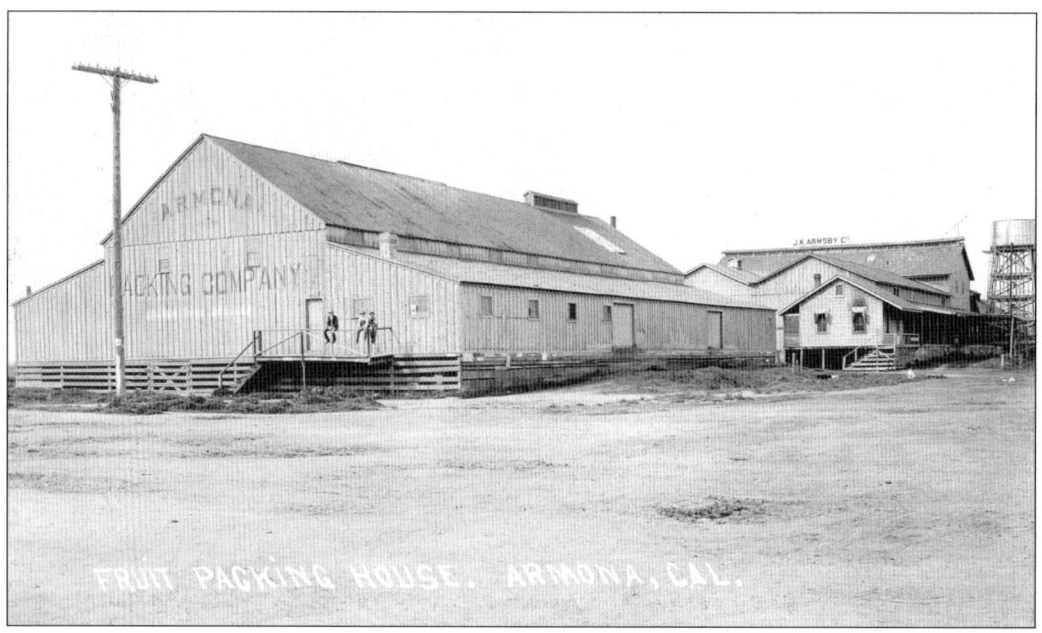

FRUIT PACKING HOUSE, ARMONA. The J. K. Armsby Company packinghouse was located next to the Southern Pacific Railroad tracks. Armona had numerous packing sheds, which serviced the local farming community. The local area was home to thousands of acres of fruits and vines and the crops grown had to be properly packed to ship to markets throughout the United States. (Courtesy James Hickman.)

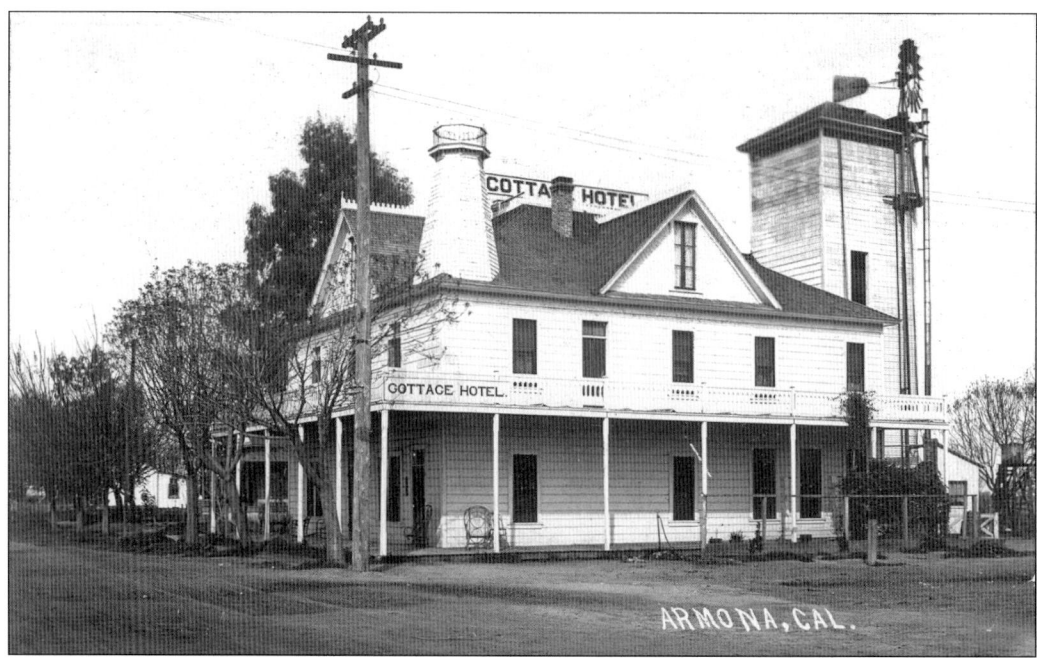

THE COTTAGE HOTEL, ARMONA. The Cottage Hotel was located on the north side of Front Street, just west of Fourteenth Avenue. The first floor of the hotel was occupied by a general store while the second floor was utilized for local dances and meetings. (Courtesy Ron Burris.)

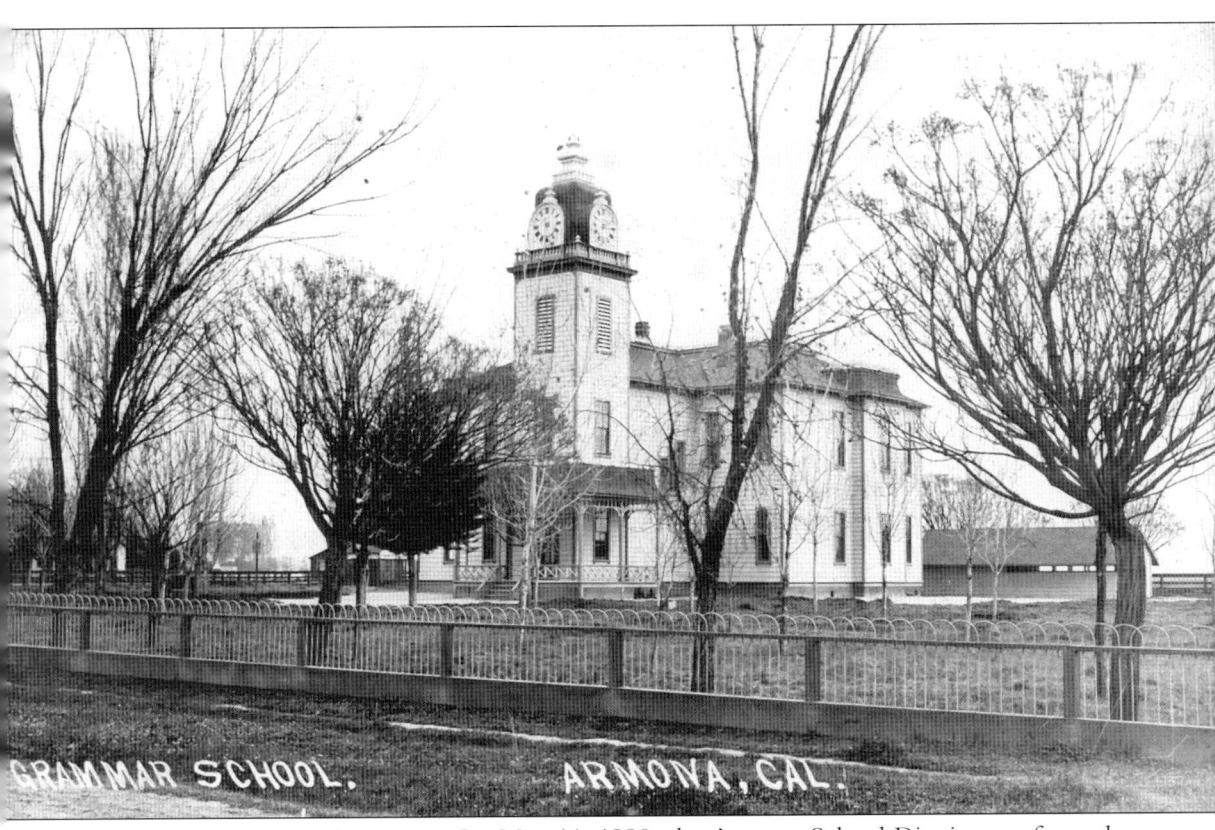

GIDDINGS SCHOOL, ARMONA. On May 14, 1880, the Armona School District was formed. The school was named after E. L. Giddings, who donated the property on which the school was built. It was located on Fourteenth Avenue between Walker and Hood Streets. It was one of the largest schools in the area at that time.

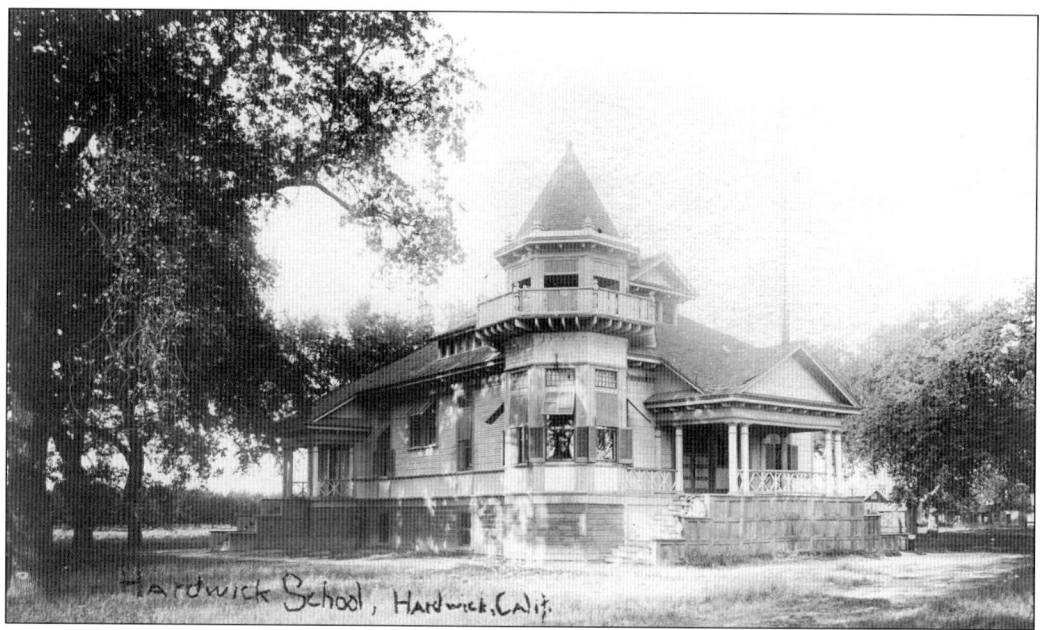

HARDWICK GRAMMAR SCHOOL, HARDWICK. This unused postcard portrays the original Hardwick School around 1910. Built between 1893 and 1895, the building was used as a school until 1914, when a newer school was built. The building was purchased by a local farmer, moved several miles, and used as a residence until recently.

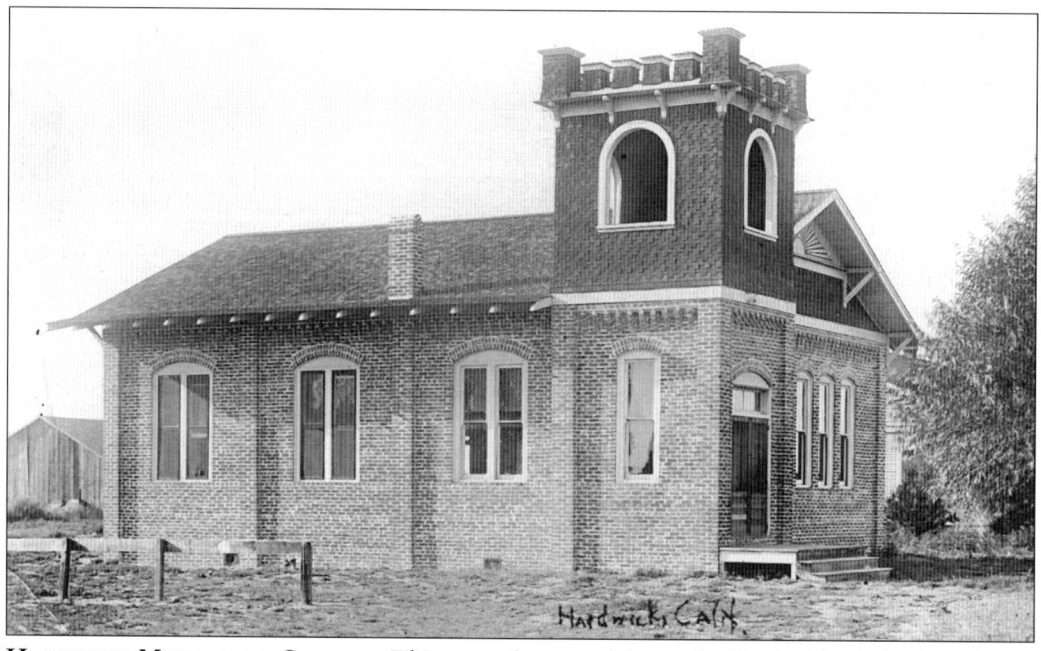

HARDWICK METHODIST CHURCH. This unused postcard shows the Hardwick Methodist Church around 1910. Originally constructed in the late 1890s, it was acquired by Kings County in 1925 for $1,700 to house the Hardwick library collection. In 1973, the building was demolished.

Six

AGRICULTURE

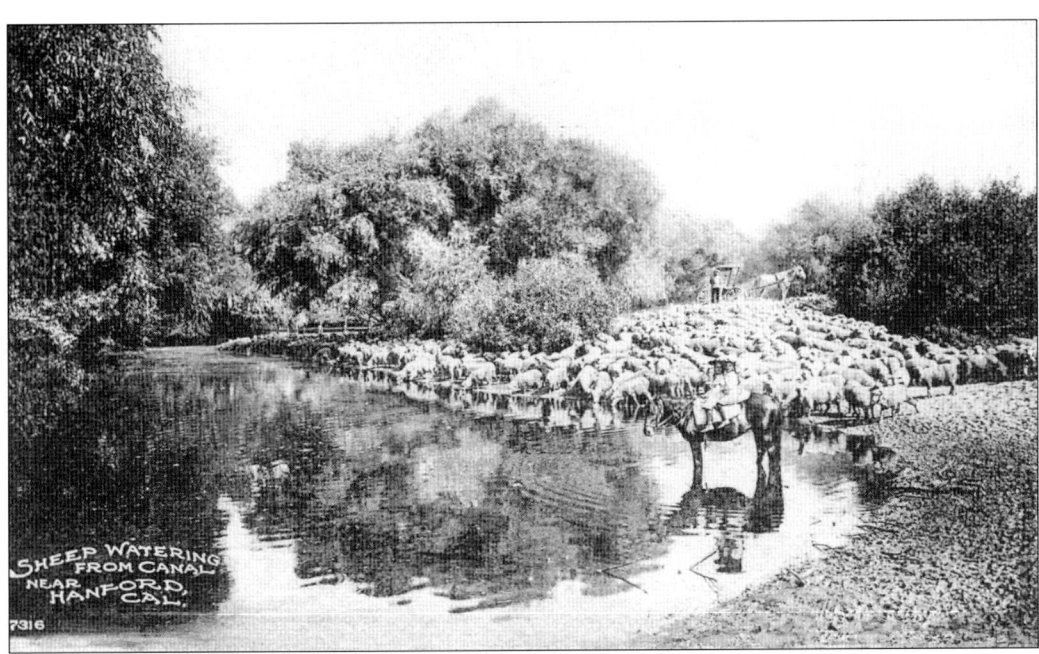

SHEEP WATERING FROM CANAL, HANFORD. The picture on this 1905 postcard originally appeared in an 1898 publication called *Kings County Resources Illustrated*. It depicts Merino sheep watering from a canal on the John Sigler Ranch, which was located six miles south of Hanford. Sheep were raised for their wool and meat, and they served a double purpose of minimizing the growth of weeds in the vineyards and orchards of the area.

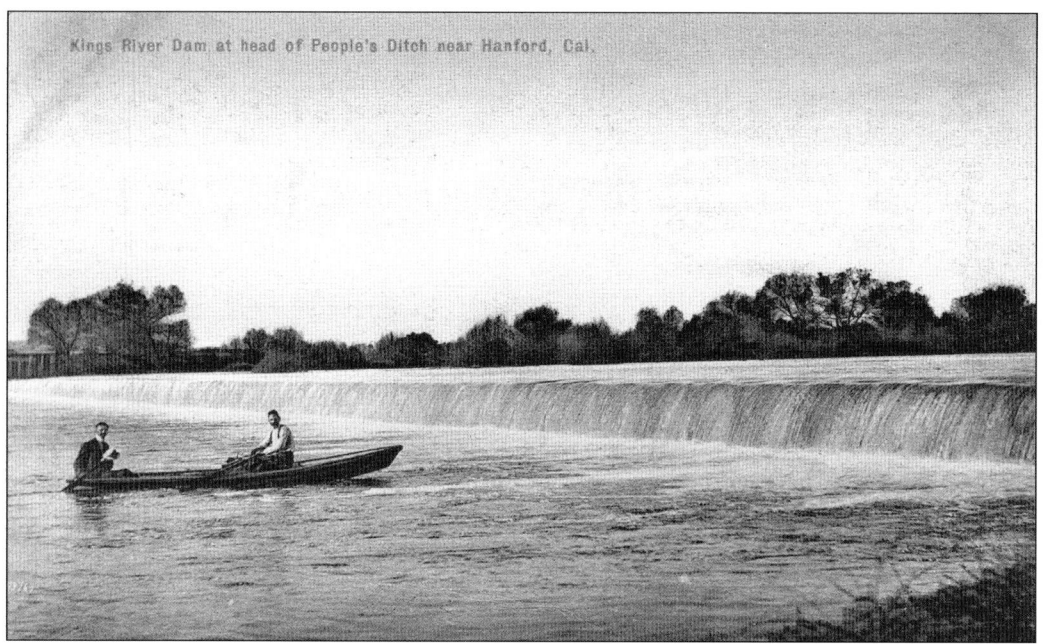

KINGS RIVER DAM AT HEAD OF PEOPLES DITCH NEAR HANFORD. Weirs, rudimentary dams that hold back the water on a river and force it to flow outside its natural channel, on the Kings River diverted water into irrigation canals. This weir was built in 1877 and was instrumental in transforming the dry, arid land into productive farmland.

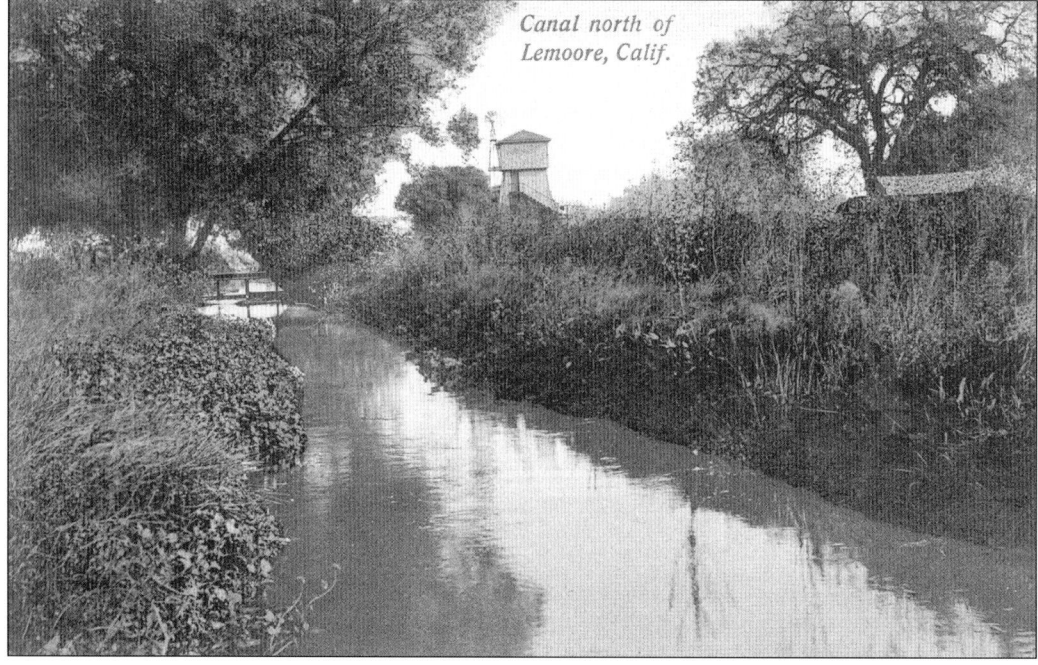

CANAL NORTH OF LEMOORE. Ditches, such as the one shown here, crisscrossed the local landscape. These ditches were dug by the early settlers using horse-drawn scrapers and by hand using picks and shovels. Trees and other vegetation sprouted along the banks of irrigation canals creating cover for the wildlife of the area.

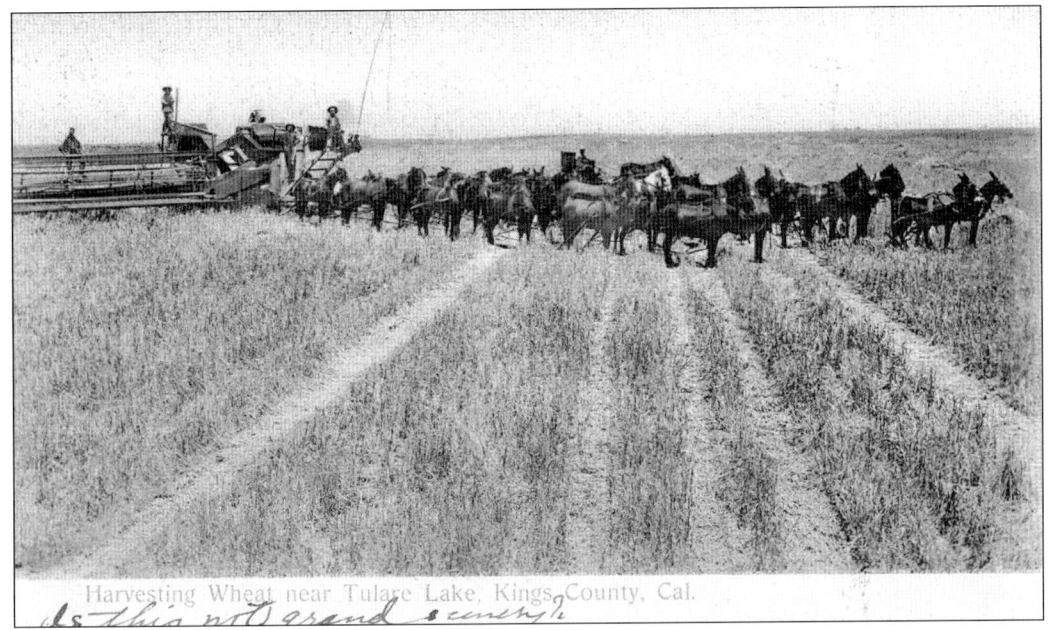

HARVESTING WHEAT NEAR TULARE LAKE, KINGS COUNTY. In this 1907 postcard, a harvest crew poses for the photographer. The first major agricultural crop grown in county was wheat. More wheat was shipped from the area from 1880 through 1895 than from anywhere else in the world at that time. Wheat was harvested by mule-drawn reapers that crawled along the landscape.

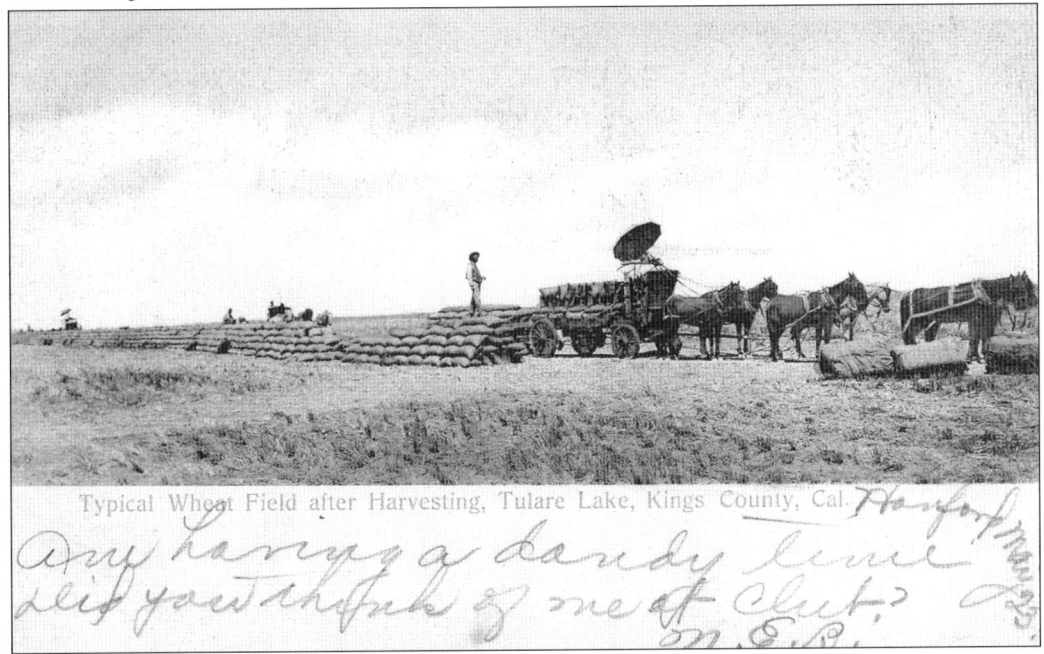

TYPICAL WHEAT FIELD AFTER HARVESTING, TULARE LAKE, KINGS COUNTY. After the wheat was harvested, it was threshed to separate the grain from the chaff. The wheat was bagged and placed in large piles at the ends of the fields. This 1906 postmarked card shows the bounty of harvest from a particular field.

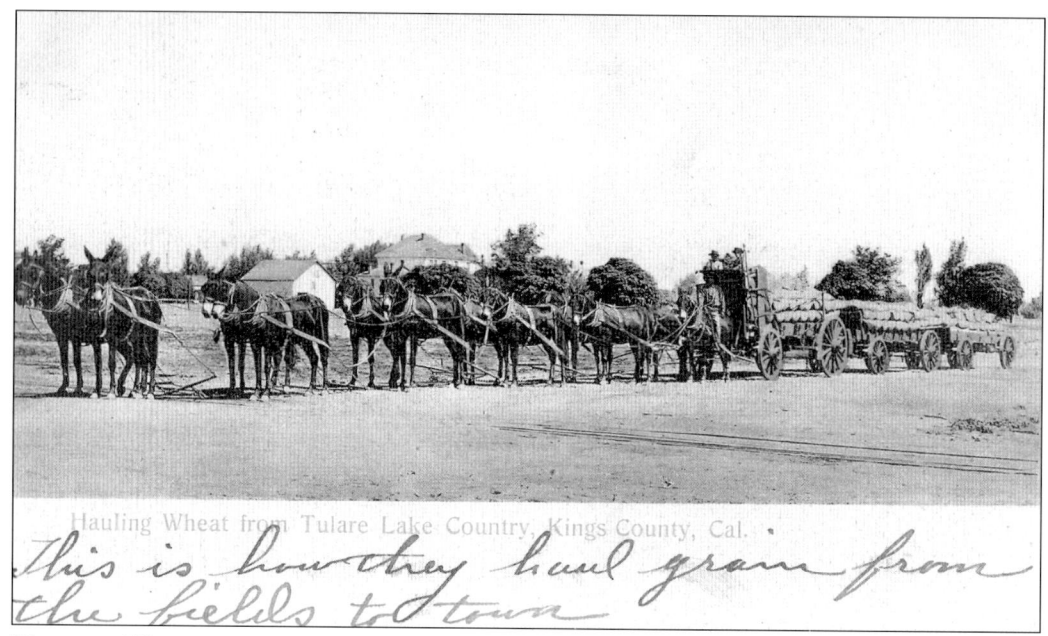

HAULING WHEAT FROM TULARE LAKE COUNTRY. The sender of this card wrote "this is how they haul grain from the fields to town." Grain sacks were loaded onto wagons and hauled into town by large mule teams. This 12-mule wagon train was a common sight in 1908, when this card was mailed to Nebraska.

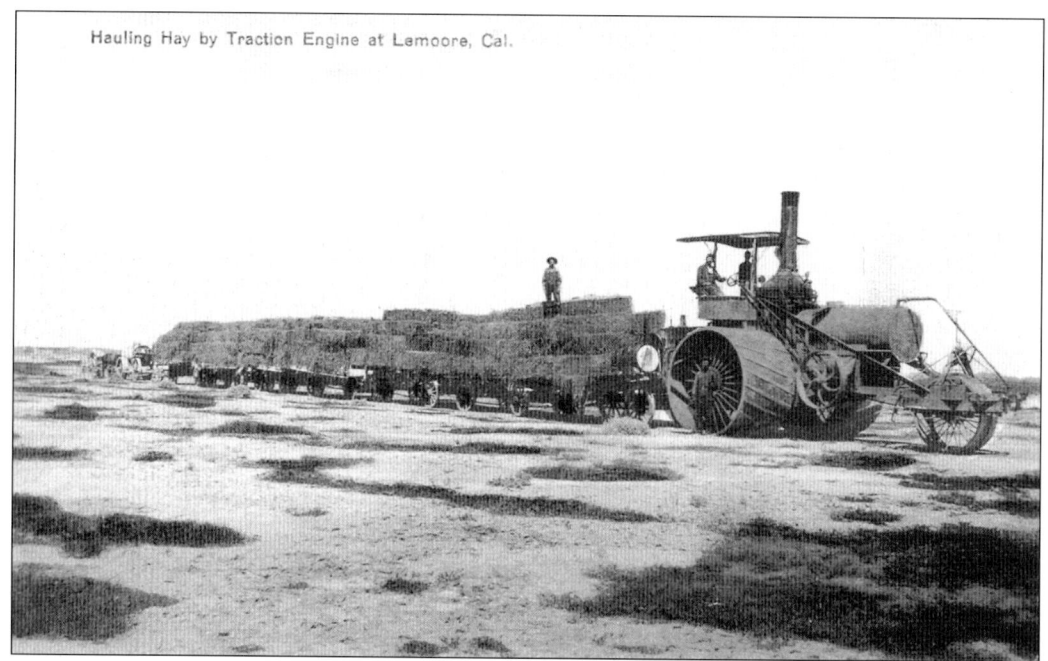

HAULING HAY BY TRACTION ENGINE, LEMOORE. This unused postcard shows the immense size of the mechanized equipment at that time. Steam powered tractors were not a common sight because of their cost. Note the water tank being towed behind the hay wagons. (Courtesy Ron Burris.)

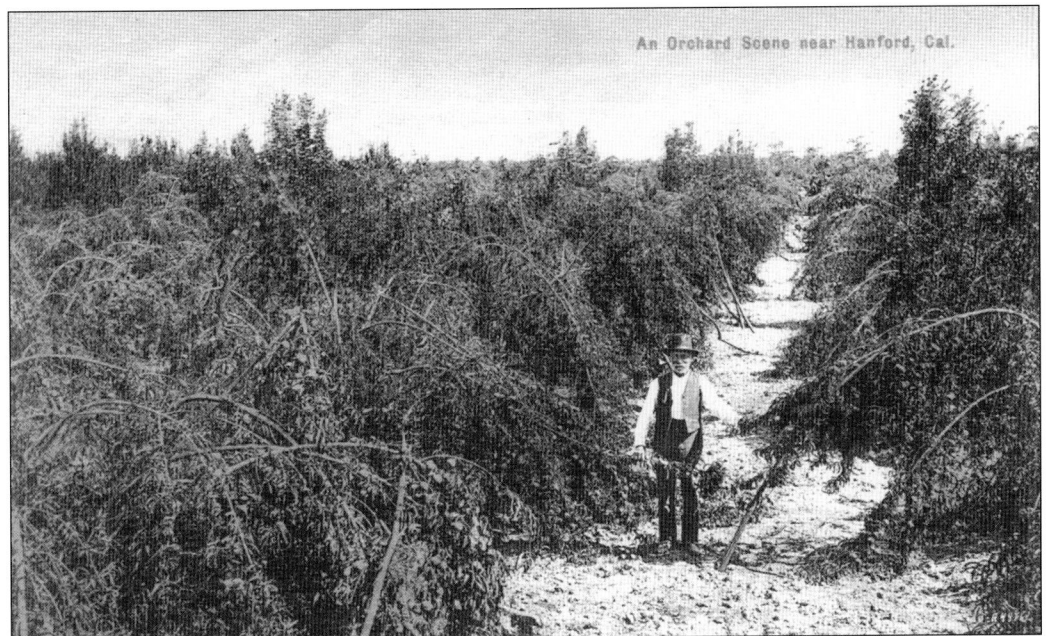

AN ORCHARD SCENE NEAR HANFORD. With the introduction of controlled irrigation, permanent crops were planted. Vast orchards of plums, peaches, pomegranates, persimmons, almonds, pecans, and walnuts were established. The trees flourished in the mild climate and moderate soil, and the wealth generated from these endeavors was a boon to the county as a whole.

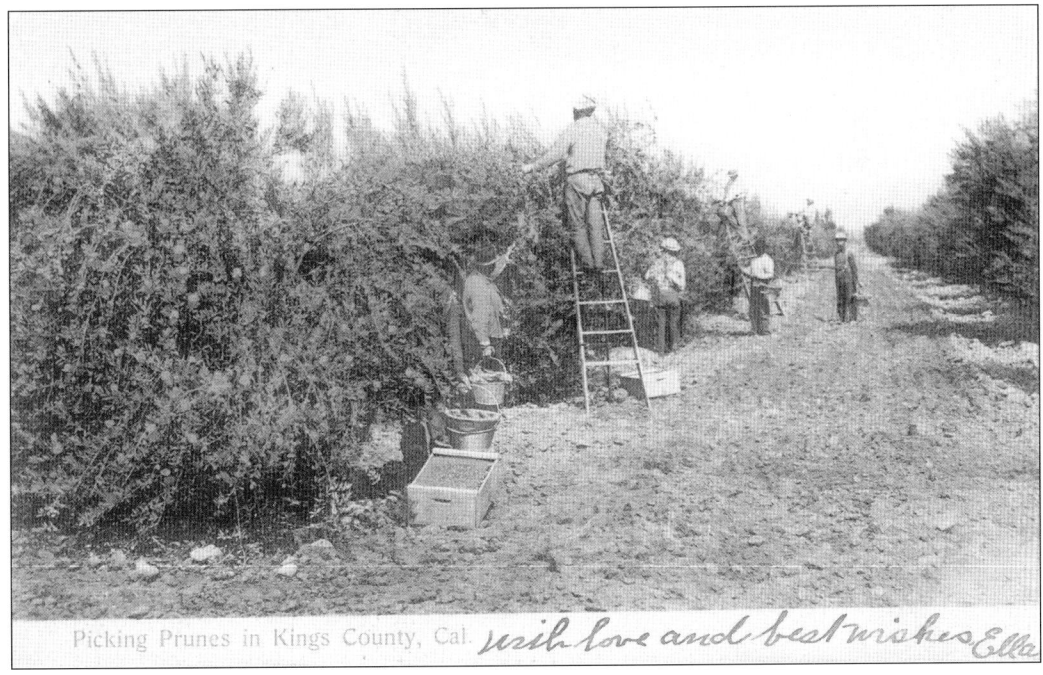

PICKING PRUNES IN KINGS COUNTY. The caption on this card is a misnomer, since prunes are dried plums and can only be dried after they are picked from the tree. This card was postmarked in 1907 and mailed to Seattle.

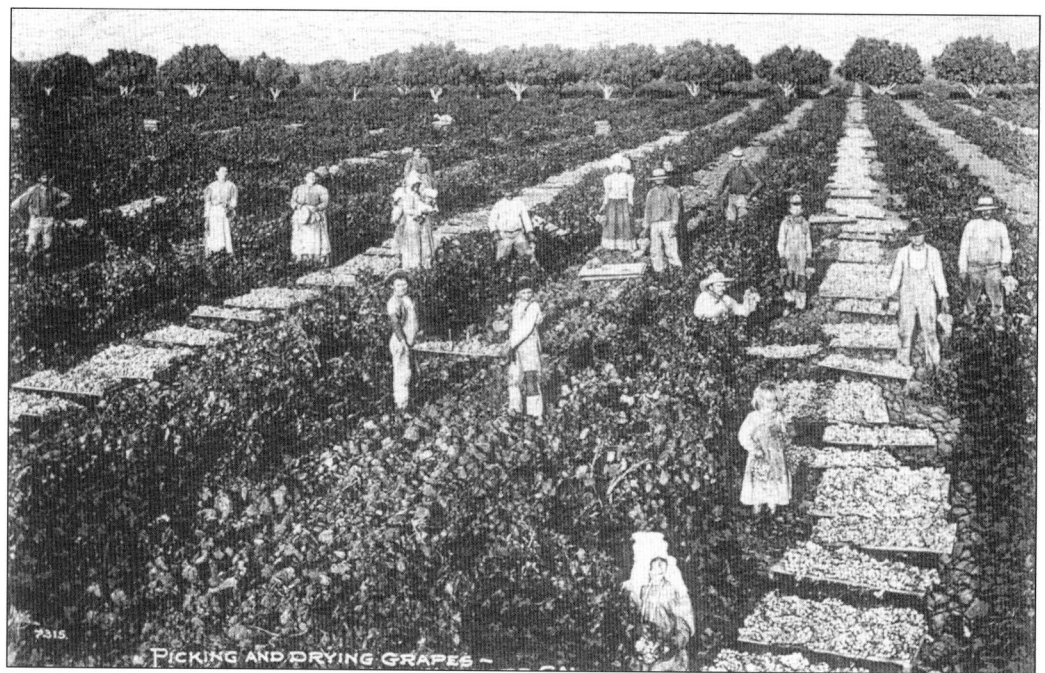

PICKING AND DRYING GRAPES, HANFORD. Vineyards became an early crop of the county since the soil and climate were ideal for the vines. It was the transformation from growing wheat to more permanent crops that created a stable job base, which attracted many immigrants to the area in the early 1900s. Note the numerous children working in this photograph.

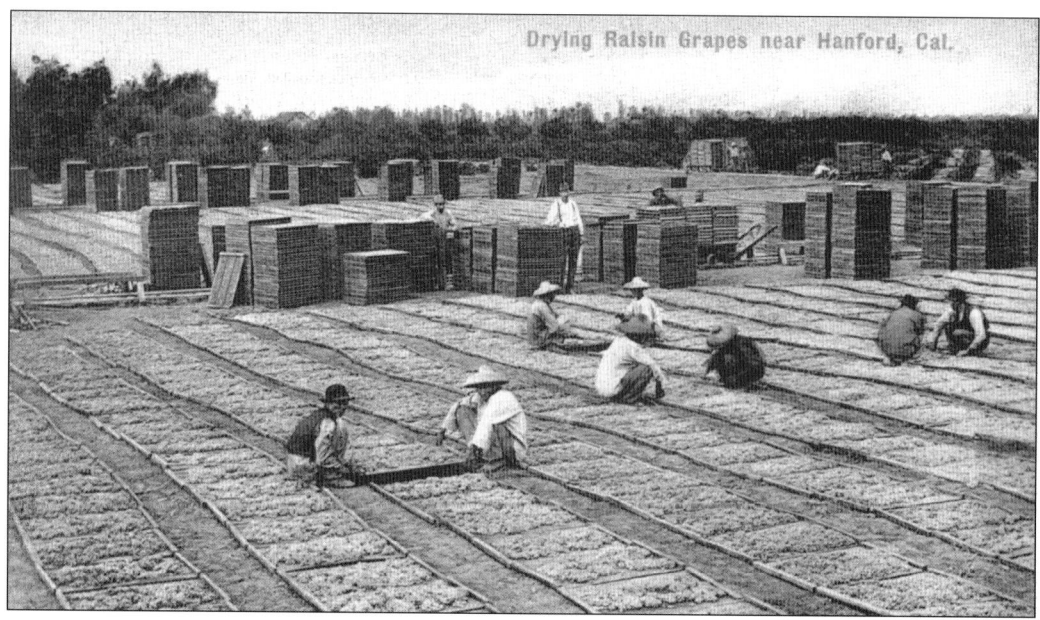

DRYING RAISIN GRAPES NEAR HANFORD. After the grapes were harvested, they were laid out on wooden trays and placed in the sun where they would dry. Raisins were a very profitable crop of the time. This unused postcard shows the drying yard being attended to by Chinese laborers.

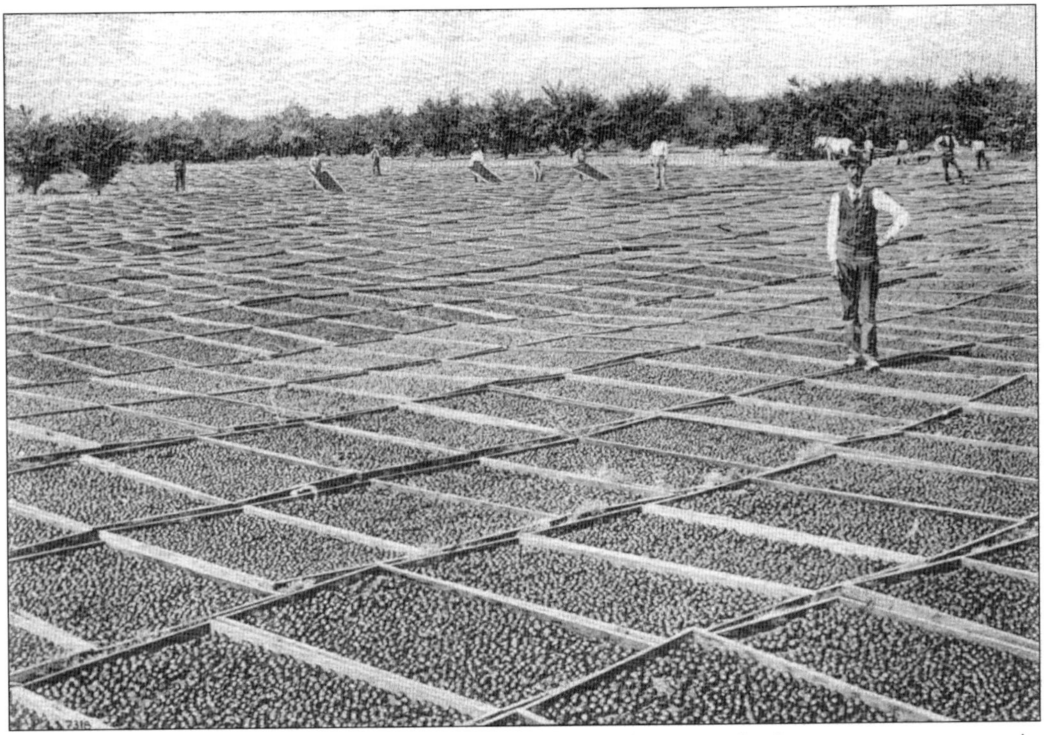

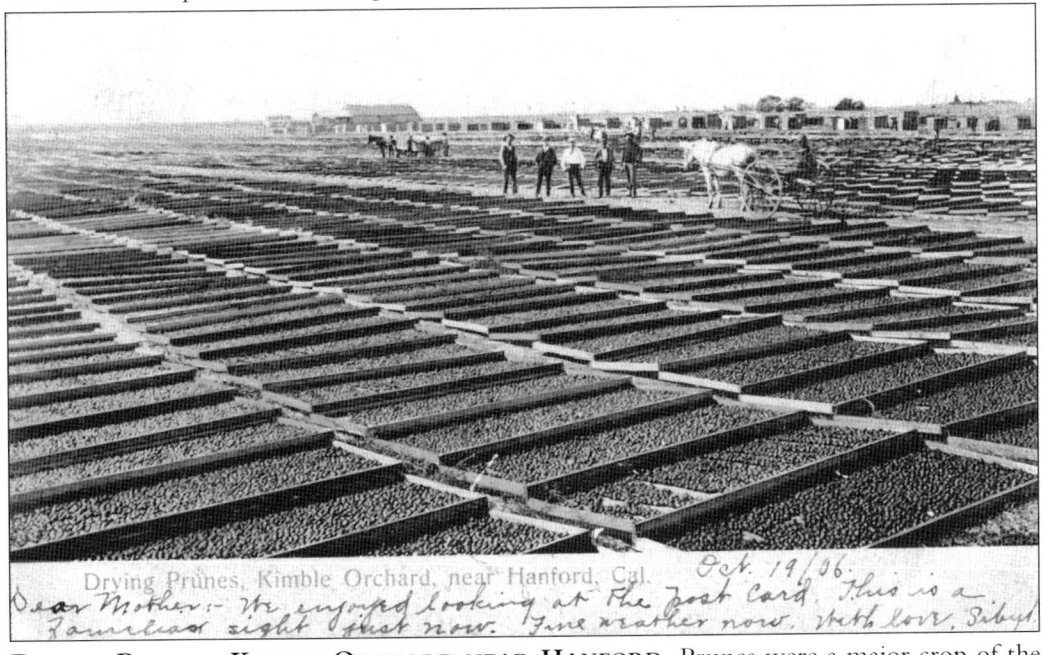

PRUNE-DRYING NEAR HANFORD. Kings County was home to the largest prune growers in the world. This postcard shows a proud man standing in the middle of his bountiful harvest.

DRYING PRUNES, KIMBLE ORCHARD NEAR HANFORD. Prunes were a major crop of the county during the early 1900s. The fruit was recognized as a mild laxative and was in great demand. The county's climate was ideal for the trees and the plentiful sunshine simplified the drying process. Pictured in this 1906 postcard is the Kimble Prune Orchard.

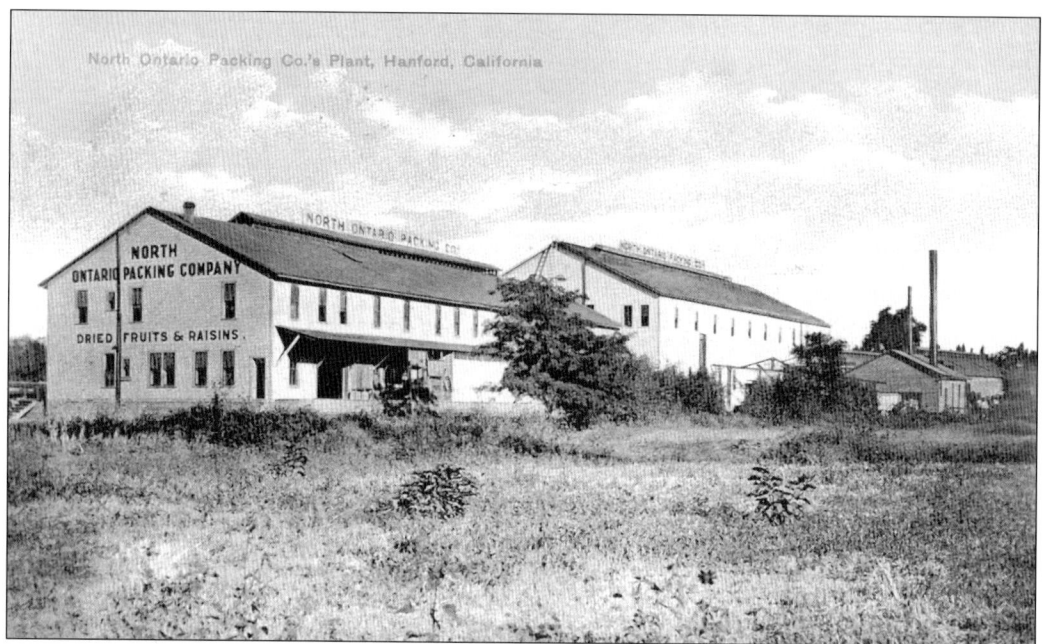

NORTH ONTARIO PACKING COMPANY. This 1912 postmarked card shows the North Ontario Packing Company that was situated north of the Santa Fe Depot in Hanford. This building was gone by 1920.

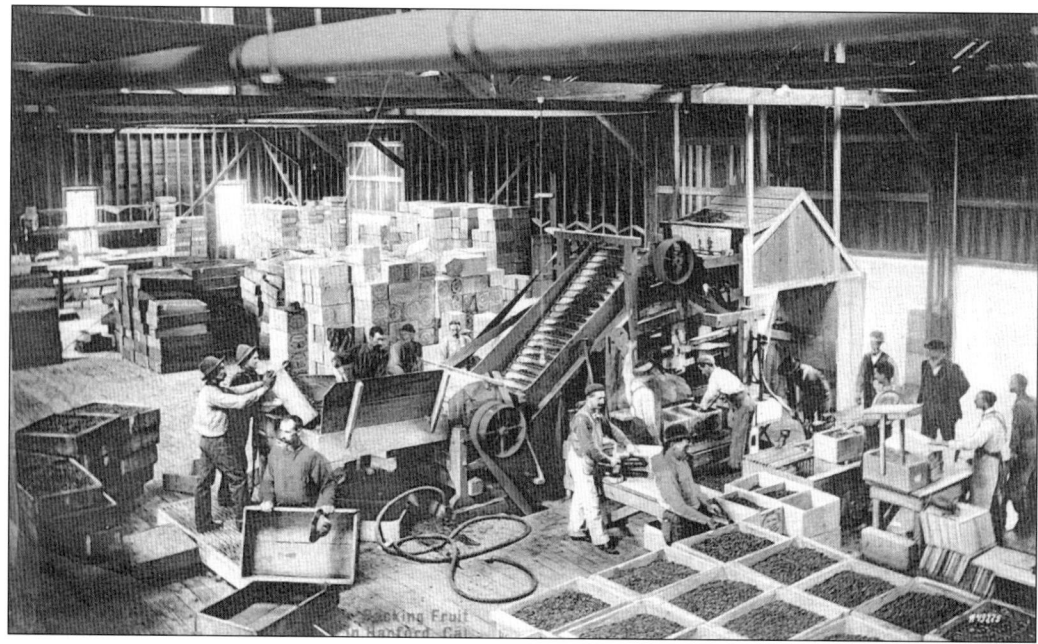

PACKING FRUIT IN HANFORD. This 1912 postcard shows the interior of the North Ontario Packing Company.

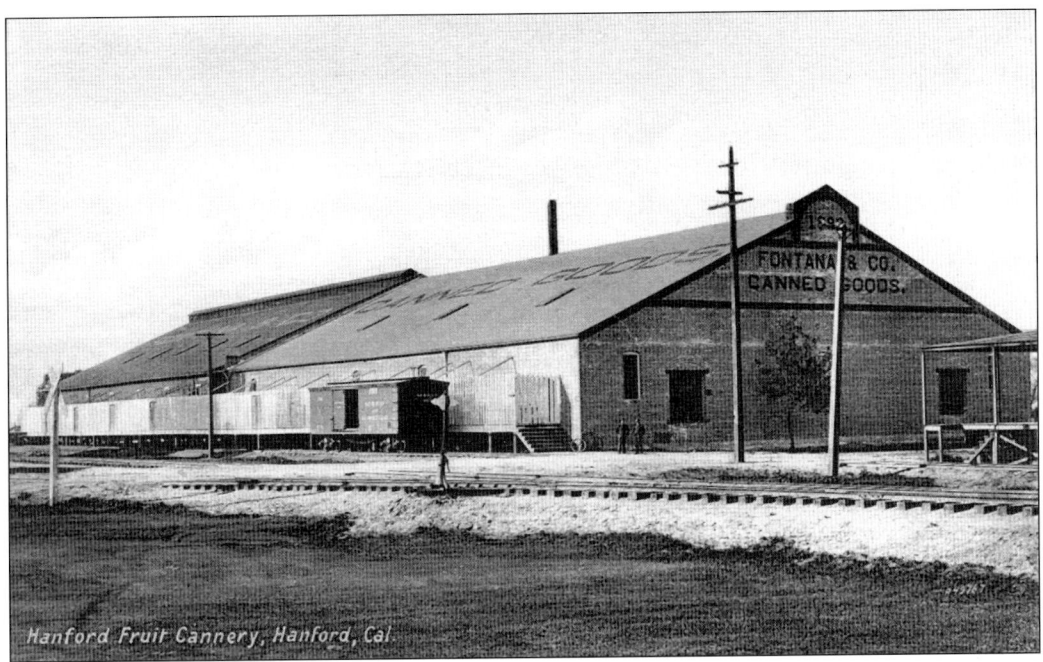

FONTANA AND COMPANY FRUIT CANNERY, HANFORD. This building originally was located on the west side of the Santa Fe tracks between Fourth and Fifth Streets. It was one of many canneries that were located in the county to pack the local fruit harvest.

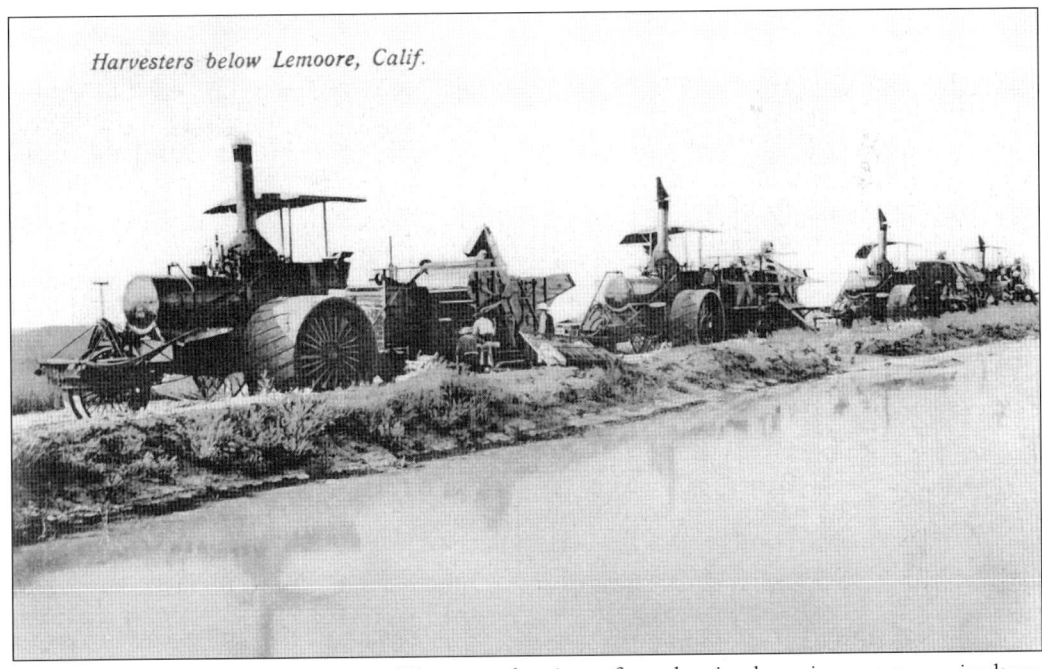

HARVESTERS BELOW LEMOORE. The introduction of mechanized equipment to agriculture transformed the local economy by increasing farm yields and acreage farmed. The steam-powered tractors pictured in this 1914 postcard were used to cultivate large tracts of farmland in the Tulare Lake bottom south of Lemoore.

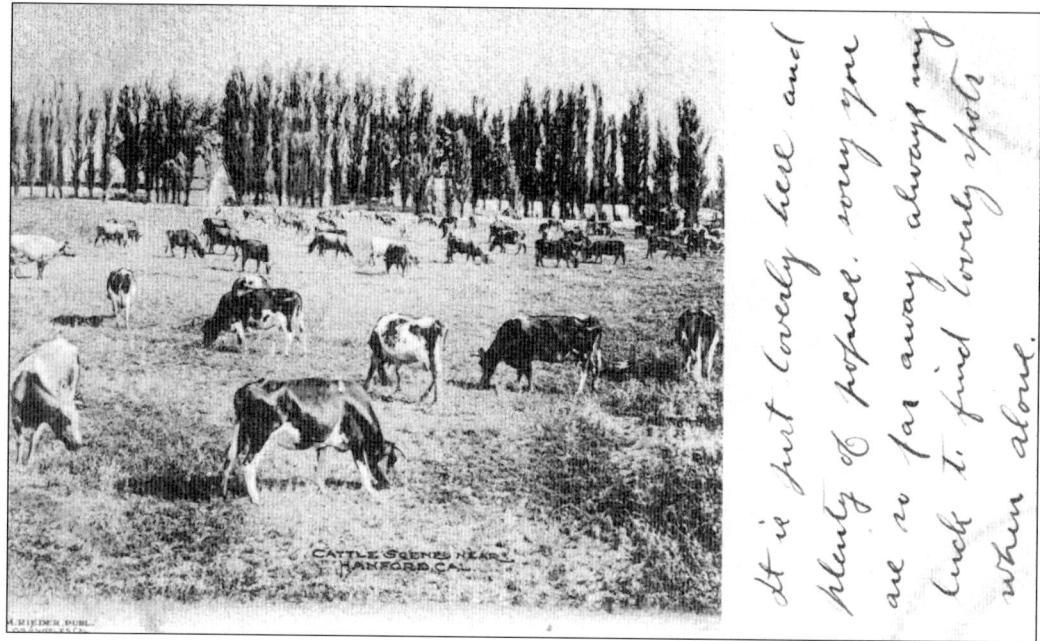

CATTLE SCENE NEAR HANFORD. Dairy animals were a common sight in the county. Plenty of feed was available in the area and the mild weather allowed the animals to flourish. Dairy is still one of the largest agricultural industries in the county today.

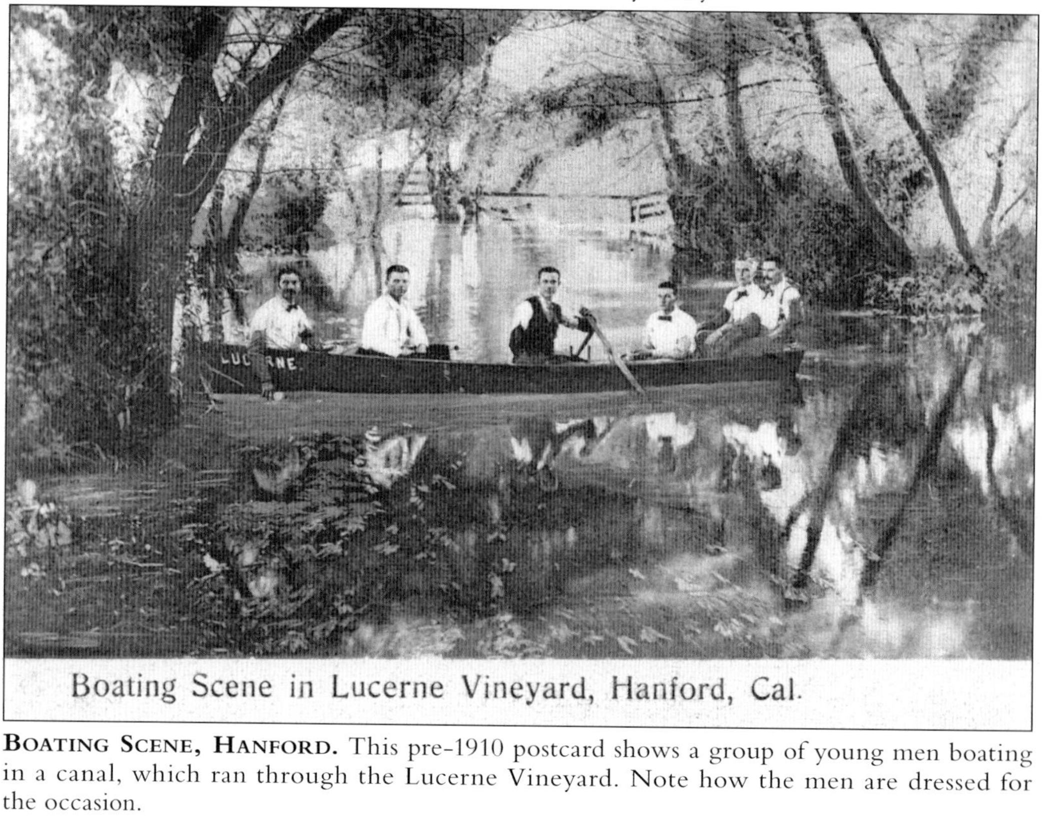

BOATING SCENE, HANFORD. This pre-1910 postcard shows a group of young men boating in a canal, which ran through the Lucerne Vineyard. Note how the men are dressed for the occasion.

Seven
Kings Kounty Karnival Parade, 1911

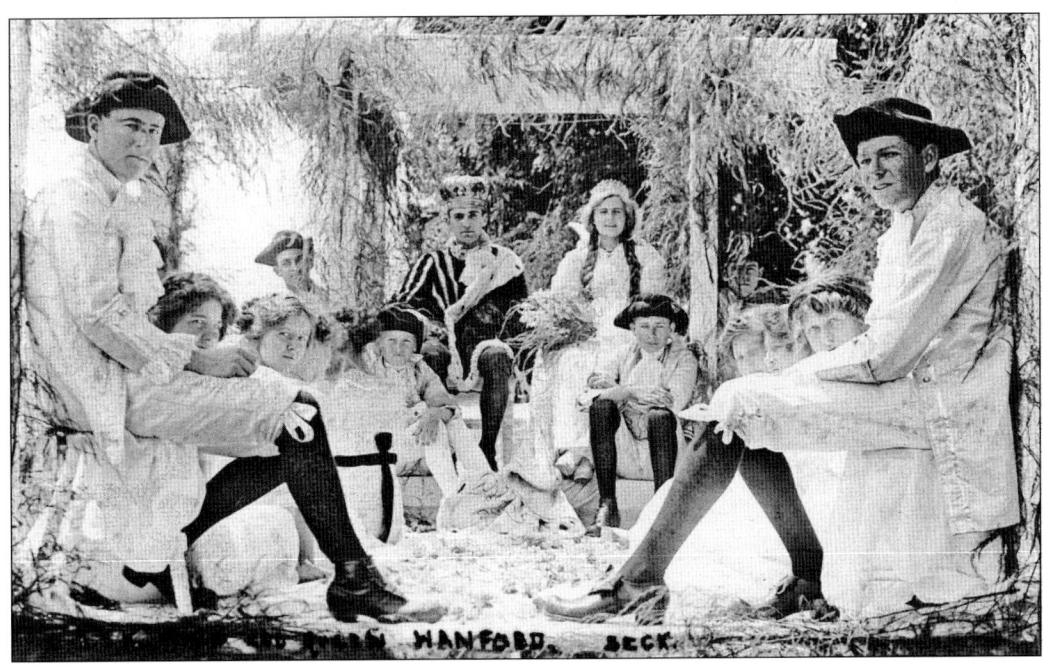

Kings Kounty Karnival, Hanford. During the week of May 23 through May 27, 1911, Kings County celebrated its 18th birthday with a series of parades. This postcard depicts the parade's king and queen, who were coronated on May 23, 1911.

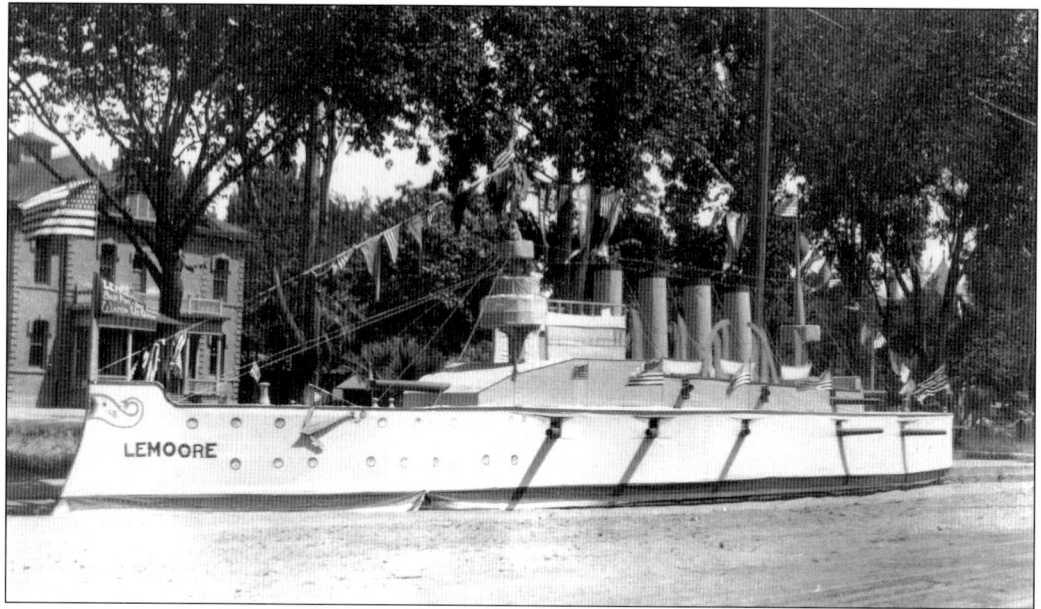

Lemoore Parade Float. The Lemoore parade entry, that of a battleship, honors the travel of the Great White Fleet, the flotilla of United States battleships that sailed on a world tour to demonstrate America's military might.

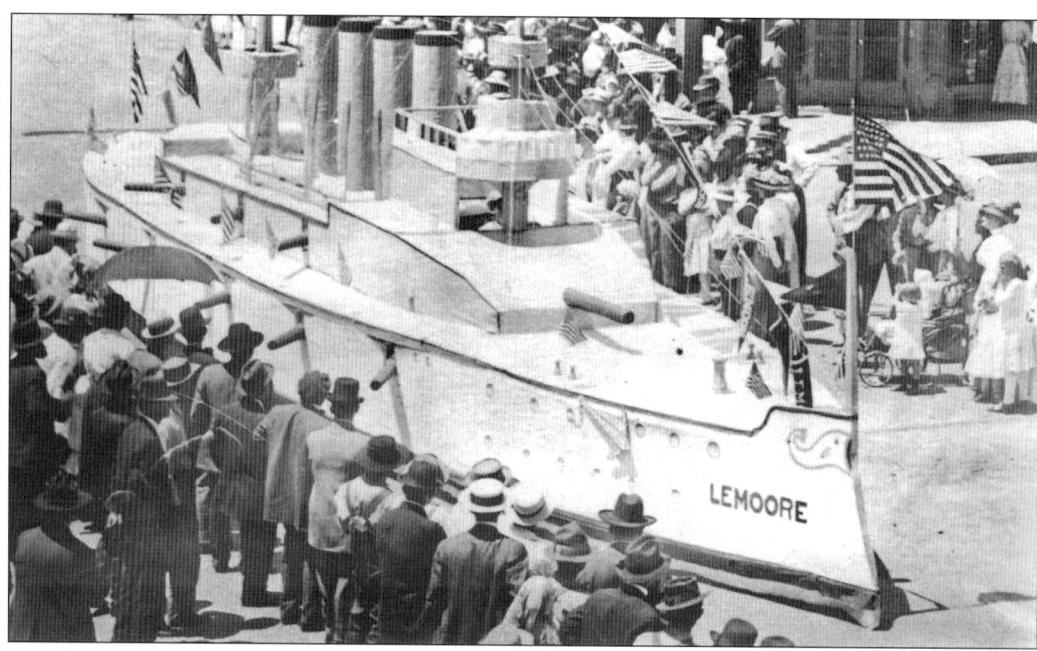

Lemoore Float. A crowd watched as the Lemoore float passed through the intersection of Douty and Seventh Street.

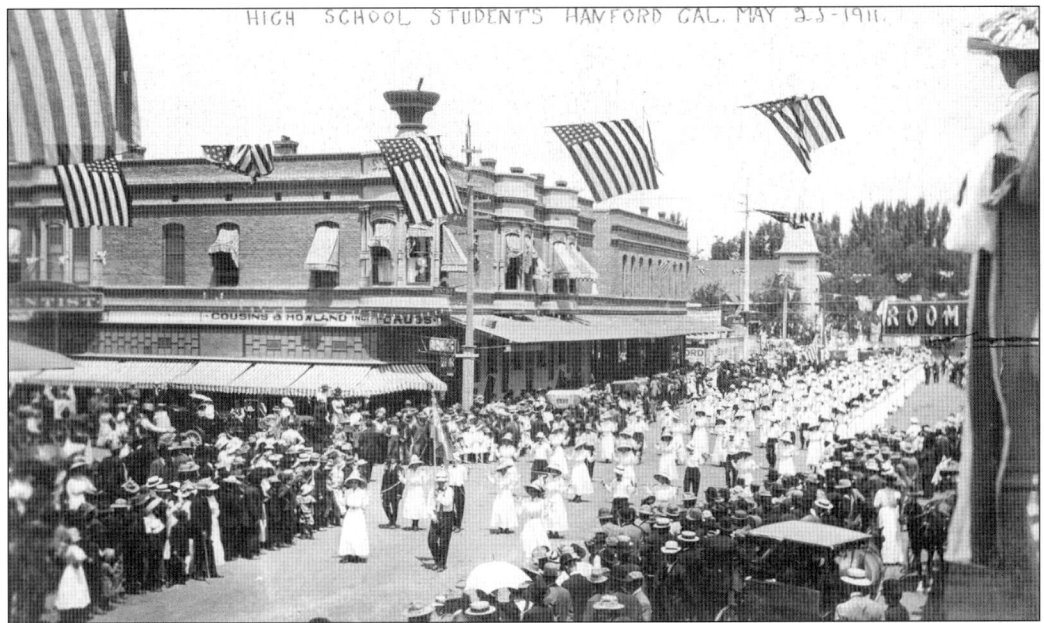

HIGH SCHOOL STUDENTS. This view shows the parade marching south along Douty Street. Hanford High School won "Class Number One" in the parade. The prize was a $10 picture.

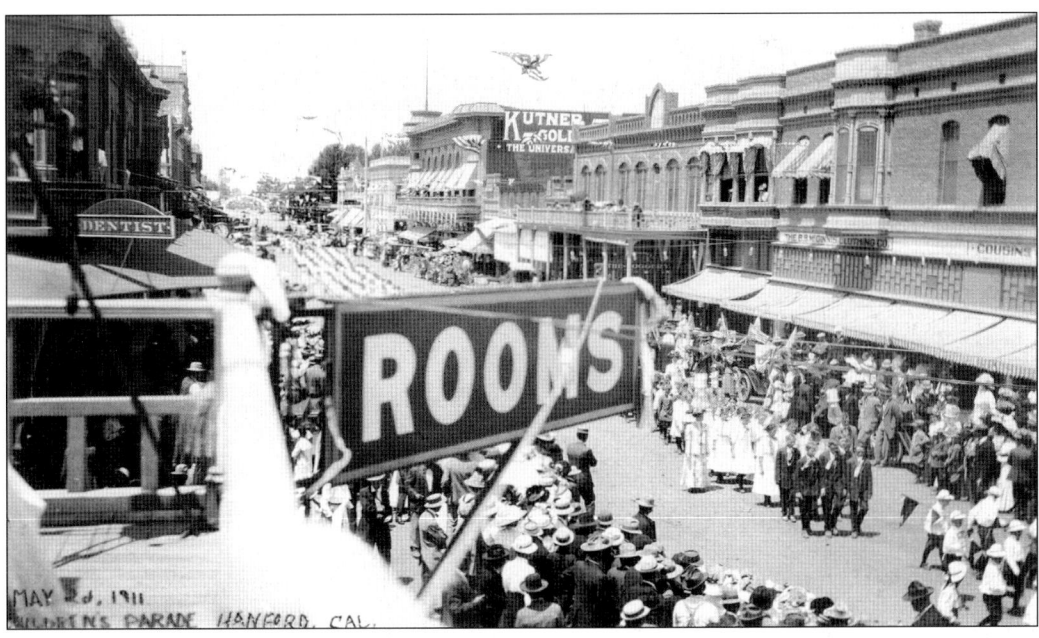

CHILDREN'S PARADE. This image, taken from the second floor balcony of the Hanford Hotel, looks west on Seventh Street. According to the local newspaper, over 1,800 children from all of the county schools participated in the event.

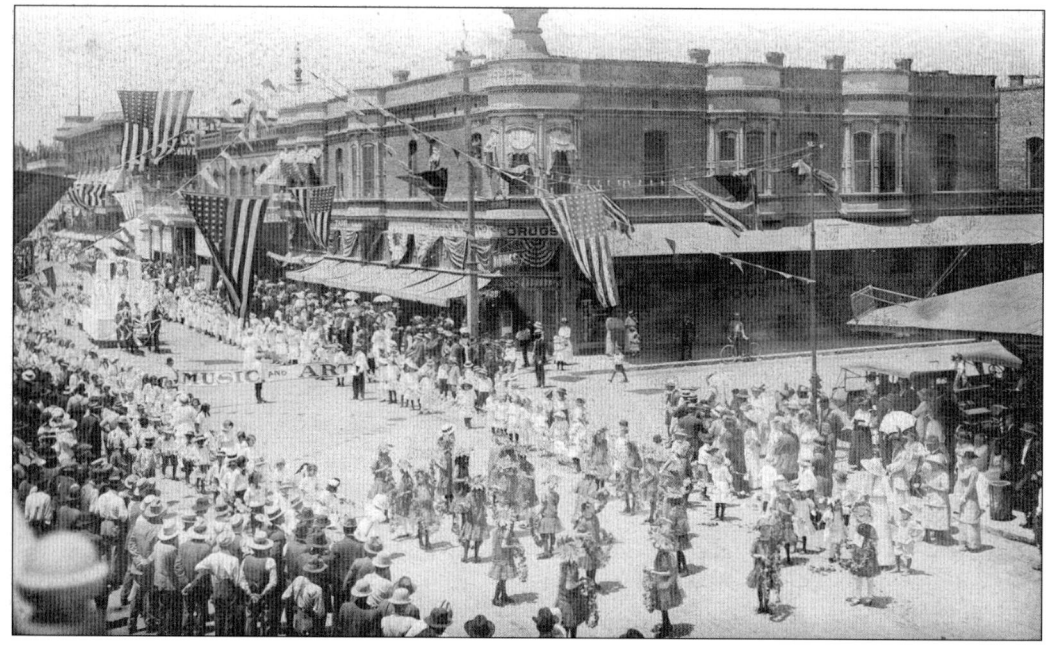

KINGS KOUNTY MUSIC AND ART. This postcard shows a parade float entry depicting music and art.

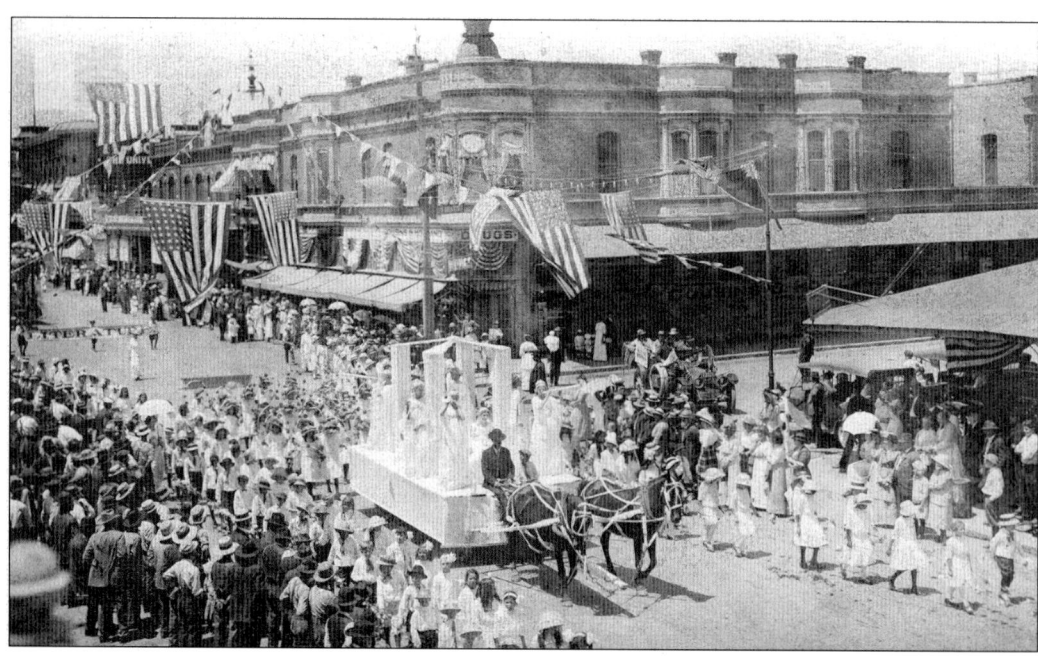

KINGS KOUNTY KARNIVAL PARADE. Here is another view of the music and art parade entry as it advanced further down Seventh Street.

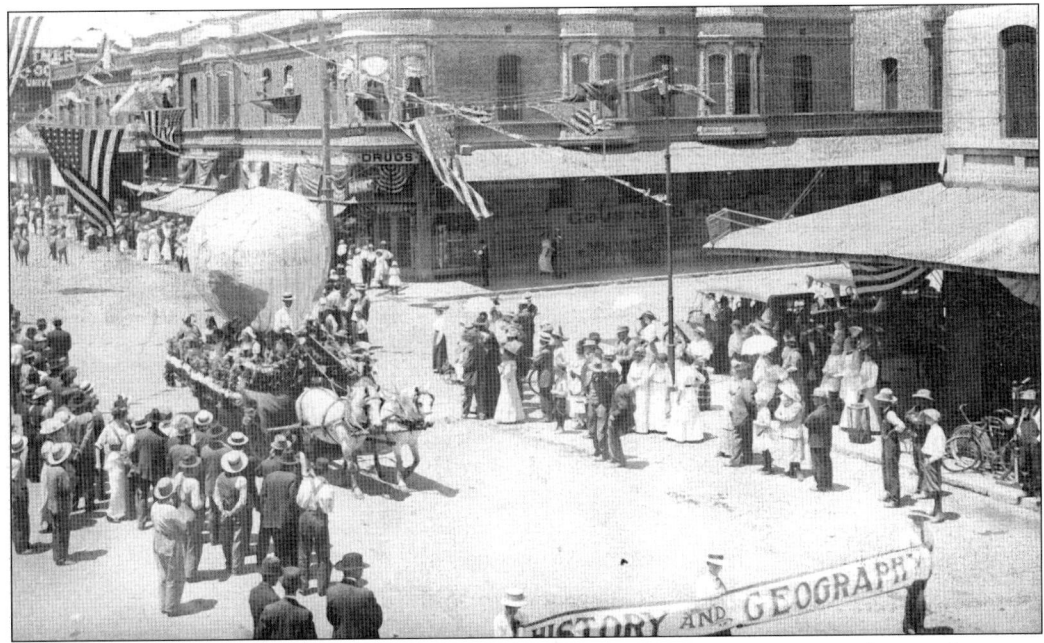

KINGS KOUNTY HISTORY FLOAT. This postcard shows the history and geography parade entry.

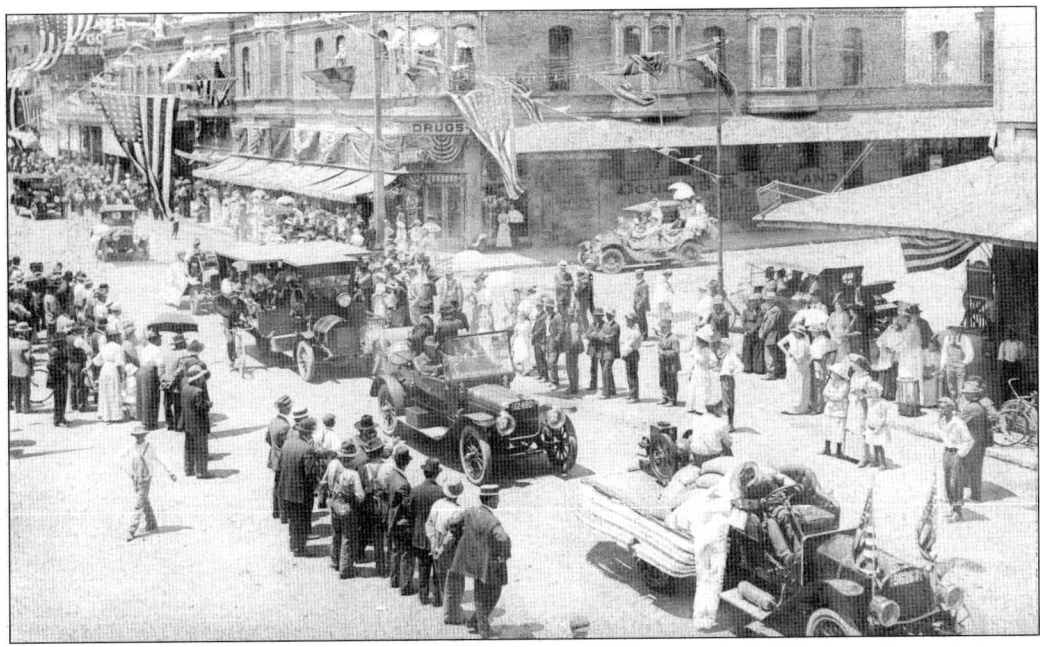

FUN AT THE KARNIVAL. This postcard shows the jovial mood that the parade participants displayed. Spectators were on their honor to stay out of the parade route.

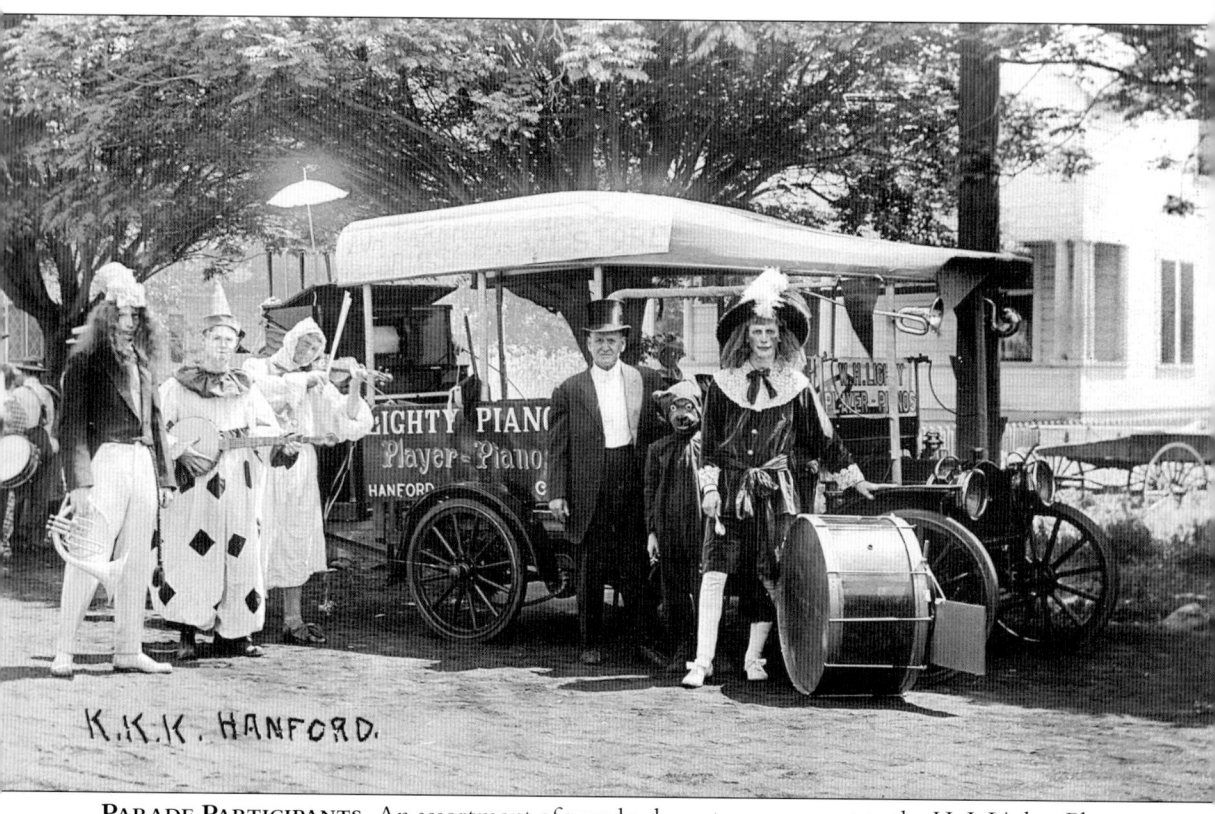

PARADE PARTICIPANTS. An assortment of parade characters pose next to the H. J. Lighty Player Piano Car. H. J. Lighty's store was located in the 100 block of West Seventh Street.

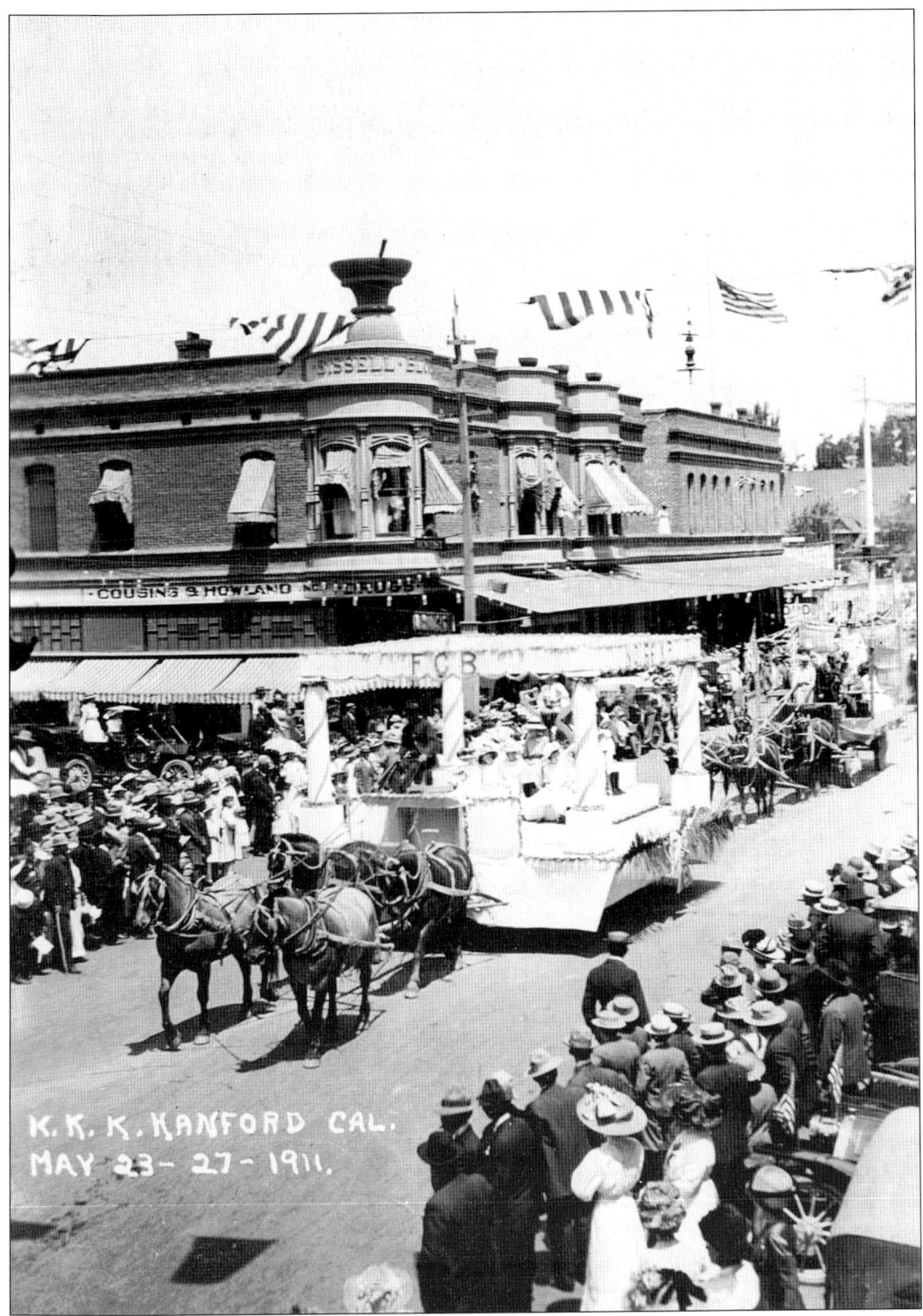

EARLY TIMES IN HANFORD. The caption on this card reflects a more innocent time of Kings County's early history.

BIBLIOGRAPHY

Armona American Revolution Bicentennial Committee. *The Armona Centennial 1876–1976, One Hundred Years of History.* Armona, CA: Armona American Revolution Bicentennial Committee, 1976.

Corcoran Journal, Bicentennial Edition. 1976.

Gibson, Harold H. *History of Kings County Public Schools, California.* Hanford, CA: Copy Connection, 2004.

Hanford Centennial Committee. *Hanford, Hometown America.* Hanford, CA: Hanford Centennial Committee, 1990.

Hanford Journal. *Resources of Kings County.* Hanford, CA: 1898.

Hanford Lodge F&AM No. 279, Centennial Committee. *Hanford Lodge F&AM No. 279 1885–1985, Centennial Edition.* Hanford, CA: 1985.

"Kings Kounty Karnival Celebration." *Hanford Journal.* May 27, 1911: 1.

Latta, Frank F. *Tailholt Tales.* Santa Cruz, CA: Bear State Books, 1976.

Lemoore Centennial Committee. *Lemoore Centennial 1873–1973.* Lemoore, CA: Lemoore Centennial Committee, 1973.

Lemoore Union High School. *Nuntius, 1918 Year.* Lemoore, CA: 1918.

Preston, William L. *Vanishing Landscapes; Land and Life in the Tulare Lake Basin.* Los Angeles, CA: University of California Press, 1981.

Smith, Wallace. *Garden of the Sun.* Fresno, CA: Linden Press, 2004.